I AM A DICE CONTROLLER

I AM A DICE CONTROLLER

Inside the World of Advantage-Play Craps

Frank Scoblete

TRIUMPH
BOOKS

Library of Congress Cataloging-in-Publication Data

Scoblete, Frank.
  I am a dice controller: inside the world of advantage-play craps / Frank Scoblete.
     pages cm
  ISBN 978-1-62937-072-9 (paperback)
  1. Craps (Game) I. Title.
  GV1303.S389 2015
  795.1'2—dc23

                              2014042494

This book is available in quantity at special discounts for your group or organization. For further information, contact:

Triumph Books
814 North Franklin Street
Chicago, Illinois 60610
(312) 337-0747
www.triumphbooks.com

Printed in U.S.A.
ISBN: 978-1-62937-072-9
Design by Amy Carter

To the Captain and the Arm

Contents

PART I:
The Captain

CHAPTER 1

Dice Control:
The New Frontier

I met my future wife, the Beautiful AP, when I was part owner of The Other Vic Theatre Company on Long Island in New York. Responding to an ad I had placed, AP applied for the job of stage manager. I have to be truthful—I loved her at first sight. She got the job.

She was a good stage manager and a good actress too. After she did several shows with us, she auditioned for the role of depressed chorus girl Fran Walker in the play *The Only Game in Town* by Frank D. Gilroy. I was the lead, Joe Grady, a degenerate craps player with a good heart. It was a powerful, funny, intense play about lives first lost and then found and the life-changing power of love. It also showed the degenerative power of a gambling addiction. I guess another title of the play could have been *Losers in Love!*

I faced a big problem, though. I had no idea what I was talking about when it came to casino gambling. I'd have these really dramatic monologues about casino play, my good and bad streaks, and I wasn't sure what the words I uttered meant. The final monologue of the show, an uplifting David and Goliath story of one incredible night at the craps tables, had me emoting like crazy about...what? I had no idea what the words meant.

This was in the mid-1980s. I had never been in a casino, nor had AP. We decided we'd better take a trip to Atlantic City to learn what casino gambling and craps were all about.

We went to the Claridge because I had a personal interest in the historic hotel. In November 1946 I was conceived there. The Claridge was built in 1930 and became known as "the Skyscraper by the Sea." The Claridge had an old-world charm. It also had the Captain and his high-rolling Crew.

Unquestionably the Captain had the most profound effect on my gambling life. Without his ideas and mentoring, I never would have become an advantage player or a successful writer of gambling articles and books.

We met the Captain at the Claridge. What the great Paul Keen was for me in blackjack (see my book *I Am a Card Counter*), the Captain was even more for me in craps. He was the master, the conductor, the genius of the game, and I learned more from him about craps and casino gambling than I ever learned from any book.

It just so happened that during that period of time, the Captain and his Crew of 22 high rollers called the Claridge their home. So in a sense I was conceived in the Captain's Atlantic City home—the very hotel that would launch my casino playing and writing career. My late father-in-law, Don Paone, would call that "divine providence."

The Beautiful AP and I walked through the casino. I noted some interesting facts about blackjack, and then we headed over to the craps tables. I observed what was going on and was totally confused by the multitude of bets a craps player could make. Chips were flying all over the place.

"Give me a yo!"

"Craps check!"

"How about snake eyes?"

"Hard 8, my man."

"Any craps!"

"Big red!"

"Everything across."

The dealers were moving like lightning—taking chips and putting them on various numbers and symbols, paying off winners, taking from losers. It was mind-boggling, and then mind-numbing, and I wondered how people could play what appeared to be the most confusing game I had ever seen. Even the layout looked like some space aliens had designed it.

The Captain was about 65 years old then, and he could see that I was totally confused. He also heard me say to the Beautiful AP, "I'll never learn this game. It's insane."

"Yes, you will," he said. "Most of the bets you are hearing players yelling, you can ignore. They are bad bets; I call them Crazy Crapper bets, and they should never be made. They sound good, but they stink. What you are hearing is a symphony in chaos."

That sold me: "a symphony in chaos." The Captain could have been a writer if he so desired.

The way the Captain played the game was anything but chaotic. Eschewing all the bets he called Crazy Crapper Bets—such as the Horn, the Whirl, the craps numbers, the Hardways, the Field, and others—the Captain instead focused on the Pass, Don't Pass, Come, and Don't Come.

"It isn't enough just to bet these bets, you must have some rhythm with the dice," he said. "Every bet has a casino edge on it, and to win you must overcome that edge. There is no other method to beat the casino at craps than good bets and rhythmic rolling."

The Captain firmly believed in this "rhythmic rolling" idea, the ability of some players to change the probabilities of the game based on the way they handled the dice. Today, we call such shooters dice controllers or dice influencers. He was convinced that if you made the right bets and threw the dice in a rhythmic way, the game could be beaten. In fact, he *knew* the game could be beaten because he had been doing just that—in a big way—for more than a decade.

Dice control critics want to know why there aren't dice controllers making millions playing the game. The critics present their arguments in a sarcastic way, not to win over those who are on the fence but merely to amuse those who already agree with them. The Captain made millions, as did Jimmy P. and several others that I know. The Captain was also a great teacher; he taught me everything I needed to know about advantage play.

Certainly, casinos try to protect themselves against dice manipulation by putting rubber pyramids against the back wall where the dice must hit. These pyramids supposedly randomize each and every throw. But for a good rhythmic roller, the pyramids just reduce the control; they do not fully randomize the results of most rolls.

"The pyramids are a nuisance, nothing more," the Captain said. "You can have some control even with them there. Your edge goes down when the dice hit them, but you can still have an edge. The casinos probably have no idea that their pyramids are not fully protecting them against rhythmic rollers."

The Captain also believed that many rhythmic rollers were not aware that they were changing the nature of the contest from one of randomness (which favored the casinos) to one of control (which favored the players). "If you take a look at rhythmic rollers, there are certain things that they all show. They carefully set the dice the same way each time. They aim. They take care with the speed of the dice, with the slowest speed being the best. If you throw the dice in a slow way, when those dice hit the back wall they will not scoot all over the layout as a regular dice thrower's will. They will tend to settle down in basically the same relationship with each other. It doesn't happen on every throw—many throws are random—but this happens with enough throws that some control is created. That control gives the player the edge if the player bets right."

Some rhythmic rollers in those days often said that they had great success at craps when they threw, never realizing that their "luck" was self-made because they were exerting some control over the outcome. In short, true skill could beat the game of craps. The Captain thought such rollers had helped him win since Atlantic City's Resorts Casino first opened its doors in 1978.

From my more than a quarter century of personal experience at the craps tables, I can see that everything the Captain said about rhythmic rolling was correct. In those heady days of Atlantic City's childhood, the Captain did the supposedly impossible—he won *a lot more than $1 million*. Naturally those wins did not come in one night, one month, or even one year. Having an advantage at craps does not mean you will win every time you play. Much like in blackjack, the edge a player has is small but it *is* an edge, and the longer you play, the better chance you will be ahead.

The Captain was well ahead when I met him that first night at the Claridge. He was well ahead of the casinos until the very day he died on February 10, 2010, during a huge snowstorm in New York City, where he lived. There is a myth that when great men are born or die, nature goes into turmoil—wild swings occur in weather, moving stars appear in the sky, and the dead walk the Earth. The Captain was a great man, and nature seemed to reflect his death during that great snowstorm.

When he was alive, the Captain had two strong factors in his favor: he was an excellent dice controller with a beautiful backspin and landing, and a truly soft throw, and perhaps even more important, he had his not-so-secret weapon, a woman everyone in his Crew called "the Arm." The Arm's roll was not a "slide" or "carpet roll," meaning a roll that stayed on the felt all the way down to the back wall. She had a unique lob of a toss, the dice going into the air without any spin, as if they were stuck in time and space, landing softly, and then *skidding* to the back wall, where they died. Indeed, despite the fact that I have seen some of the best of the modern dice controllers, no one has matched the Arm.

Still, who was this Captain, this greatest of all craps geniuses, the teacher who taught me everything and has influenced hundreds of thousands of craps players for more than a quarter of a century?

The Captain was born in 1922 in Brooklyn. His immigrant father was a fruit store owner whose common-law wife was a descendant of some of the earliest Americans. When his father and mother decided to *officially* get married in 1953, his mother was quite nervous and said, "I'm worried I might be rushing into this." At that time their five children were grown with families of their own. The Captain's life was a mixture of skill, chance, good fortune, and often the inability to see that others took advantage of his generous spirit and willingness to forgive transgressions against him.

He was a newspaper delivery boy in the 1930s and later volunteered for the Army Air Corps during World War II, during which he saw combat in the Philippines. During this combat period, his plane was shot down and he spent more than 10 days behind enemy lines, catching malaria, losing 33 pounds, hallucinating wildly, and carrying a dead companion around (he thought the guy was alive) before being rescued. He saw the Enola Gay, the plane that dropped the atomic bomb on Hiroshima, sitting secure on the runway as the officers and airmen ate their meal before taking off on a mission that would see the first use of an atomic weapon.

It was during that time period that the Captain learned to play craps and started tinkering with controlling those cubes. The craps game the soldiers played was different from the casino game as it exists today, but the idea was basically the same: make your numbers; avoid the 7. The players booked their own games; there was no house. The Captain banked quite a high percentage of those games.

During the 1950s and 1960s, the Captain tried his hand at various businesses; some succeeded and some failed. He became the neighborhood go-to guy if you wanted a no-interest "loan" that you could skip out on without fear of having your head bashed in as would happen with a loan shark. That was the Captain. If you needed money, he would give it to you and tell you to pay it back when you could. Many of the people who soaked him never paid him a dime.

But one such act of generosity set the Captain on the course of earning enough money to establish himself in the bigger business circles in Brooklyn.

During the 1950s the Captain ran a television store, one of the first stores of its type in the neighborhood. He sold Admiral TVs, and he kept a television in the window so people walking by could see this new marvel of entertainment technology.

A young man named Johansen would get off the subway near the Captain's store. He'd watch the television in the window. Finally the Captain talked to the young man and told him to pick out whichever set he wanted and pay the Captain when he could.

In the mid-1960s, competition in the television field became intense as department stores started to carry TV sets as well—sets they could price much lower than an independent store such as the Captain's. The Captain then partnered up with a "good friend" in convenience stores spread throughout Manhattan. The friend turned out to be a crook and bankrupted the stores. He borrowed money from loan sharks and one day just vanished as the loan sharks were closing in on him...and by association the Captain.

The Captain had no idea what was going on, but he did manage to pay back everything his vanished partner and "friend" had borrowed. But his career selling televisions and sundries was over.

"It was horrible, that betrayal by a friend I trusted," the Captain said. But the Captain paid the money his partner had borrowed from the mob. Some friends are only friends in name, not in deed—a sad fact of life. The Captain never saw that "friend" again.

He went to work for the airlines and decided to become a commercial real estate broker. He got his first property with his savings from his airline job and a loan. It was an empty lot in New York City. He put an advertisement in the paper showcasing the lot as a great property on which to build an office tower.

A few days after the ad appeared, the Captain got a call from an investor. The investor did not ask any questions about the property. He just wanted to know if the man selling it was the same man who used to own the television store by the subway station. The Captain said yes, and the man said—without even looking at it—that he would buy the property. The man on the phone was Johansen, who had been the young man to whom the Captain had given the television set many years before. Johansen had become a millionaire.

That sale launched the Captain on a successful career as a commercial real estate broker that he continued until his early eighties.

When Atlantic City's Resorts Hotel and Casino opened in 1978, the Captain took a trip down to the shore. That started him on his second career, that of the greatest craps player who ever lived. I'll let him tell the story of what took him from a gambler to an advantage player.

"My one great failing as a young man was playing the horses. I was a decent player, but still, during the course of my career I took a beating, as do just about all horse players. I quit cold turkey when I went into real estate, but I always had that urge to try my luck.

"I went down to Resorts and watched the [craps] games. The place was always packed with players. I didn't actually play at first. I made many trips and just watched.

"It took me a while of watching and then playing to realize that craps was a devastating game against most players. They would go up on numbers, make really bad bets, and often lose everything really quickly when a 7 showed.

"That's when I decided that I didn't want to go up on shooters right away—why take the chance? I started to wait a few rolls and finally I decided that five rolls would be sufficient before I risked my money. This idea ultimately became known as the 5-Count, and over the first half decade I tinkered with it in different ways. I figured the 5-Count eliminated maybe half the rolls." [NOTE: Mathematician Dr. Donald Catlin's study of the 5-Count showed it eliminated 57 percent of the random rolls, thereby allowing the 5-Counter to bet on just 43 percent of the random rolls.]

The Captain continued: "Simultaneously, I really studied the shooters. It didn't take me too long to see that the shooters who took care with the dice tended to have better rolls or to hit repeating numbers before sevening out. I started to look for these shooters and I started to call them 'rhythmic rollers' because I could see that they got into a kind of rhythm when they rolled.

"I also wondered why others were not noticing what I was noticing. I would look around the table, and most of the players just weren't watching closely. They were concerned with their bets for the most part. A shooter was just a shooter. Other players basically thought—if they thought at all—*If the shooter has form, so what?* Despite the fact that craps is a communal game with many players betting the same bets on the same shooter, it is still solitary because you are concerned with your own bets. Still it did surprise me the lack of focus other players had on the form of the shooters in the game.

"Of course, if shooters sevened out early, there was a lot of grousing on the part of the players who had lost money, but being miserable at a craps table is part of the fun for many players. I don't understand why it is fun for them, but it is.

"As time passed, I started to make friends with various guys at the casinos. I also had a bunch of friends from the neighborhood that enjoyed going to the casinos. The Arm was one. She is the one that solidified my theory that some players could control the dice because over two decades she was either the luckiest craps player in the history of the planet or she had a profound ability to control the dice. I opt for the second one. She was a marvel.

"I worked on my shooting, too. My form and style were completely different from the Arm's, but it worked for me. My style was also a lot easier than the Arm's. I really don't know how she could do what she did. Those dice looked like slow motion in the air, and they rarely bounced when they landed on the table. They just slid to the back wall and died.

"I guess by the time we met at the Claridge, my friends had become known as the Crew. We were big shots in Atlantic City because of the Crew's high-roller betting, and for some reason or another I had been chosen as their leader. They are the ones who started calling me the Captain. I was never a captain in the military. "Everything just kind of evolved."

While the Captain used the word "evolved," it took a man of great insight to see the possibilities in the game. His powers of observation brought together two important factors:

1. The need to prevent random rollers from draining a player's bankroll, and thus he created the 5-Count as a protection
2. The need to change the inherent probabilities in the game, which gave rise to his idea of rhythmic rolling

Over the years the Captain and I spent a lot of time together in the casinos. He was my coach in craps and my mentor. In the early 1990s, I started trying to control the dice as well. It took me three years of red-chip casino craps play to begin seeing positive results, but see them I did. (I'd go to casinos between 100 to 130 days a year during that time.) Even though I was primarily a relatively high-stakes blackjack player through the 1990s, my blackjack play began to decline as my dice control ability started to peak. Craps then became my game of choice. Since 2002 I've played craps about 95 percent of the time.

In addition to the impact he had on my playing career, the Captain also had a profound effect on my writing life. My first book, *Beat the Craps Out of the Casinos: How to Play Craps and Win!* is the best seller of any craps book in history. Although the book is now outdated, it is a nostalgic tour for me because most of the Captain's Crew have passed, with two exceptions—Satch, who was the youngest member of the Crew, and me. My more recent craps book, *Casino Craps: Shoot to Win!*, is a far more complete and powerful work, but it too is built on the foundation the Captain laid.

As Paul Keen was to blackjack, the Captain was to craps—"the greatest of all time" to quote Muhammad Ali. How good was the Captain as a controlled shooter? Amazing. He is the only player I have ever heard of who had two hands that went 100 or more rolls before sevening out. In 2004 he rolled 100 numbers and in 2005 he rolled what was then a world-record 147 numbers (recounted in greater detail later in this book).

Over the years I have written many articles and books about the Captain. During that time he has become a controversial figure in the "gaming community," and I have become a controversial figure for writing about him.

Some bellicose writers, backed by absolutely no knowledge of the Captain, the Arm, or the Crew, have confidently written that the Captain was merely a figment of my imagination created to sell books. He's been disdainfully called the "mythical" Captain, the "phony" Captain, and the "crazy" Captain. Other unknowledgeable writers do credit his existence but as an exaggeration—again for the purposes of selling books. Those who say such things have the supreme confidence of individuals who know nothing of what they speak.

Naturally, those who have played with the Captain know him and see him for what he was. I remember once in 2003 when the Captain and I were playing at Wild Wild West in Atlantic City, one of my students, Vegas Ray, came to the table. He had no idea who the "old man" playing next to me was. But when that old man rolled and rolled and rolled, hitting number after number, Vegas Ray mouthed to me, "Is that the Captain?" I nodded, and Vegas Ray beamed. When we were finished with our session, I introduced Vegas Ray to the Captain. Even making loads of money on the Captain's roll was not as exciting to him as meeting the man himself.

Still other critics acknowledge the Captain's existence but challenge the notion that he is responsible for the ideas behind modern dice control. I have even been accused of stealing those ideas from other writers and popularizing them through my own books and articles. All I can say is: check the publication dates. I began writing about dice control in the late 1980s, well before other writers. But I owe even my early involvement with dice control to the Captain.

Indeed, the very first dice-control school, PARR—created by author Jerry Patterson and taught by Chris "Sharpshooter" Pawlicki —used the term "rhythm roll" to describe what they taught. This was a compliment to the Captain's definitive contributions to advantage-play craps. They just changed *rhythmic* to *rhythm*.

In fact, in 1996 the Beautiful AP and I met Pawlicki for the first time at Tropicana in Las Vegas. During that lunch he poured on the accolades for the Captain and how the Captain inspired him to really study the field of rhythmic rolling. I autographed copies of several books for him too. These books (*Beat the Craps Out of the Casinos, Guerrilla Gambling*, and *The Captain's Craps Revolution*) opened the dice control doors.

Without a doubt, Sharpshooter and Patterson had a profound effect on controlled shooting, as Sharpshooter was the first engineer to really study the physical dynamics of the skill and Patterson saw a way to market such a skill to the casino gambling public. The PARR course attempted to teach a throw that was similar to the Captain's. Although that course was mostly lecture, it set the stage for the development of more sophisticated schools. Without PARR, the world of dice control education probably would not have developed.

Sharpshooter is not the only writer who had the utmost respect for the Captain. In the early 1990s I met with Sam Grafstein, author of the enjoyable book *The Dice Doctor*. Upon first reading Grafstein's book, the man seemed a little harsh, the gambling equivalent of Archie Bunker. It turned out he was nothing like that.

Beat the Craps Out of the Casinos had just come out, and I was in Las Vegas visiting the Gambler's Book Shop for an autograph session. Howard Schwartz, the irrepressible manager of the store and the Gambler's Book Club mail-order company, told me that in a few minutes Grafstein would be there. I was quite nervous when I heard that because even in those days Sam was a known craps celebrity. What would he think of the book—that is, if he had read it?

Then Sam entered the bookstore and went over to Howard, who nodded in my direction.

"You Scoblete?" asked Grafstein.

Crap, what was he going to say? Would it be: "Kid, your book sucks!

You call yourself a craps expert? Who is this idiot the Captain? Don't quit your day job. And you're ugly"?

Instead, he was gracious and friendly. "That Captain is a genius. I loved the 5-Count. I loved the book." He was nothing like what I thought he would be. "Let's go play when you finish your book signing," he said.

And we did. We headed to the Horseshoe in downtown Vegas.

Sam was primarily a Don't player when I was with him, but he never rushed onto a shooter. He'd qualify the shooter in the interests of picking the one he felt would seven out quickly or, if betting the Rightside, would make some numbers. His method of "qualifying" was a typical gambler's approach since there is no such thing as qualifying a random shooter; still, the more time spent qualifying shooters, the less time the house has to grind down your bankroll with its edge because qualifying keeps the player out of the action

I got to play at the same tables with Sam for several days and I enjoyed every minute of those sessions. Over the years I really don't know if he lost or won (based on his philosophy, I would guess he was a long-term loser), but I can say he had a winning personality and I really liked the man.

Perhaps the greatest compliment for the Captain by a writer on the inside of the casino industry came from Robert Renneisen, who was president of the Claridge Hotel and Casino in Atlantic City during the early 1990s, when the Captain and his Crew played there. His book *How to Be Treated Like a High Roller...Even Though You're Not One* references the powerful impact the Captain had on his casino.

He writes, "We had a host, I'll call him Mike [author's note: interesting because I believe his actual name was Mike, and he was the Captain's host at several casinos in AC over the years]. He had a large following of players who knew how to take advantage of the system. They came frequently and would quickly leave when they were unlucky, rarely losing much. When they were winning, however, they would bet enormous sums and rack up a lot of 'points' in the rating system...Frankly, they were smart players...Mike said this: 'The Captain is killing us.'"

The Captain's followers actually leaving the casinos when things weren't going well happened not to be my experience with the majority of them.

Only the Captain, Jimmy P., the Arm, Satch, and I would leave if things were going poorly. Still Renneisen sums up how the Captain played.

The Claridge was the Captain's paradise for several years until Mike moved on to the Castle in the Marina District. The Captain then moved his whole Crew to that casino-hotel. The Castle went through many incarnations over the years. It became Trump's Castle, Trump Marina, the Marina, and now the Golden Nugget.

I spent many nights at the Castle with the Captain and his Crew. I remember one Saturday evening the Captain and the Crew and their significant others had a huge party in the Harbor View Grill (now the Chart House Restaurant), a beautiful restaurant overlooking the marina with a wonderful view of the skyline of Atlantic City. Even though it was a Saturday night, the executives closed the restaurant for the Captain's private party.

Why did casinos such as the Claridge and the Castle and numerous others treat the Captain so well? Simple. While the Captain won boatloads of money—as did the Arm and (eventually) Jimmy P.—the rest of the Crew tended to be crazy bettors. They liked to play, and they liked to bet big money. Their losses over time were immense. The Captain's wins could not touch those losses.

I also think the casinos did not fully appreciate the concept of rhythmic rollers. It almost seemed that the Captain had exclusive rights to this brilliant idea until I opened—as Ralph Kramden said—my "big mouth" by writing articles and books about it. Only then did the idea of controlled shooting (now also called dice influencing) make its way into the consciousness of craps players. The smart ones learned how to do it, or at least tried to learn how to do it, while others pooh-poohed it. Keep in mind that just "setting" or "fixing" the dice is not enough to give a player the edge; it is merely the first step. So all those "dice setters" out there have no impact on the house edge. About the only thing some of them do is slow down the game because they have no idea how a die's pips are laid out. But I digress.

I promised the Captain I would never reveal his name and I have kept and will continue to keep that promise. I keep such promises. For example, I promised Dom "the Dominator" that I wouldn't reveal his last name in this book and wouldn't mention another embarrassing fact about him. I've kept that promise as well.

Why some critics try to diminish the Captain's contributions to advantage-craps play—or even to deny his very existence—puzzles me. Perhaps it is a heavy dose of jealousy or the mistaken belief that if they knock someone superior, they elevate themselves. Who knows?

But long after the self-described experts and Internet gurus are totally forgotten and their criticisms lie in the dust like Ozymandias' ruined statue, the Captain's ideas will live on.

He started it all.

He was and still *is* the man.

CHAPTER 2

The Captain, the Arm, and Jimmy P. vs. Atlantic City

Heady days for me, the 1990s, when I was a part of something unique: the Captain's Crew of 22 high rollers. Atlantic City was thriving in those days. Weekends brought out mega-high rollers.

Frank Sinatra, Dean Martin, Sammy Davis Jr., and a host of other well-known entertainers played the Boardwalk. I saw it all. Sinatra and Martin even played in the casinos, amongst mere mortals such as me.

Atlantic City's casinos were on the shores of the Atlantic Ocean on one side and the edges of a slum on the other side. But inside Lady Luck's domain was another world—of sparkling lights, well-dressed men and women, and fine food and services. It was a world apart from the sordid landscape just a block away and from the mundane existence in which many gamblers live their normal lives.

The Captain had a practical philosophy of gambling. He said, "Never bet too much money in relation to your bankroll and always have a lot of money in your total bankroll, much more than you ever need." The Captain believed you should have a separate account for your gambling money. Since he said it—and since one disastrous trip that wiped me out—I have done it. I took his lesson and coined the term "401(g)" based on the 401(k)—but the *g* stands for *gambling*.

The Captain told me, "When you are rolling the dice, you never want to be thinking about the possibility of losing money. Even when the Arm rolls, I do not bet so much that I ever worry about losing. Worry creates a bad player. If you want to play with the winning edge over the house, you must be cold-blooded. Keep your bets low and your bankroll high. Money should never come between you and winning. If you don't have a big bankroll, make your bets so low that even a small bankroll is big in relation to it. If you think about money, you are in trouble if you really want to have an edge over the house."

The Captain eschewed just about all bets at the craps tables. He termed bets such as the 2, 3, 11, and 12; the Horn; the Whirl; Any Craps; the Hardways; and the Field "Crazy Crapper bets" because "you have to be crazy to make them."

He religiously played the 5-Count, saying, "I really think you have to reduce drastically the number of shooters' rolls you bet on. Even with rhythmic rolling you just can't win if you keep pumping bets out there on non-rhythmic rollers who have no control of what they are doing. That's ultimately taking a match to your money."

The 5-Count, as I mentioned earlier, eliminates about 57 percent of the random rolls. The Captain said that if you bet really low on the 43 percent of the other rolls, "your bankroll will not be hit that hard and you can, by using a decent rhythmic roll, beat the house over time."

As strange as it might sound, the very act of *thinking* is bad for a controlled shooter. The Captain said, "You do not want to be think-ing when you roll the dice. You don't even want to be thinking when you bet on others. The 5-Count is a mechanical way to play. You don't need thought to do it. It is automatic. You don't have to spend time thinking whether the shooter you are watching has talent or is just the same as a slot machine: random. You just let the 5-Count do what it does. Thinking tires you out, and that will affect your shooting. A shooter who makes it past the 5-Count, you bet on. No thought needed. Thinking tires out a rhythmic roller, and there is no need to do it. You do not want to think when a Bob Feller fastball is heading for the plate because the split moment when that thought rises up, the ball is by you and you've struck out."

While the Captain and the Crew went to Atlantic City almost every weekend, the Captain, the Arm, Jimmy P., and some others also enjoyed day trips or overnight trips during the week. The most money was made during those trips because the Captain did not have to play with crowds. "Most of the Crew," he told me, "are just gamblers, and all of them want to shoot. I play the 5-Count on all of them. I don't even think most of them notice how I play. But it is a long wait for me or for the Arm to get the dice. During the week, there might be only six or so players at a table. It is easier to win money that way."

While most of the Crew were—as the Captain once told me—"wild gamblers," Jimmy P. began to see that over time the Captain was winning money, unlike his fellow members of the Crew. Jimmy P. had an epiphany in the early 1990s and asked the Captain exactly what he did to come out ahead.

The Captain taught him. For quite some time, Jimmy P. practiced his rhythmic roll in the casinos. I did the same thing. It never dawned on me to create a practice station at home. I just kept going to the casinos. It took me three years to get competent at it. It took me 10 years to get *good* at it.

The three of them—the Captain, the Arm, and Jimmy P.—soon became the bane of Atlantic City's casinos. Here was a city quite close to their homes where they could play their game and bring home the bacon.

I do have to put the Arm's play into a somewhat different perspective. She did not gamble at all. She rarely made a bet. When she shot the dice, the Captain or Jimmy P. put up her Pass Line bet. When other players shot, the Captain or Jimmy P. would put up a single table-minimum bet for her, should a shooter make it past the 5-Count.

She wasn't selfish—after all, she made them a fortune with her rolls—she just didn't care for gambling. She enjoyed going to the casinos, to gourmet dinners, shows, walks on the Boardwalk, but gambling as such was not her thing. I know that sounds strange. I guess you could say she was the equivalent of the nondrinker who enjoys hanging out in clubs.

How great was the Arm? I can remember incidents at the table that stand out. I remember rolls of repeating numbers that boggled my mind. She once came down on New Year's morning and saved the Captain and Crew from rather large losses by taking several turns with the dice in a row—all of them monsters. I recall how seas of people would sometimes part when she headed toward the craps tables. That was especially true at the Claridge, a small compact casino where it seemed as if everyone knew her or at least knew about her. Sometimes you could hear people say, "That's her; that's the Arm." She was like Moses when those seas of people parted to let her through. The casino was like Pharaoh's army— about to be destroyed, about to be drowned.

Yes, I admit that my memory highlights this past in glowing colors. As time goes by, that glow becomes brighter, not duller, and I was a part of that brightness. The Arm stood out to me the way the Statue of Liberty stands out to Americans and immigrants alike. The Statue of Liberty exists in its own brilliant light. So did the Arm. She was the queen of craps, by far the best shooter I ever saw. I do see an ethereal glow about her. I do see her eccentric throw. I do see chips overflowing into everyone's chip racks.

I realize that I see her—and the Captain and Jimmy P.—in the light of joyful memory. I do think of them as mythical figures, but nothing I have written about them is false. But I know what I experienced back then was magic; I was a part of the very myth I have written about.

Certainly, the Arm did not have epic rolls every time she took the dice. I just remember it that way. But she usually won on her turns with the dice because she had the knack of hitting repeating numbers—*bam! bam! bam!* I have snapshots in my head of her rolling, snapshots of the Crew cheering, snapshots of the Captain smiling and collecting his wins.

In those days, long rolls were counted in time: "So-and-so rolled for a half hour" or, "This person rolled for an hour." We had no idea how many numbers were actually rolled before a seven-out. I did not start counting actual numbers until the turn of the 21st century. I wish I had counted actual numbers to see how high the Arm's counts were.

The Captain's technique was the form that many dice controllers use today. It is the form that Sharpshooter taught. The Captain generally stood at stick left one (SL1) or two (SL2), or stick right one (SR1) or two (SR2), though sometimes he shot from straight out. He threw the dice backhand. The dice had a backward spin. His throw was soft and went right down the center of the table. The dice hit and went to the back wall with very little energy left in them. Those of you who play craps have probably seen some form of this throw from many players nowadays. In the Captain's day, it was he and then Jimmy P. who were the sole players I saw do it, while I was attempting to learn it.

The Captain set the dice in the classic 3V set. So did Jimmy P. Note that the pips add up to 6s and 8s all around it. I use the very first one on the top left.

3V Sets:

T3F5:T3F1

T2F3:T6F3

T4F2:T4F6

T5F4:T1F4

T3F6:T3F2

T1F3:T5F3

T4F1:T4F5

T6F4:T2F4

The Captain put his three front fingers level on the front of the dice with the thumb in back equidistant between each die. On SL1 or SL2, he had that backswing, just like today's dice controllers, but he did do a slight jerk as he brought his hand forward. On SR1 or SR2, his throw was more of an underhand or sideways throw with not very much backspin. He seemed to be equally good from either side.

I have no idea how the Arm set her dice. Her hand covered them completely. Today some floor people or box people might tell her that they must see the dice. In those days no one bothered her. Of course, that could also be a pleasant payback for the deluge of tips the dealers got when the Crew played or the opulent gifts the box people, the floor people, pit bosses, and hosts received from the Captain and the Crew. I really don't know. But I do know that you could not see the Arm's dice until she released them. Strangely enough, in those days I hesitated to ask her how she set her dice. I guess I felt I was in the land of the giants and I must not barge in on them. Indeed, back then I was a man amongst the giants.

CHAPTER 3

TropWorld: Screwing the Forest for Three Trees

I have many tales of the Captain's adventures in Atlantic City, but there is one that has become legend: the events leading to the Captain's withdrawal from TropWorld (now Tropicana).

The Captain followed his Claridge host Mike to TropWorld, as did the 22 members of the Crew. The Crew played mainly on weekends, but the Captain, Jimmy P., and the Arm made frequent midweek visits. I made some of those visits as well.

I remember the spectacular ocean-view suites the three of them got, and the Captain would always make sure I had a suite as well. Those were some great midweek excursions.

Any time I had a day off from teaching, I would join the Captain if he was going to the shore. Since the Captain and Jimmy P. worked for themselves, and the Arm was totally free from such daily drudgery, those trips were frequent.

By 1993 or so, the Arm was in her glory, Jimmy P. had become a proficient rhythmic roller, the Captain was—as always—*the* Captain, and even I was beginning to get the hang of some control, though I tended not to shoot when I was with those three. I have to say, I am not an easily intimidated man, but being in their company was almost like being in an alternate universe. I knew they were doing what gaming writers, casino personnel, and casino mathematicians thought to be impossible: beating the supposedly unbeatable game of craps.

The traditional thinking when it comes to craps is really simple. It is the exact same thinking as with slot machines or any other random game. If the game is indeed random, the casino wins either because it wins more decisions or because it pays back less than the true odds of a bet. If a bet should pay 35-to-1 at craps, the casino might pay back 30-to-1. No betting system can overcome a random game where the house manipulates the payouts; you just can't bet yourself out of randomness and you can't bet yourself out of a fixed house edge. It is mathematically impossible. When the casino changes the real mathematical paybacks, the players are ultimately doomed to lose. The worse the changes in paybacks, the more players lose. You might call that a true law of nature.

Yet dice control changes the underpinnings of the game. By moving the game away from randomness, the probabilities change. Some bets can then be beaten, and the money flows from casino to player. Although very few dice controllers can beat the outrageously high house edges on the Crazy Crapper bets, a competent dice controller can certainly gain an edge on the lower-house-edge bets. And that is exactly what the Captain, the Arm, and Jimmy P. did. Essentially they were playing a different game of craps from the run-of-the-mill craps player—even though they played at the exact same tables.

The three played TropWorld for about six months when someone in management began to realize that they were not only winning money— those wins were more than $1 million—but were hauling in comps galore. At the time, TropWorld had a shopping area where you could get meats, fruits and vegetables, electronic equipment, and various sundries. Comps could be used for all of those things, not just the rooms, limos, entertainment, and restaurants. The three of them went comp crazy.

Jimmy P. was a purple and orange chip player (keep in mind this was the early 1990s, when money and chips were worth far more than they are today), the Captain was black and purple, and the Arm was whatever Jimmy P. or the Captain made her. The Captain and Jimmy P. took their comps in the form of food and gadgets, including stereos, televisions, and the like. They gave most of the electronic stuff away as gifts to relatives and friends—including me. Winning money and getting truly free stuff; now that is every casino player's dream.

On certain days Jimmy P. would bring in one of his trucks, and they would fill it with meats from the butcher, electronic equipment, and just about anything else they wanted. It was delightful to see them taking everything they could get. There were times I laughed as I saw all that free stuff being hauled off to Brooklyn.

In those days, during midweek in Atlantic City, it was practically a World War II reunion: veterans enjoying the game they played when they were saving the world from fascism and Imperial Japan—the Greatest Generation playing the most exciting game in the house.

Many of the players tended to be somewhat cantankerous; I guess that was a combination of age mixed with being Northeasterners. The Captain and Jimmy P. were in their element. The other players were the guys they fought alongside, though the fight had become against the casino. Sadly, their friends-in-arms tended to get killed at the craps table despite the fact that they had survived World War II.

The management guy who first noted that the Captain, the Arm, and Jimmy P. were clobbering them immediately made two basic (and stupid) moves. He eliminated their comps—in fact, he came down to the casino as the three of them were playing and with a sneer on his puffy red face grandiosely informed the Captain and Jimmy P., "You no longer have any comps at TropWorld." He couldn't ban them, but he could take away all comps—including comped rooms, dinners, and entertainment—which he did.

The second move was the one that (I hope) cost the man his job. He sent a picture of them to the other casinos, warning those casinos that the Captain, the Arm, and Jimmy P. had worked out some method of winning money at the game. He never really figured out how they were doing it; he must have thought they had manufactured luck in some way with their intermittent betting methods.

Just as it never dawned on me to create a practice rig to develop my controlled throw, it was really not in the air at that time that players could control the dice if those dice hit the back-wall pyramids. To this day, many casino folks still think that the pyramids automatically make all dice that hit them randomized. Not so. My book *Cutting Edge Craps* explains exactly the various ways the dice hit the back wall. The executive never thought in those terms. He never thought at all.

Many casino executives don't know their games. Back then some did; today fewer do. In controlled shooting the general opinion of most casino folks is that the skill is geared to missing the back wall. In fact, just the opposite. The modern controlled dice throws are geared to hitting the back wall; if they miss, the game is random. Strangely enough, casino floor people and box people should be encouraging dice controllers to miss the back wall so that the game reverts to random. I doubt that we will see this happen.

The Captain was soon alerted that a picture had been sent to various casinos when one high-level executive at the Sands casino (a man the Captain had helped several times over the years) called to tell him that the TropWorld management was spreading the photo. The Captain informed the Crew—which had lost much more money in aggregate than the Captain, the Arm, or Jimmy P. had won or gotten in comps—and all of them left TropWorld and trouped to another casino, following their host Mike. Obviously that TropWorld executive who irritated the Captain was penny-wise and pound-foolish—a ploppy of the first order.

CHAPTER 4

The Captain's 12 Precepts

The Captain had fundamental principles when it came to playing craps.

1. It was essentially a waste of time to think you would win money on the average shooter who was a random roller. The casino has an edge on these shooters, and over time, the players who bet on these shooters will lose. There is no betting system that can overcome the house edge.

2. Money could be won only on rhythmic rollers (dice controllers, dice influencers)—those shooters who had some control over the dice.

3. Players had to bet correctly and not try to win money on Crazy Crapper bets. He also didn't think it was a good idea to go up on too many numbers, since he thought controlled shooters would have the tendency to hit repeating numbers. Today we call this tendency "on-axis rolling."

4. While the Captain was not an expert on the various dice sets that have by now been studied extensively, he knew that the 3V set allowed him to go for the 6s and 8s—the two most frequently thrown numbers other than the 7 in a random game. By using the 3V and being on-axis, he felt this was the way to beat the house. He was right, as SmartCraps software has shown us. While the Captain did not discuss things such as axis control in the language of today, he was well aware that he tended to hit those 6s and 8s. From my appraisal he had great axis control.

5. You had to reduce the hit on your bankroll when you bet on random

rollers, and he created the 5-Count to do that. That method allowed the 5-Counter to look like a gambler who "qualified" shooters when in reality what he did was limit exposure to such shooters. While the Captain estimated that approximately 50 percent of all random rolls were bypassed by this method, we now know that approximately 57 percent of the random rolls are not wagered on.

6. The Captain used to bet on three numbers when a random roller made it through the 5-Count. You will see me reference that method in my early craps books. As time went on, he changed his mind and started to bet on only one number when random rollers were shooting. The Captain figured (correctly) that every bet against a random roller was an ultimate loser, so why bet more than one? I have now adapted that to my own play. One bet on one random roller. That now reduces the hit by two-thirds on such shooters. Keep in mind that every bet you make at craps is a separate game against the house. One bet is one game, two bets are two games, and so on. Why play multiple losing games?

7. The Captain believed in style. He felt that all craps players, whether rhythmic rollers or random rollers, should develop a style of shooting that had some grace. He disliked when players just winged the dice down the felt. He said such players "lacked class." He would always tell me, "Even if you do not have the skills to beat the house, you should at least look good and *act* as if you are *trying* to beat the house." He thought that players who pretended not to care about whether they made money or not were making a big mistake. "Look like you want to win. Let everyone at the table know you want to win," he said.

8. The Captain thought it was fine to cheer when a point was made or when numbers hit, but he was a firm believer in never bothering a shooter, even if that shooter was just a random roller. "Give the shooter his space," he said.

9. The Captain rarely argued with the calls of the box people, saying, "They are in charge, and even if they make a mistake, what is the point of continued arguing? You can say your piece, and then they make the decision." Many a long roll by a controlled shooter

has gotten that shooter out of his rhythm when another player starts a heated argument over a trivial bet. Most of the time, in my experience, the player is wrong. Also such arguing seems to occur during many long rolls.

10. The Captain would say, "Don't criticize other players if they seven-out early. It is part of the game." If you have ever played craps, you know that many players weep and moan, and some will even yell at shooters who lose them money. The shooters are just playing a random game—they can have long rolls, short rolls, and everything in between. The Captain felt that a friendly craps table was more conducive to a rhythmic roller being able to actually achieve an edge over the house. The less tension, the more relaxed a shooter, the better the chances he can perform.

11. Bet low in relation to your total bankroll and have a separate account for your gambling funds. Being wiped out is the worst feeling in a casino player's career. Again, I recommend that you create a 401(g). Only use the money in your 401(g) to play with. Over time, as you win money (*if* you win money), you can take some and treat yourself to something you want.

12. Emotions count. The Captain said: "Any athlete will tell you his mental state has a lot to do with his success. An uptight ballplayer is one who is ready to screw up. The same holds true for a rhythmic roller." The Captain knew that any tension, any thinking, any upset during a rhythmic roll could undo a good shooter. A calm mental state is a fundamental foundation to a good throw. The Captain wisely summarized: "Screw up the mind, screw up the throw."

CHAPTER 5

Satch and Me

It took me about three years to get somewhat competent at dice control. During the 1990s it was not unusual for the Beautiful AP and me to spend upward of 130 days a year in the casinos of Las Vegas, Atlantic City, and, toward the late-1990s, Tunica, Mississippi. We were a great blackjack team, and it was during those years that I worked on my controlled throw.

I practiced in the casinos on most days after my blackjack sessions, betting a $5 Pass and a $5 Don't Pass. When I reached the 5-Count on myself, I'd take the odds on the Pass Line. This method of betting, also called the Doey-Don't, was advocated by the Captain early on. He called it the Supersystem. It was anything but. It is not the best way to bet, and the Captain abandoned it after a while.

When I played at the same tables as the Captain and the Arm, I rarely shot the dice. I would pass them to the next shooter. I was nervous about looking bad, but more important, I wanted the dice to get to the Arm and the Captain. I realize that not taking the dice was silly on my part, because even after I had some control, I still backed off from shooting. Such are nerves. Worry and skilled shooting are anathema to each other.

The other Crew members did not feel that way. With the lone exceptions of the Arm, Jimmy P., Satch, and me, I doubt that any of them had any idea of exactly how the Captain played or even if the Captain was winning a bundle over time. I am also sure they merely thought the Arm's great turns with the dice were caused by good luck or real magic or God's grace or just some unfathomable something that she had. Gamblers are the ultimate believers in luck, and sadly for most gamblers, that luck turns sour. Luckily it did not turn sour for the Arm, the Captain, or Jimmy P.

I am sure that some of you might wonder why all the Crew didn't win loads of money when they had such shooters as the Arm and the Captain in their midst. The major reason was that neither the Captain nor the Arm played for long periods of time. The Crew tended to play all day and most of the night. They were wild players and just couldn't stay away from the tables. While the Captain (and sometimes the Arm) would take long walks on the Boardwalk each day, the Crew would be at the tables almost as if they were attached by crazy glue. The Crew played with abandon. And they played long hours. They'd hop from casino to casino. The Captain would take the dice a few times, and if he didn't have it, he'd take a break. His intent was not just to play; his intent was to win money.

I was also astonished when my books started coming out that even those members of the Crew who read them didn't follow the advice. I guess that is similar to other craps players out there right now. The good information is available, but craps players are essentially gamblers and want to do what they want to do—even if doing it costs them money. I guess they call that "fun."

During those days of the 1990s, Satch and I would go to Atlantic City and occasionally Las Vegas to play craps together, just the two of us. For two straight years and many, many sessions together, we couldn't win a damn thing. As those two years plodded on, we both became somewhat depressed and humorously wondered if we were cursed.

"How is it when we are at the table with the Arm and the Captain and the Crew, we win, but when we are alone together, we consistently lose?" wondered Satch.

"Beats me," I said.

Satch has a nice throw now, but in those days he wasn't a controlled shooter, and I was just a marginal one.

Yet sheer blind, dumb luck should have allowed us to win at least once during that two-year period. I mean we played *a lot*. Neither of us had a single decent roll in that time together. It was truly mind-boggling.

Okay, to be sensible, there was no magic involved in our stinking up every joint we played in together. In any gambling activity—even in advantage-play gambling—you are going to experience streaks of losses. But it is easy to get the feeling that somehow the Olympian gods are deliberately screwing around with you when you are involved in a negative streak. You'll also experience streaks of wins when you'll think to yourself that *you* are an Olympian god. In short, Satch and I—when we played together—were just hitting a prolonged negative streak.

That ended at the Horseshoe Casino in Las Vegas when I broke out for an hour-long roll (remember we counted time in the 1990s, not actual rolls) and then Satch followed up with a 50-minute roll. Those rolls occurred just before the Beautiful AP and I were banned by a gun-toting security guard several weeks later. That horrifying adventure, if you can actually call it an adventure, is fully recounted in my book *I Am a Card Counter*.

The Plaza casino and one table at the Horseshoe had 25¢ games, and the characters surrounding those tables came right out of *Mad* magazine. The "mixed nuts quotient" there certainly surpassed that quotient in the general population. It would be a psychiatrist's dream. Some of those individuals could take up a whole psychiatric conference.

Watching those games, I saw for the first time people who had black teeth; I mean, my lord, *black teeth!* I also saw a rogue's gallery of people with *no* teeth, people with clothes that had more holes than cloth, people who probably hadn't bathed in days, and people wearing weird-looking hats in 115-degree weather. It was an education on the down-and-out end of the gambling spectrum; although, to be clear, many of the players were just your average players, many senior citizens, who preferred low stakes.

Of course, the Golden Nugget—right across the street from the Horseshoe—was a whole different world. The Nugget had some high-rolling craps players. The casino was bright and clean, as opposed to dim and dingy like the Horseshoe. The Plaza was in between the Nugget and the Horseshoe in decor. Sadly, the Beautiful AP and I were banned from the Golden Nugget before we were banned at Horseshoe.

The first real monster roll I ever had came at the Horseshoe in Vegas. I was at the table with Peter Nathan and best-selling author Bill "Ace-10" Burton. I rolled between 40 and 45 minutes. It was heaven. I felt as if I were in another world—a slow-motion, random-thought world. Since then I have experienced that sense of timelessness on many occasions. It is the best experience in casino craps play; it involves being in a zone, and just as important, it means winning money, sometimes a lot of money.

By the mid to late 1990s, I was beginning to get better than just marginal. I was starting to have some truly noticeable control. I was not great, but I knew I was on my way to being able to do (in a smaller way) what the Arm did consistently. Those days made me exuberant. The better I got, the more money I began to bet on myself when I rolled the dice.

By 1996 I was even rolling the dice when I played with the Captain, the Arm, Jimmy P., and the Captain's Crew. I was no longer worried that I would fail.

CHAPTER 6

Jerry Patterson's PARR

J ust before I helped start Golden Touch Craps in November 2002, I was primarily a shooter from the right side of the stickman, usually at SR1 or SR2. I had good control by 2001 and was slowly leaving intense blackjack play for more time at the craps tables.

While I had stayed in contact with Sharpshooter, who wrote for my now-defunct magazine *Chance and Circumstance*, I had never taken a course in dice control, so I figured I'd give PARR a shot.

Jerry Patterson comped me to the April 2002 course if I would be the guest speaker. I happily agreed.

The PARR course was quite good on the theoretical level. Sharpshooter did hours of lecture showing the physics and mechanics of a controlled throw, but unfortunately we got to shoot the dice only a few times the whole weekend. I stuck with shooting the dice from stick left since that was the side where I needed work.

The instructors were quite good, but many of them were disenchanted with the way PARR and Patterson treated them or how PARR structured the course. In fact, the instructors would travel the country to help out with PARR without being paid. Patterson and Sharpshooter made the money. The instructors' dismay and eventual dislike of PARR would become the underpinnings of the Golden Touch Craps company, composed of many PARR teachers who happily fled Patterson the first chance they got.

After the April PARR class, I went home and started to really practice my throw on a makeshift table. At first I stunk from stick left, but endless hours of practice started to pay off. My stick left throw overtook my stick right throw. I became better from that side.

The Captain was somewhat interested in finding out how the PARR school was going. Many of his Crew had passed away by 2002, and he told me that talking about "youngsters" learning rhythmic rolling "revitalized" him. Although he didn't want to get involved with any schools of dice control, he was happy that others were learning about rhythmic rolling.

In November 2002, during a trip to Atlantic City during a PARR weekend, three PARR teachers—the late Bill "Ace-10" Burton, Bob "Mr. Finesse," and Dom "the Dominator"—asked if I would meet with them at a small bar at the casino.

The three PARR teachers put their cards on the table. They were totally unhappy with PARR, with not getting paid, with not being appreciated by Patterson. They also didn't particularly like the way the course was run and that Sharpshooter was being treated like a god when he was in fact a boring lecturer. Would I be interested in helping to form a new company? Certainly they flattered me by saying that my name alone would bring in plenty of students.

So we negotiated.

I had retired from teaching in June 2002, and I had plenty of free time to devote to a company that would teach dice control the way it should be taught, with plenty of hands-on instruction and far fewer long lectures. I also knew that in any activity involving skill, a very small student-to-teacher ratio is paramount—no more than four or five students per teacher. Hands-on personal attention is the key to learning dice control.

One instructor came up with a phrase that I have used repeatedly since he said it. "Students are not coming to class to learn how to build a clock; they are coming to learn how to tell time," he said. That was true. While some knowledge of the mechanics of how a throw actually worked was important, endless hours of lecture about physics and mechanics were essentially a waste of valuable time.

I agreed, and the four of us created this new company, to be called Golden Touch Craps. Patterson got wind of this and said to me, "You are making a mistake. Dom will screw you. Mark my words. Don't trust him." I ignored Patterson, who had an iffy reputation in advantage-play circles by that time. Many advantage blackjack players and writers thought of Patterson as a scam artist. Why should I believe him about Dom? After all, Dom was leaving him and moving into a better position.

Dom and I became the majority partners while Bob "Mr. Finesse," John Robison (a non-player), and Howard "Rock 'n' Roller" became the secondary partners. Tertiary partners were Jerry "Stickman," Billy "the Kid," Daryl "No Field Five," Arman "Pit Boss," Bill "Ace-10" Burton, and Doc Holliday. Dom immediately took over the business aspects of the company and the handling of the money. The only thing I had to do with money was to put my name as the primary cardholder on the Golden Touch Craps American Express account. That was at Dom's insistence. The Beautiful AP wondered somewhat why Dom wanted me as the primary since I would not be handling the money, but neither of us had much of a problem with it. I was just too excited to give it much thought.

I took over developing the curriculum, the teaching style, and the publicity. I made arrangements with most of the magazines for which I wrote to exchange my articles for advertisements. Although I took a big hit in my writing income, I was just so excited about Golden Touch Craps that I really didn't think twice. I got the word out to players that a dazzling new company had been formed to teach players how to beat craps by learning a controlled throw—the Golden Touch throw.

I would also incorporate all of the Captain's ideas into the curriculum. There would be a high level of competency needed to teach in our school. We'd have categories of teachers from interns to assistant instructors to full instructors to instructors/partners. Everyone would be paid for their time and effort. We'd hold the classes in Vegas, Atlantic City, Tunica (after we fled Mississippi we went to Memphis), and Chicago.

It worked.

In the 10 years between 2003 through 2012, Golden Touch Craps was the premier dice-control school in the country. At our height during those years we had 22 teachers, and our classes in Vegas and Atlantic City would have upward of 60 students per weekend with somewhat fewer in Tunica and Chicago. To steal a phrase, we were rolling.

And it was during that time with the growth of Golden Touch Craps that the Captain did the almost-impossible. In 2004 he rolled 100 numbers and in 2005 he rolled 147 numbers before sevening out. I had the great good fortune to be on the 147-number roll. I've written about that roll before, but it is always worth reading because it gives you a privileged insight into the greatest craps player of all time...and the single-greatest session I ever experienced in a casino.

CHAPTER 7

The Captain's Greatest Roll

[I wrote this immediately after that trip to Atlantic City. I have left it basically the same as when I wrote it, though I have edited it somewhat. Since this was written, the Captain and the Arm have passed away.]

July 2005: the Captain of Craps called me at 11:00 last night, which is late for him and late for me, and he wanted to know if I wanted to make a trip with him to Atlantic City very early this morning. It would just be a single day—to play, to talk, to walk, to reminisce. Of course I said "Of course!" I never miss an opportunity to meet with the Captain, even if it means a day trip that takes three and a half hours. From Long Island to Atlantic City is a long haul.

I had just gotten back from a graduation party for my niece, Melanie, and I was tired. I had not practiced my dice throw since May when we did the Frank Scoblete Gamblers Jamboree in Canada. I'd been working on a new book and I had not planned to play craps until I got to Vegas in mid-September—so, sad but true, I got lazy. I decided that a late night's practice would probably not help me much, since I had to get up at 4:00 this morning. Better to go to sleep and dream that I wouldn't embarrass myself in Atlantic City.

By now just about all savvy craps players know who the Captain is. Aside from being the greatest craps player of all time, the Captain is my mentor—the man who taught me more about proper gambling in practice and in theory than I have learned from all the books and articles I have ever read.

I have met most of the greats of casino gambling, but the Captain stands alone. I am reminded of Hemingway's *The Old Man and the Sea*, when the young boy, Manolin, is expressing fear about the Yankees not being able to win the pennant. The old man, Santiago, states, "There are many good ballplayers and some great ones, but there is only DiMaggio."

DiMaggio wasn't just a great ballplayer; he was *the* ballplayer.

There is only the Captain.

The Captain is the true master of the game of craps. Long before I wrote my first words about how to beat the modern casino craps game with dice control in the late 1980s, the Captain and the Arm had been beating Atlantic City casinos steadily since the late 1970s.

I was happy that the Captain shared his secrets with me, that he allowed me to write about how to succeed at craps, and I was privileged to see him and the Arm shoot countless times over those years. The Captain is a great shooter, but the Arm was the greatest I ever saw, and I have seen the great ones.

The Captain, now past the 80-year-old mark and heading, I hope, for 90, has lost just about all of his high-rolling friends, his Crew. Jimmy P., Little Vic, Russ the Breather, Frank the fearful, the Doctor, and the Judge are all now playing craps in the heavenly kingdom where dice control isn't necessary since all rolls are perfect but still thrilling.

One remaining Crew member of the Captain's, now known as Satch, is an instructor in the Golden Touch Craps dice control seminars (he has since retired). He was the youngest of the Captain's Crew before most of the members went to the great game in the sky. (The Captain died in 2010.)

Thankfully, I did not have to drive down to Atlantic City. The Captain had the limo pick me up at 4:30 AM, and then we picked him up in New York City. Usually the Captain drives down to Atlantic City with his wife, or he takes the high-roller bus where all the "old guys" (as he calls them) play poker on their way to the shore. What I find fascinating about him is the fact that despite his staggering wins at the game and his success in his businesses, the Captain doesn't have that high-roller "gimme, gimme" attitude. He is a humble man. Greatness and humility are a rare combination in the gambling world, where the biggest morons and the lightest-weight minds often have heavy egos. That bloat can also be found in some Internet dice gurus willing and able to mislead the gullible into gambling traps and poor techniques in betting.

In the limo on the way to Atlantic City, the Captain said, "I'm sad, Frank. The Arm is very sick, and it doesn't look as if she is going to improve. Her husband thinks she is preparing to go." [The Arm passed away on June 6, 2007.]

The Arm is also in her mid-80s, but the years have not been kind to her. I saw her about a year ago, and she was shrunken, bent, and a little distant, as if she were having a hard time holding herself together. The Captain can walk eight miles up and down the Boardwalk in Atlantic City, but the Arm now can barely walk across a room. I don't know if it was my father or the Captain who first said to me, "Getting old is a slow process, but one day, you fall off a cliff." The Arm seems to have fallen off the cliff.

"What does she have?" I asked him.

"Age," he said.

The Captain had a wistful look. I changed the subject.

"You've been keeping track of your rolls?" I asked.

"Most times, now, I use chips like you said."

In order to tell how many numbers you've hit during a roll at the craps table, the easiest way is to put chips aside as you roll. You use $1 chips (usually white) for one through four, then a red chip for a five, add white for six through nine, then two reds for 10, and so on. When the roll gets to 25, use a green chip. It is an easy way to count your rolls without actually having to count your rolls. If you are playing with a friend at the table, the friend can do the counting. Seeing one or two or three green chips set aside is exhilarating. When I had my 89-roll hand, seeing three green chips almost took my breath away. I was hoping to get to a black chip, but as the dice gods would have it, I sevened out before that happened. Dom "the Dominator" scolded me: "You couldn't get to a hundred?"

"In the old days," smiled the Captain, "the fun of going to Atlantic City was that I played with a whole bunch of friends and I also was able to win money. I had friendship and a challenge all wrapped together. It went very fast. The time, it flew."

It does fly. I am at the stage in my own life where I see that time has flown. My sons—my *little* boys whose small hands I could consume in mine—are now men. I see pictures of them when they were little and I can still feel the *feel* of them from those times. I can almost go back in time, almost but not quite. I am a grandfather, too, of John and Danielle.

Time.

"You know," said the Captain, "I live more in the past now than in the present. I watch the old movies. Cary Grant, Ingrid Bergman, Ronald Colman. I don't even know today's stars. My generation merely lingers now. We fought Hitler, the Japanese, and Mussolini. We defeated the great enemies of mankind and now we just linger."

In Atlantic City the time was only 8:30 AM when we checked in, but the casino had a suite ready for us. One of the Captain's good friends is a high-ranker at one of the biggest casinos, and he made sure that the two-story suite was ready for the Captain's day at the Queen of Resorts.

"Let's put our stuff in the room," said the Captain. Room? It was six rooms! But to the Captain it was a room.

"Then let's take a little walk," said the Captain.

"Fine," I said.

We put our bags in the suite. The Captain took one of the bedrooms; I took the other. Mine was actually the better bedroom, as I had my own Jacuzzi in it.

We took a walk along the Boardwalk. The Captain and his departed Crew once owned this town. They were $1,000 and better bettors. And that was way back when. "Atlantic City is actually nicer now than it was in 1978 when it was really a ghetto," said the Captain. "The buildings in those days were falling down all over town. It isn't Vegas, but Vegas isn't Vegas anymore either."

We walked for about an hour and a half, and the Captain recommended that we go back to the room, rest a little, and then hit the tables. The Captain is a firm believer that you have to play rested and that you must never allow the casino's 24-hour-a-day rhythm to overwhelm you. I learned that lesson the hard way when my wife, the Beautiful AP, and I lost all our gambling money on one trip because I had played stupidly—

overbetting my bankroll and going on tilt. The Captain taught me then how to keep my normal human rhythm in the face of the 24-hour *bam, bam, bam* of the casino.

In the suite, the Captain went to his room. I lay down on the bed in my room. The Captain did seem wistful. His perkiness was not at the usual level. The Arm's deterioration must be weighing heavily on him. He and the Arm had won millions together. They had been on the crest of the first wave of the dice-control revolution, a revolution he created.

It's funny, but I never think of people dying. I never think of myself as dying. I just counted up the people I have been close to who have died. I number 20, and that includes my grandparents. [Note: that list has grown much longer since 2005, when I first wrote this.]

The Captain went to a high school class reunion a few years ago, and there were only five of his classmates left alive.

Now we just linger.

The Captain was a part of the Greatest Generation. He was in the Army Air Corps in World War II. He was shot down behind enemy lines in the Philippines and had to survive for more than a week hiding from the Japanese soldiers who scoured the jungle looking for Americans who had been shot down; he caught malaria to boot. He saw the Enola Gay land at his army air base. He served in Japan during the occupation. He's a fascinating guy. I think of him as a hero.

Now we just linger.

An hour or so later, we were heading for the casino floor. The Captain said he had actually fallen asleep. I must have, too because the time went by in the blink of an eye.

Time.

The casino was crowded, but we found our two spots open at a 12-foot table. I was on stick left one, and the Captain was on stick right one. Something else I noticed: the Captain has gotten shorter in the past few years. He used to be my height, now he is an inch or two shorter. He is in good shape, but time has also diminished him somewhat.

The pit boss came over and said hello to him. The Captain took out a marker. The Captain's betting in the past few years has decreased somewhat from his glory days of the 1980s. I took a marker as well.

In Atlantic City, it usually takes a while for the marker to arrive. Unlike Vegas, you don't get your chips until you actually sign the marker. So we had to wait. While we were waiting, two hosts came over to say hello to the Captain. They knew him as the Captain, too. What interests me all the more is why haven't the people who know who the Captain is told others? These two hosts, longtime Atlantic City people, knew him. Three of the casinos' biggest honchos in Atlantic City know who he is, too. Indeed, he has some good friends in Atlantic City who work for the casinos. They were kids when he started his craps career, some of them craps dealers, and now they run places. And they still come to him for advice.

Time.

We waited for our markers as the hosts departed.

No big deal. The dice were two people to my left with a squirrelly fellow. He established the 5 as his point, rolled a couple of times, and sevened out. I wanted the markers to come to us just as the Captain was about to roll. Then we wouldn't be wasting any money on random rollers.

When the shooter just before the Captain got the dice, our markers came. "Sorry this took so long," said the floor woman. "We're a little understaffed today."

The Captain signed for his marker. I signed for my marker.

We were playing at a 5X odds table with a $10 minimum bet. Both of us 5-Counted the shooter next to the Captain. He made it to the 4-count and sevened out.

Then it was the Captain's turn. I placed a $15 Pass Line bet, and the Captain placed a $30 Pass Line bet. The Captain rolled a 6 as his point. The Captain sets the 3V set at all times, even though he keeps his bets off during the Come-Out roll, which is perhaps not the optimal way to play when setting dice that way. However, the Captain thinks of the Come-Out roll as a rest period when he shoots.

I studied him a few times during his rolls today, and indeed on the Come-Out roll, his intensity is not as great. He is *resting.*

He put up a $300 bet on the 8 and he bought the 4 for $55, paying a $2 vig. He put $250 in odds behind his Pass Line bet of 6. His betting today was more than I had seen him bet in the past few years, and I wondered why he had upped his action. I had $125 in odds behind the point and I had $150 on the 8. I also bought the 4 for $55, as I would mirror the Captain's betting. If you are going to imitate, you might as well imitate the best.

By betting $15 or $30 on the Pass/Come at a 5X odds game, the casino we were playing in allows you to "push the house" up on the odds. So you can take $75 for $15 on the Pass/Come or $150 for $30 on the Pass/Come on the 4 and 10, $100 or $200 on the 5 and 9, and $125 or $250 on the 6 and 8. The Captain is a master at pushing the house, as he was the first player to get Atlantic City casinos to allow you to buy the 4 or 10 for $35, paying just a $1 vig. He even pushed some casinos to allow you to buy the 4 or 10 for $39 for the same $1 vig. [I doubt the AC casinos allow that anymore.]

The Captain rolled a 5, a 10, and then sevened out.

It was my turn.

I took the dice and set for the 7. I hit 11, then two 7s in a row, then a 5. That was my point. I took $100 in odds on my point of 5. I placed $150 on the 6 and $150 on the 8. I also used the 3V set. I rolled a 6; was paid $175 for it. I rolled another 6. Then I rolled a third 6. Then I sevened out.

My dice were looking good, and I figured I would have a good roll next turn. Little did I know there would be no next turn.

We 5-Counted all the shooters. Four of the eight at the table made it through the 5-Count and we put up $10 Come bets on them with double odds. We lost money on them, as they all sevened out soon after we had some bets up.

A lot of players don't realize that the 5-Count really does not reduce the house edge on random rollers. It just reduces by 57 percent what you bet on random rollers, thus saving you money. However, as Dr. Don Catlin showed in a massive study of 200 million simulated shooters, if you are at a table with controlled shooters, even if you don't know they are controlled shooters, the 5-Count gets you on them 11 percent more often than a normal player will be. That's where you can make some money.

Smart dice controllers use the 5-Count to reduce the number of rolls we bet on, and on random rollers we also bet much lower than we will on controlled shooters. The 5-Count is a wonderful tool in a controlled shooter's arsenal if he has to play at the same table with random rollers, which most of us do. As you can see, my total risk on the random rollers who made it through the 5-Count today was a mere $30. Odds don't count, since they are a break-even bet with the house.

The Captain got the dice again. The Captain is a calm shooter, second in calmness to the Arm herself. Nothing gets to him. I have rarely seen him lose his temper at the tables. He doesn't practice Zen, but he is very Zen-like.

The Captain set the 3V and rolled. It was 1:15 in the afternoon. He hit a 2. Then he hit a 3. Then he established his point, a 4. We were going up the number scale! The Captain put up $300 on the 6 and 8 and $150 in odds behind his point. I had $150 placed on my 6 and 8 and $75 behind my Pass Line bet.

The Captain rolled a few numbers we weren't on and then hit a 6. Then he hit the 8. Then the 6 again. Then he made the 4. The table gave polite applause. The Captain added a $55 buy of the 10 to his bets. I did the same.

In Atlantic City, if you want to buy the 4 or 10 for $55, you pay a $2 vig, but if you put up both numbers at the same time, you must pay $5 in total. So the way to bet to save that $1 is to make a bet of one number, then after a roll, bet the other number. Those dollars add up. Unfortunately in Atlantic City, you must pay the vig up front on buy bets, which means you pay that vig on winning and losing rolls. In many casinos around the country, the vig is only extracted on the buy bets after you win but not on any losses. That cuts the house edge down considerably.

The Captain established his point, a 6. We both bought the 4 for $55. We took our 6 Place bets down and took odds behind the Pass Line point of 6.

So we were up on four numbers—the 4, 6, 8, and 10. And the Captain rolled. He was focused because he could seven out. And he started hitting numbers. At a certain point, he made his point of 6. He then made several more points and many numbers.

The Captain was hot. Other players joined the table.

At the 25-minute mark, the Captain had rolled 32 numbers—one green chip, one red chip, and two white chips—and he was on another Come-Out roll. Then he did something that was unusual for him.

"Frank," he said. "Can you get me a chair?"

Since the mid-1980s when I first started to play craps with the Captain, I don't think I ever saw him sit down. I was startled. But I quickly went over to an empty blackjack table and grabbed a chair. I set it behind the Captain, and he sat on it right away.

The young floor woman came over and said, "I'm sorry, you can't sit there." Just as quickly, the pit boss came over and touched the floor woman on the arm and said, "He's the exception. Let him sit if he wants to." The floor woman looked confused but obeyed her boss. The two of them walked away, and when they were on the other end of the pit, they started to talk. I have no idea what they were saying, but they both kept shooting glances our way.

On the Come-Out roll, all our bets, except our Pass Line bets obviously, were off. The Captain gently lofted the dice down the table. He rolled a 7 and then established a point of 6.

From there on in, it started to get blurry. The Captain rolled numbers and points. I was counting the rolls, putting white chips down, then reds, and then a second green. We were at 45 minutes and the Captain had rolled 54 numbers. On his Come-Out rolls and when the dealers were paying off the bets, he would sit in the chair and just stare straight ahead. He was locked into some kind of meditative state. I never said a word to him. I had bets on all the numbers and had pressed them once, twice, or three times depending on how often they had hit.

The third green chip went down. The Captain was at 75 numbers. I looked over at him. He did not look at all tired, just reflective, sedate, as if he were in another world. In January 2004 the Captain had rolled 100 numbers—an amazing roll. I wondered if he could reach that plateau again. One hundred numbers is a magic roll.

76 numbers.

The Captain has a very easy throw. There is no strain in him when he shoots. He is focused. He is in total control of himself.

77 numbers.

He is in total control of the dice. His roll is the model for a controlled throw.

78 numbers.

The Captain made another point. I had three green chips and three white chips for the 78 numbers. The cocktail waitress came over, and the Captain ordered an orange juice, no ice, and I ordered bottled water. "When you come over with the drinks," I said to the waitress, "bring me his drink if he's still rolling, okay?" I put $5 on her tray. "Okay," she said.

Kenneth Frasca appeared. I squeezed over so he could get next to me. The table was packed.

"How's he doing? How did he do last roll?" Frasca asked.

"It's the same roll. He's at 78 numbers," I said.

"Oh, man!" he whispered in my ear.

"I thought we were going to walk the Boardwalk," Linda said.

"Not now," said Kenneth, who bought in. Linda did not seem pleased, but she wandered away. The Captain had no magic for her.

As the Captain shot his Come-Out roll, new chips were brought in. We had seriously damaged the casino's chip area, and new chips, both big and little denominations, were being counted on the table.

The Captain ignored it. He rolled. He established a point.

79 numbers.

Most of the other players were betting green and black chips. Somewhere around roll 45, most of the players started to press their bets. Some had become almost insanely aggressive. The table was full of players—13 players altogether, seven on my side with Frasca squeezed in, and six on the Captain's side.

80 numbers (three green chips, one red).

81 numbers (three green chips, one red, one white).

There were only a few Hardway bets, an unusual situation during a big roll. It was almost as if no one wanted to slow down the game with bets that take too long to pay off. Most of the players were good bettors—a rarity at a craps table but one that was making the game progress at a nice pace.

The Captain was in his rolling zone for sure.

82 numbers.

83 numbers.

84 numbers.

85 numbers (three greens, two reds).

The Captain is a rarity. I am not. As a writer, a teacher, a speaker, and a former actor, I crave the public performance. I want a readership, an audience. I like the spotlight on me.

86 numbers.

The Captain doesn't care about those things. He was the leader of the Crew because they made him the leader; he didn't ask for it. His nature must make other men and women want to follow him.

87 numbers.

He never asked to share in the glory or profits of the books or tapes I wrote. He never asked to be on television or radio. He never asked me to write about him. He does his thing, and he lets the world do its thing.

88 numbers.

Best-selling gaming author Henry Tamburin asked me, "How come the Captain doesn't want to go out in public and be recognized?" I told Henry the Captain is the guy everyone wants *us* to be. "You see, when we are criticized, some of it is, 'Well, if they are so good, why are they writing about it? Why aren't they just doing it?' Well, the Captain is the guy who did it and is still doing it. He doesn't crave the public attention like we do."

89 numbers.

I had hit 89 numbers. I wasn't keeping track of them, but Dominator and one of our Golden Touch students were. I had two students at the table that day.

90 numbers.

So much for 89! The Captain was getting close to the magic 100 rolls.

91 numbers.

The Captain is happy that I became successful as an advantage player and as a writer. He is happy my books have sold so well. But he is content to do what he does.

92 numbers.

He has slowed down now. His investing in real estate is over. He lives off his past investments and his once-a-week play in Atlantic City.

93 numbers.

The Captain used to play several times a week. I can recall him in those days. He was probably 65 when I first played craps with him at the tables. He was not much older then than I am now. I first played craps at the Claridge, which was a great casino for players.

94 numbers.

"Pay the line!" shouted the stickman.

It was another Come-Out roll. I remember this clearly. I put several stacks of black chips on the table to color them up. I was completely out of room in the chip rack in front of me. The Captain was sitting for all the Come-Out rolls. Kenneth Frasca kept whispering in my ear, "I can't believe I'm playing with the Captain."

"Believe it," I said.

95 numbers (no point established—he rolled an 11).

96 numbers (another 11).

I noticed that the Captain's bets were with purple and orange chips.

97 numbers (point of 4 established).

We were getting close to 100 numbers. Would he make it?

98 numbers.

99 numbers.

I looked over at the Captain. He had no idea how many numbers he had rolled, but the time was 2:45 in the afternoon. He had rolled for one and a half hours.

He set the dice carefully. He aimed. I noticed that there were several suits behind the box man. Big money was being wagered at our table, and it was the job of the suits to make sure that no mistakes were made with such big money in play. I could see another cart loaded with chips being wheeled to the table. Some players think that the suits gather on a hot game to cool it off. That is not so. They gather to make sure the money is being handled properly. With $500 and $1,000 chips in play, a small mistake can cost a lot of money—to the casino and to the players.

"This is number 100?" asked Frasca.

"Yes," I whispered.

"Oh, man," he whispered.

The Captain lofted the dice, giving them a gentle backspin. They hit the table, moved slowly to the back wall, and died, flat, dead at the base of the pyramids, having barely glanced off the back wall.

"Five! Five!" shouted the stickman. "No field five!"

That was 100 rolls. That was one black chip. That was—my God!—100 numbers for the Captain.

No one other than Frasca and I knew what a monumental moment it was, but they all knew they were on one hell of a roll.

101 numbers.

102 numbers.

103 numbers.

The new chips were brought in. One of the suits laughingly said, "This is it, guys, these are our last chips. Don't take them all from us."

104 numbers.

105 numbers.

106 numbers.

Then a bloated man at the end of the table started an argument. "I had a $5 yo bet! Where's my money?" [For some reason this always seems to happen during long rolls—one ploppy can't keep track of his bets.]

"That was the roll before this one, sir, not this one. It's a one-roll bet, sir," said the dealer.

"Call over the floor man," said the bloated one.

I took $80 in chips and threw them over to the man.

"Forget the floor man," I said.

"I, uh, I..." said the large one.

"Take the chips and let this man roll for God's sake!" I said. The dope took the chips.

"Move the dice," said the box man. "We don't want this table to cool down."

The stickman pushed the dice over to the Captain. He had been seated while the bloated one had stupidly slowed down the game. The Captain stood, set the dice, aimed, and released.

107 numbers.

That was nice of the box man to say he wanted the hot roll to continue. He would not be able to share in the massive amount of tips the Captain, several players, and I were giving the dealers on each and every roll, but he looked genuinely happy that he was watching such a great afternoon session.

108 numbers.

Several players and the Captain had reached table-maximum bets on some of the numbers.

109 numbers.

110 numbers.

111 numbers.

Which got me to thinking: Stanley Fujitake! The *record*.

112 numbers.

Fujitake held the dice for three hours and six minutes. He did this on May 18, 1989, at the California Club in downtown Las Vegas. That feat earned him the title of "the Golden Arm." A whole inventory of spectacular tales has grown up around the man who holds the record for the longest craps hand in history.

113 numbers.

Sure, others have claimed anonymously that they have seen shooters surpass that record, but only Stanley Fujitake's record is taken seriously by anyone the least interested in craps. He did his feat in front of scores of witnesses, and the time was verified by them and by the casino.

114 numbers.

Fujitake's *is* the record.

115 numbers.

How incredible is *the* record? Take Joe DiMaggio's 56-game hitting streak, Wilt Chamberlain's 100 points in an NBA game, Muhammad Ali's upset of big George Foreman, Secretariat's winning of the Triple Crown in stunning blowouts, and wrap them all up in a knot. Fujitake's record is more spectacular.

116 numbers.

Three hours and six minutes! That might have been 200 rolls of the dice.

117 numbers.

Fujitake. *The record*.

118 numbers.

I looked over at the Captain just as he looked at me. A smile played on his lips. "I feel good," he said to me.

119 numbers.

Of course, Fujitake was a random roller and not a controlled shooter like the Captain. His great feat is the great feat of luck, while the Captain's great feats—and he has had many great feats—are the result of skill. While the Captain was rolling, I had no idea that he had actually beaten the number of rolls Fujitake had in 1989—which was 118 rolls before he sevened out.

120 numbers.

Each stickman at the casino was courteous and moved back as the Captain threw. That gave him a clear vision down the table. The player at the end of the table never put his Pass Line bet down where the Captain landed his dice. That was very smart of him. The table was behaving as you would want the table to behave to help create and perpetuate the monster roll.

121 numbers.

There were maybe 30 people standing around the outside of the table watching. Frasca kept whispering "Holy shit" in my ear. That was his day's religious mantra. An aggressive-looking guy with slicked-back black hair was about to try to squeeze in next to the Captain as the Captain was lifting the dice. The guy next to the Captain pushed the aggressive one and said, "Don't even think about it." The guy next to the Captain sounded and looked like a "wise guy," and the aggressive guy slunk away, his girlfriend hanging on his arm, saying, "Why can't we get in and play? Why can't we get in and play?"

122 numbers.

123 numbers.

124 numbers.

For almost 20 years, the Captain and his Crew owned Atlantic City. High rollers, fun lovers, 22 of the most interesting men and women one could ever meet. Strangely only one of them ever really understood that the Captain was winning all those years. His name was Jimmy P. In the early 1990s, Jimmy P., the Captain, and the Arm hit TropWorld for millions in wins and comps.

125 numbers (one black chip and one green chip).

126 numbers.

This roll was the longest roll I have ever seen. Even the Arm never had a roll that was this long. At 126 numbers the Captain was approaching two hours of rolling. I remember one of the hosts, who worked at the Claridge, saying in 1992, "The Captain is killing us." Even the former president of the Claridge wrote about the Captain and his Crew in a book.

Yet no one has revealed the Captain's name. Interesting.

127 numbers.

The length of a hand kept in time is not as descriptive as the length of a hand kept in number of rolls.

128 numbers.

129 numbers.

This roll was in the mega numbers.

130 numbers (one black, one green, one red).

We were at the two-hour mark. Two hours of rolling the dice. The Captain would roll, sit in the chair as the payouts were made, then stand when the stickman moved the dice to him. He constantly set the 3V. He was a machine. No, in fact, more accurately, he was in a gambling ballet. His every move was smooth and beautiful.

131 numbers (one black, one green, one red, one white).

How much luck did the Captain need to create this monster of monsters hand? He had rolled some sevens on the Come-Out. The 3V is not a set for rolling sevens, and those sevens were therefore mistakes. That was good luck for him and for the rest of us at the table. He rolled at least four sevens on the Come-Out that I remember. Had any one of those sevens been during the Point Cycle of the game, he would have sevened out.

132 numbers.

133 numbers.

Good luck? I have had great luck in my life. I have wonderful parents, a wonderful wife, wonderful children, wonderful grandchildren, a wonderful writing career, and I have a friend, too.

134 numbers.

135 numbers.

I also have some people who—for God knows what reason—hate me and hate my writing. The late Walter Thomason, the gambling writer, used to tease me by sending me Internet posts by people who were attacking me. One famous, though highly pompous, gambling authority whose books are poor sellers once said he would kill himself if he woke up and found out he had turned into me. As I have become better-known, the attacks have become even fiercer. As the Beautiful AP says, "No one kicks a dead dog."

136 numbers.

137 numbers.

138 numbers.

139 numbers.

The Captain was in a rhythm.

140 numbers.

Bing!

141 numbers.

Bing!

142 numbers.

Bing!

143 numbers.

Bing!

144 numbers.

Bing!

We were at 144 numbers! *There is only the Captain.* The very Captain who was now banging away at two hours and 15 minutes in a roll that will become legendary.

145 numbers.

Bing!

146 numbers.

Bing!

I looked over at the Captain, who was as calm then as he was when he first got the dice. *There is only the Captain. There is only the Captain. There is only the Captain.* Could he go to 200 numbers? Could he go for more than three hours and six minutes?

147 numbers.

Bing!

The Captain is the greatest craps player who ever lived. He is more than a master, more than a mentor. *There is only the Captain.* He was at two hours and 18 minutes and had hit 147 numbers.

Now we just linger. Time. There is only the Captain.

He lofted the dice into the air. One die lagged a little, and when they came down that lagging die just stopped dead. The other die went to the back wall, hit, and gently rolled over.

There was a pause. Time stopped.

"Call it," said the box man.

"Seven," said the stickman, "Seven out! Line away, pay the Don'ts."

There were no don'ts. There was only silence.

Now we just linger.

Time.

There is only the Captain.

"That was a great roll," I said.

"Oh, God," Frasca said.

"Great roll, sir," the box man said.

"Great roll, Captain," the pit boss said.

"Great roll, Captain," one of the other suits said.

And then the applause started. The players and the spectators started to clap. It became thunderous. Even the box man clapped. The stickman, with the stick under his arm, clapped too. Then people cheered, and some yelled, "Bravo! Bravo!"

That roll lasted two hours, 18 minutes. It was 147 numbers, with the 148th number being the seven-out.

The guy next to Frasca said to us, "They called him the Captain? Is that *the* Captain? *The* Captain?"

"Yes," said Frasca, as if he had known the Captain for a long, long time.

"You know him?" the man asked.

"Yes," I said. "We know him." I included Frasca in the "we." Frasca smiled.

"My God, I can't believe it," the man said. "I saw the Captain himself. Oh, my God," he said as he put down his stacks of black, purple, and orange chips.

"Yes, you did," I said. "That is the man himself."

"Amazing," Frasca said. "One hundred forty-seven numbers."

"One hundred forty-seven numbers," said the man. "God."

No one can take that achievement away from the Captain—147 numbers; two hours, 18 minutes of rolling. The man who first realized that rhythmic rolling, a synonym for dice control, was the way to beat the house in 1978, the man who figured out how to win money playing craps, had just completed a Babe Ruthian roll. It's been said that Ruth once hit a baseball 626 feet, the longest home run in history. And this was the longest craps roll in history—147 numbers.

There is only the Captain.

We colored up our mound of chips, and security escorted us to the cage.

"We'll have a late lunch in the suite and then we'll head back home," said the Captain.

"You rolled 147 numbers, Captain," I said.

"It was a great roll," he said.

Yes, it was.

There is only the Captain.

[On May 23, 2009, random roller Patricia DeMauro rolled 154 numbers, breaking the Captain's world record. Her achievement is completely chronicled in my book *Casino Craps: Shoot to Win!*]

PART II:
Gambling Strategies That Work, Gambling Strategies That Don't Work

CHAPTER 1

Proof Dice Control Works

Dice control is now the "in" thing among many craps players—it is talked about, written about, argued over. Some say it can be done; others say that it is a fool's errand. The fact is that dice control can be tested, has been tested, and those tests have shown that some players not only can get an edge over the house practicing at home, but they can exploit that edge in real casinos.

It is not difficult to determine whether a shooter is changing the game to favor the player; the SRR (meaning seven-to-rolls ratio) and the software program SmartCraps, which measures on-axis control, are the two main tests. The normal random SRR is one 7 per six rolls on average (1-6), and anyone who can get around 1-6.2 or 1-6.3 has a slight edge over some bets. As the SRR gets stronger (1-6.7; 1-6.8), the advantage over the house increases. Naturally, you need a significant number of practice rolls—at least 10,000—in order to establish that the edge belongs to the shooter and is not just the variance of a random game.

SmartCraps measures on-axis performance, a more advanced skill. Unlike the SRR, which analyzes rolls based on avoidance of the 7, SmartCraps looks to see if the shooter can go after select numbers; for example, the Captain's 3V set tries to hit a disproportionate number of 6s and 8s. In such a case, the SRR is probably irrelevant. One can win money on extremely short rolls by hitting a repeating number. I have been using the 3V for my entire career. On rare—really rare—occasions I will use the Hardway set, which shows Hardway numbers all around.

Hardway Sets:

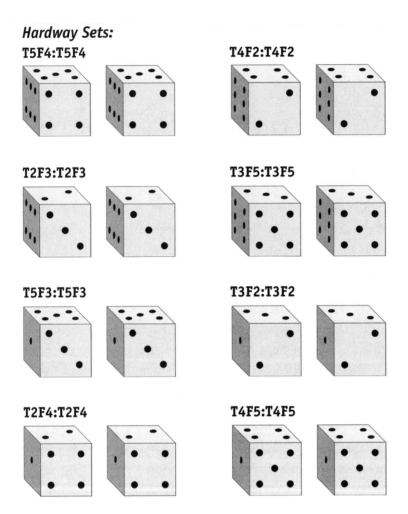

T5F4:T5F4

T4F2:T4F2

T2F3:T2F3

T3F5:T3F5

T5F3:T5F3

T3F2:T3F2

T2F4:T2F4

T4F5:T4F5

Although I am like all dice controllers and love epic rolls, I realize that such epic rolls are not the norm; winning requires hitting those repeating numbers, and being able to set the dice a certain way in order to hit specific numbers is the premium skill.

Plenty of dice controllers have passed these tests; just about anyone who works at it can have a winning SRR. Being a good on-axis shooter is harder. SmartCraps shows you clearly where you are in the on-axis realm. Sadly, too many would-be dice controllers think they have on-axis skill, and you see these players constantly changing their sets thinking it is helping them win. It isn't. You must pass the SmartCraps tests to see what your skill level is and what dice set you should use.

Dice-control skill is real even if controversy surrounds it. Generally those who are critical of dice control remind me of most movie critics—they have never made a movie but are expert at pontificating. Dice control is real even if most critics have never tried it or, if they have, couldn't master it. In addition, many players who set the dice and have no skill are confused with real dice controllers. Setting the dice is just setting the dice.

A controlled shooter must do the following:

- Set the dice in a proper set (usually the Hardway set for most shooters).
- Properly pick up the dice. The best way is to have three fingers straight across the front of the dice and the thumb equidistant in back of the dice.
- The dice must be aimed at the landing zone—maybe six to 10 inches from the back wall.
- A gentle backswing and then a forward swing with the dice released at the end of the forward swing. The release will happen naturally.
- The dice are released creating a 45-degree angle (can be less for some shooters and for some types of layout material that cause the dice to bounce a lot).
- The dice should be close together in the air—the hope is to have them look almost as if they are glued.
- There should be a backspin that causes the dice to slow down when they hit the layout surface.
- The dice should hit the back wall softly and do the same basic movements as they come to rest.

How many players can actually be successful at this activity? Just about anyone who works at it. Gaining a controlled throw takes dedication, discipline, and practice—almost daily practice. Just as Major League Baseball players take batting practice before almost every game, the skilled dice controller must practice regularly. The saying "You don't practice, you won't get it" aptly applies to dice control.

So why aren't the casinos crumbling under the aggregate losses they must be suffering because of such skilled players? Sadly, the overwhelming majority of dice controllers bet improperly on their rolls. In short, they make bets where their control can't overcome the house edge. They are losers, just like pitchers with blazing fastballs who can't throw strikes.

CHAPTER 2

Proper Betting
for Dice Controllers

The hardest thing that novice dice controllers must accomplish is the reining in of their desire to get into the *riot* that is a craps game. As soon as they see other players winning on those long-shot, big-payout Crazy Crapper bets, the desire to get into the action becomes almost overwhelming. When they see certain numbers hit in streaks, they think they should Place-bet those numbers. Some still buy into hedging systems.

Getting "into the action" when translated by the casinos means, "That player over there throws his money away. We want him! He's an *action* player." The word *action* here means *stupid* to the casinos, which in turn court action players.

The betting pitfalls are legion; so many novice dice controllers fall flat on their faces by not being able to control *themselves*. If they can't control themselves they are no longer dice controllers, just failures.

Let me add one more thing that is just as important: if you bet on all the other shooters at the same levels that you bet on yourself, most likely you will end up deep in the red. You have to limit your betting on random rollers; they destroy your bankroll. The best way to limit your betting on them is *never* to bet on them. Figure out the time of day when the tables are empty and play then.

If you must play with random rollers at your table, I urge you to use the Captain's 5-Count, which I will go over soon. Again, you'll reduce

63

the number of random rolls by about 57 percent. If a random roller gets through the 5-Count, only make one Come (or Pass Line) bet on such a shooter (take odds if you have a decent bankroll, since this is a normal way to play). Make your bet on a random roller as low as you can go.

So here are the best bets:

- Pass Line = house edge 1.41 percent (expectation is to lose 14¢ per $10 Pass Line bet)
- Maximum odds on Pass Line that you can afford (see chart for how odds reduce the house edge)
- Come bets = house edge of 1.41 percent (expectation is to lose 14¢ per $10 Pass Line bet)
- Maximum odds on Come bets you can afford (see chart for how odds reduce the house edge)
- Placing of the 6 and/or 8 (1.52 percent house edge; expectation is to lose 18¢ per $12 wagered)
- Buying of the 4 and/or 10 if the commission is taken on wins only—house edge 1.3 percent on buy of $25 for $1 commission with buy of $50 for $2 in commissions

The Odds is a great bet with no house edge, even though you have to make the Pass Line and/or Come bets, which do have a house edge, in order to bet the Odds. The Odds will reduce the house edge on the *total amount* wagered with one catch; you will always lose 1.41 percent of your Pass Line and/or Come bets no matter how much you put in Odds. However, if you intend to bet $30 on the 6 and/or 8 as a Place bettor, instead of doing that you are always better putting the least on the Pass Line or Come and the most in Odds. In such a case, you are really smashing down the overall house edge on that $30.

Watch: the house edge on a Place bet of the 6 or 8 is 1.52 percent. If you bet $30 on either of those numbers, your expectation is to lose 46¢. If you play a 5X odds game with a $10 Pass Line or Come bet with $50 in odds, your expectation is to lose 14¢. That is a big difference!

Number of Odds	House Edge	Losses & Added Information
1X	0.85 percent	85¢ per $100 wagered
2X	0.61 percent	61¢ per $100 wagered
Full 2X Odds	0.57 percent	Allows 2.5X Odds on 6 and 8 57¢ per $100 wagered
3X	0.47 percent	47¢ per $100 wagered
3X—4X—5X	0.37 percent	3X on 4/10; 4X on 5/9; 5X on 6/8 37¢ per $100 wagered
5X	0.33 percent	33¢ per $100 wagered
10X	0.18 percent	18¢ per $100 wagered
20X	0.10 percent	10¢ per $100 wagered
100X	0.02 percent	2¢ per $100 wagered

I caution everyone reading this book that if you want to be a winning dice controller you must bet perfectly. That's it. There is no argument otherwise. If you have an excellent on-axis performance, then SmartCraps will tell you what set(s) you should use and what type of edge you have. My SmartCraps results indicated that I should continue to use the 3V set to get my highest edge.

Don't Betting
The Don't Pass

Now we go to the Darkside of craps, which the Don't players inhabit. While 95 percent of the craps players are making their Pass Line bet, the Darkside/Don't player puts up his Don't Pass bet. On the Come-Out roll, this bet will lose on the 7 and 11 but win on the 2 and 3. The 12 is a push (bar/tie), except in some casinos that use the 2 as the bar/tie instead of the 12. Although the Darkside player bucks big odds on the initial placement of the bet (he faces an 8-to-3 house advantage), once the point is established he has a decided edge over every number.

Still, the Don't Pass bet is only marginally better than the Pass Line bet as the casino wins 976 decisions; the player wins 949 decisions, with ties making up 55 decisions. The house edge, if you count ties, is 1.36 percent; if you don't count ties it is 1.40 percent. Thus, for a $10

Don't Pass wager, your expectation is to lose 13.6¢ or 14¢. The difference between those two figures is just how you decide to do the math, whether you count the ties or not.

Laying the Odds on the Darkside

The Darkside/Don't bettor can also take advantage of the Odds bet, only this time he *lays* the Odds since he has the better of the game once a point or number is established. In short, he lays the long money to the casinos' short money. Again, the Odds bet can only be made once a point is established.

Here are the Odds you can lay on the various point numbers:

1. If you have a 4 or 10 with a $10 Don't Pass bet, you can lay $40 in odds to win $20.
2. If you have a 5 or 9 with a $10 Don't Pass bet, you can lay $30 to win $20.
3. If you have a 6 or 8 with a $10 Don't Pass bet, you can lay $24 to win $20.

The Odds on the Darkside is how much you want to win, which in the above case is $20, double your $10 Pass Line bet.

The Don't Come

The Don't Come bet, like the Come bet, can only be made after the shooter's point is established. It functions just like a Don't Pass bet, winning on the 2 and 3, losing on the 7 and 11, and pushing (tying) on the 12 (or 2 at some casinos). Once up on a number, a 7 will win the bet; the hitting of the number will lose the bet. As with the Don't Pass, you can lay Odds on the Don't Come as well. The house edge on the Don't Come bet is 1.36 percent (or 1.40 percent, depending on how you count ties), which means you will lose $1.36 or $1.40 for every $100 you bet. This is a good bet.

Don't Pass and Don't Come bets can be taken down if you desire to do so. Why? Because the house edge on the Darkside bets comes on the first placement of the bet, but the game shifts heavily in favor of the Darksider once the bet is up on a number.

Now, with the knowledge of the Pass Line, Don't Pass, Come, and Don't Come bets, along with taking or laying Odds, you can play the strongest craps game against the casinos. The house edge is small; your chances of winning will be far greater than just about all the other craps players who bet foolishly. The only way to play a stronger game is to learn how to control the dice.

Odds on the Darkside

Number of Odds	House Edge	Losses & Added Information
1X	0.68 percent	68¢ per $100 wagered
2X	0.46 percent	46¢ per $100 wagered
Full 2X Odds	0.43 percent	43¢ per $100 wagered
3X	0.34 percent	34¢ per $100 wagered
3X—4X—5X	0.27 percent	27¢ per $100 wagered
5X	0.23 percent	23¢ per $100 wagered
10X	0.12 percent	12¢ per $100 wagered
20X	0.07 percent	7¢ per $100 wagered
100X	0.01 percent	1¢ per $100 wagered

CHAPTER 3

The Captain's 5-Count

How do you position yourself to take advantage of hot rolls without losing a fortune betting on every single shooter and every single roll of the dice? How do you get the same amount or more in comps with less risk? The Captain developed a method called the 5-Count that took both these questions into consideration.

When the Captain was discovering his great 5-Count, he knew he had three imperatives:

1. Reduce the numbers of random rolls you bet on to save money
2. Increase likelihood that the shooters you do bet on will win you money
3. Increase your comps based on *body time* as opposed to *risk time*

The 5-Count accomplishes all three of the Captain's imperatives based on Dr. Donald Catlin's study.

1. It eliminates almost 57 percent of the random rolls. You will only be betting on about 43 percent of the random rolls.
2. It gets you on the controlled shooters (the Captain called such players "rhythmic rollers") at a higher frequency than bet-all players. If there is a controlled shooter at the table, you will be on him with the 5-Count 11 percent more often than bet-all players.
3. It usually increases comp value because of body time. You are usually given credit for 100 percent of the time you are at the table, but you are only risking your money 43 percent of the time.

The 5-Count also makes you look just like all those players who wait for some qualifying event to enter the game.

So what is the 5-Count? It is the method we use to decide which shooters to bet on. It starts with a point number on the Come-Out roll (4, 5, 6, 8, 9, or 10) and ends with a point/box number. Throws between rolls No. 1 and No. 5 can be any number, except if the shooter sevens out. Let's take a look at the various scenarios:

Example One: The Basics

Shooter's Roll #	Number Rolled	Count	Bet
1	7	0-count	0
2	*4	1-count	0
3	11	2-count	0
4	6	3-count	0
5	3	4-count	0
6	*8	5-count	Betting begins

This is the bare-bones 5-Count. The shooter is on the Come-Out roll and rolls a 7, which is a winner but is not the start of the 5-Count because it isn't a point number. [Remember that point numbers are also called box numbers.] His second roll is a 4. The 4 is a point/box number and is also his point. Then he rolls an 11, the 2-count, then a 6, the 3-count, then a 3, the 4-count, and then an 8, another point/box number, which completes the 5-Count.

Example Two: The Holding Pattern

Shooter's Roll #	Number rolled	Count	Bet
1	11	0-count	0
2	7	0-count	0
3	*6	1-count	0
4	5	2-count	0
5	9	3-count	0

6	11	4-count	0
7	3	4-count and holding	0
8	2	4-count and holding	0
9	*10	5-count	Betting begins

This example shows what happens when something other than point/box numbers are thrown after the 4-count. This causes a holding pattern. Roll six, which is an 11, establishes the 4-count, but then the shooter rolls a 3 and then a 2—both of which are not point/box numbers—which causes the 5-Count not to be completed. The 4-count is holding until a point/box number is rolled. Finally the shooter rolls a 10, a point/box number, and the 5-Count is completed.

Example Three: Shooter Makes Point

Shooter's Roll #	Number Rolled	Count	Bet
1	4	1-count	0
2	3	2-count	0
3	4 (point!)	3-count	0
4	7	4-count	0
5	11	4-count and holding	0
6	7	4-count and holding	0
7	11	4-count and holding	0
8	3	4-count and holding	0
9	*9	5-count	Betting begins

Example Three shows what happens when a shooter actually makes his point during the establishment of the 5-Count. His first roll is a 4, the 1-count; his second roll is a 3, the 2-count; and on his third roll, he hits his point, the 4, which is the 3-count. Then he is on the Come-Out again. He rolls a 7. Because it is a Come-Out roll, that 7 becomes the 4-count. Next the shooter rolls a string of non–point/box numbers (the 11, 7, 11,

3) before he finally hits another point/box number, the 9. The 5-Count is now completed.

How to Bet with the 5-Count

Now that you know how the 5-Count works, you have to decide how you are going to structure your betting. Remember that the 5-Count is the Captain's way to eliminate approximately six out of every 10 random rolls and save you a bundle of money. So how do we bet on the shooters who get through the 5-Count?

The best way is to make minimal Come bets and take the full Odds. The Odds bet is a wash between the casino and the player. If you can afford to take the Odds, do so—if you are a frequent player, the Odds bet will wind up being an even proposition between you and the casino.

If you go up on three Come bets of $10 each, your risk is 1.4 percent of $30, or 42¢.

So here is one example of how to utilize the Come bets in our most conservative way. You will put up a Come bet after the 5-Count is completed. This placement is favorable to you because there are eight ways to win on the initial placement of the Come bet (7 and 11) and only four ways to lose (2, 3, and 12). You have a 2-to-1 edge on this placement. If the shooter makes a point number, your bet goes up on the number and you take Odds.

Then you place another Come bet *if you wish*. If the shooter sevens out, you lose the bet on the number and win the bet just placed on the Come. If he rolls another box number, you go up on that number and take the Odds. If you wish to go up on a third number, you simply put out another Come bet. If the shooter has actually made his point, then you make a Pass Line bet. We will use $10 betting units. You can translate these into your betting units.

Example Four: Come Betting

Shooter's Roll #	Number Rolled	Count	Bet
1	4	1-count	0
2	11	2-count	0

3	5	3-count	0
4	6	4-count	0
5	*8	5-count	$10 Come
6	9 Come bet goes to 9		Take Odds on the 9 $10 Come
7	8 Come bet goes to 8		Take Odds on 8 Put up new Come bet if you wish to be on three numbers

You can also go up on the Come before the 5-Count is completed, doing so after the 3-count or 4-count, but only put Odds once the 5-Count is completed. The longer you wait, the better for your bankroll. However, many players don't feel comfortable waiting for the full 5-Count if they are going the Come betting route. I prefer to go up after the entire 5-Count is completed.

Example Five: Place-Betting
Place-betting with the 5-Count is very simple. When the 5-Count is completed, you Place the 6 and/or 8. If you wish to bet on the 4 and 10, or 5 and 9, make sure these are buyable with the vig paid *only on wins*.

Shooter's Roll #	Number Rolled	Count	Bet
1	7	0-count	0
2	8	1-count	0
3	12	2-count	0
4	6	3-count	0
5	4	4-count	0
6	2	4-count	0
7	*9	5-count	Place-bet lowest house edge bets

The 5-Count is the only shooter selection system that has been proven to work in a massive study of 200 million simulated shooters. Check out the report here: http://frankscoblete.com/articles/in-craps-the-5-count-is-100-proof/. It makes you look like a regular player but keeps your risk quite low.

What About Going Up on the Darkside Right Away?

Some players, trying to outthink the brilliant Captain's 5-Count, think that going up on the Don't Pass or Don't Come before the 5-Count is finished is a way to play almost every roll with little risk. Not so. The very moment you put that Don't Pass or Don't Come bet, the casino's edge is 8-to-3 over you because the casino will win eight times on the 7 and 11 and the Don't bettor can only win three times on the 2 and 3. So you are just giving the casino more cracks at your bankroll going up before the 5-Count is finished.

What the 5-Count *Isn't*

Some players mistakenly think that the Captain used the appearance percentage of the 7 as the foundation of the 5-Count. He wasn't looking at averages, or short-term results, at all. He was looking at the totality of the game to save us money over extended periods of time.

The 7 has about a 17 percent chance of occurring in a random game at any time—now and forever. There is no more likelihood of the 7 appearing on the ninth roll than on the first roll than on the 50th roll. Players who think a number is more likely to appear since it hasn't appeared are mistaken. A radical departure from betting several numbers is to go up on only one number versus a random roller. Use the 5-Count, use Pass and/or Come with the most you can afford in Odds, and leave it at that.

You can't trick yourself into believing you have an edge when you don't. Too many supposed dice controllers and dice gurus are living in a world of illusion...make that *delusion*.

But what if you don't want to be a controlled shooter? You still should make the bets I recommend in this section. They will save you a lot of money over time. A word to the wise!

CHAPTER 4

Bad Betting Choices

Meet the Charters

Sadly, some dice-control teachers are gamblers masquerading as advantage players. This section will give you examples of silly betting systems they loudly proclaim.

You see them everywhere in the casino, often with paper and pen, frantically scribbling down numbers or colors or cards. They study long lists of decisions at various games. They are the charters, often called "trackers"— players who think that in random games what has recently happened will be repeated in the near future. They faithfully believe such things will happen even in random games when everything we have learned about randomness for centuries cries out against such thinking. The greatest minds in mathematics have explained that truth about randomness.

Still gamblers keep thinking randomness holds past patterns that can be used to understand upcoming patterns. Betting such patterns wastes time and money.

The charters are looking for streaks, trends, indicators for things that can only happen in the "short run" because these players make strong distinctions between the short run and the long run. They believe that in the short run ("since anything can happen") one does not have to use the overall mathematics of the game to structure their betting; they need to hop on the streaks as they have just appeared. This is often called "charting tables" as if tables can have *predictive* hot or cold streaks.

There is a famous story about "the table" at Caesars. Seems one particular craps table lost money for several months. Finally, a truly disturbed casino manager had the custodians take the table out of the casino, break it up, and burn it.

One Internet writer coined the phrase "See a Horn, bet a Horn." He firmly believed and strongly advocated to his followers that charting/tracking random decisions worked because "Dice don't have a memory but they have a history." Obviously everything has a history. That is true. Then this sly soul went on to offer expensive courses that had tracking of random results (history) as an integral part of the curriculum, structuring your bets based on what just happened at the table in a random game.

That guru now teaches something called Trendmasters. You have just as much chance of predicting upcoming trends by banging your head against a wall. The same individual peddling those bogus "strategies" also sells an "Intuitive Betting Strategy" to those not intuitive enough to see how stupid it is. None of these methods is an advantage-play method.

Charters are people who sound like the confident captain of the *Titanic*, who said, "Even God himself couldn't sink this ship." Charting appeals to hopeless, hapless gamblers who believe the same nonsense that their Internet "gurus" preach.

Another Internet craps wizard sells a charting/tracking system that is advertised as guaranteeing "income for life"—in fact, that's its actual name. This system relies on hot number/hot table theory with a mixture of "intuitive" design thrown in for good measure. I spoke to the main American advocate/salesmen of this system, and he said that at least 25 percent of it is intuition. Again, this is nonsensical—and costs about $3,000!

Run-of-the-mill gamblers are looking for betting methods to turn a negative expectation into a positive one. Dice control can give you an edge over the casino—if you learn how to do it (a physical skill) and bet correctly; but charting, tracking, using your intuition, and analyzing random history cannot do it. Here is a saying you should memorize: *Random is random.*

There *is* something you can understand about random games: the probability of what will happen and how much of an edge the casinos create around those probabilities. We know that on the very next random roll of the dice (no matter what happened in the roll before or the roll before that or before that, etc.) the 7 has a 16.67 percent chance of appearing. We know what the percentages are, but we don't know exactly what will happen next.

So how should a smart casino player wager? Certainly not in any way, shape, or form to follow the charters/trackers or intuits. Bet those bets with the lowest house edge based on mathematics, not mysticism.

There are no good short-run strategies based on recent streaks. You must play the math of the game to reduce the casinos' edge over you. To do anything else is to hit an iceberg.

"Real Time" Charters

The newest attempt to repackage the oldest form of betting system has arrived, brought to you by a small cadre of self-proclaimed Internet dice "experts" whose gambling beliefs belie their expertise. It is a method of reacting to what is happening at the craps table in "real time" and then betting accordingly. This is nothing more than charting or trend betting under the misnomer "real time" to make it sound somewhat philosophical.

Here's how it works: the player watches the game, sees what has happened recently, and then decides whether to get into the game. It is not a mechanical method, such as the Captain's 5-Count, to cut down on the number of random rolls a player faces; instead, it is a method to figure out what numbers to bet on in the sadly mistaken notion that whatever random trends have been seen will continue to be seen.

Advocates of this system believe that tables have "energy," and if you can sense the energy then you can decide whether to play on that table or pass it by. For some uncanny reason that energy will continue into the short-range future. The dice gurus will explain for a fee how to plug into the energy to win against random rollers. It is nonsense of the highest order, but it is nonsense that massages the typical gambler's desire to chart tables and find trends, thinking this is the path to winning.

By using the coupling of *real* and *time* it sounds as if others are playing in some kind of fake or unreal time. Don't be shocked now, but there is no "real time" at a craps game; there is what happened and there is what will happen. When a number just hit, that is the past. It is not current time and has no current meaning for what will happen on the next roll, which is future time.

The human mind is a pattern-finding organ. We wish to look at things in the past in order to project things into the future. For the most part, this quality makes sense. Put simply: "Don't take a walk where the lions roam. Og was eaten last week."

In a random event, there are no predictions that can be made. You can figure out probabilities, but you cannot know exactly what is coming. Charting craps tables in "real time" is a waste of your time. Still, offering to teach superstitious craps players how to judge the energy at a table to make such predictions is certainly a path to making money—for the teachers and casinos, that is.

To top off this silly "new" system, lists of rolls are given from one's table charting and discussions are engineered to figure out how to bet on those rolls. This is what I call "betting backward." If you already know what happened with the listed rolls, you shouldn't get anything wrong! Projecting into the unknown future is impossible; correctly betting the past is easy. I'll bet the *Titanic* will sink on its maiden voyage. How hard was that to do?

Trend betting—or, as it is now being called, "real time betting"—is one of the ways the casino makes its money. Trend bettors have not had any effect on the bottom line unless their system causes them not to bet the same number of rolls that a non–trend bettor bets—again I reference the Captain's 5-Count, which does exactly that. Still, even the 5-Count can't predict what is coming next.

Another group will teach some kind of betting system they claim will win more than 95 percent of all sessions. The cost is $1,500 per student. *No betting method can beat a random game.* That is the truth of the matter.

Finally we must ask ourselves if these Internet salesmen are just scammers looking to milk players. Could be. Or they are wild-eyed true believers who have eaten the poisonous notions they teach. Perhaps that is worse than being a cynical scammer. Their adherence to silliness might cause others to think such adherence makes the silliness true.

If you want to get a real edge over the house, then you must learn to control the dice and you must bet your edge properly. There are no other ways to win in the long run. And dice control is not an easy thing to learn, because too many craps players can't stop themselves from gambling.

CHAPTER 5

The Essentials of Dice Control

I f you glued two dice together, the only numbers that could show would be those numbers already showing. Sadly, the mean casinos will not allow us to glue the dice together in a real game, so we must use energy and rotation to duplicate, however remotely, what gluing the dice would do.

Any moving projectile—and the dice in the air are moving projectiles—has six degrees of movement. By putting rotation and backspin on the dice, we try to eliminate three of those degrees. Eliminating half of the degrees of movement will give us a better chance of having an extended hand or hitting certain specific numbers more than probability predicts.

Thrown correctly, the dice have a gentle backspin that keeps the dice together, preventing them from randomizing in the air, and it also acts as a break when the dice hit the table. We want the dice to hit flat, to dissipate as much of their energy as possible but still have enough energy to make it to the back wall, which they'll hit softly before coming to a stop. You know the dice have hit flat because you will often hear a *smack!* when they hit the layout (if it isn't too noisy in the casino).

Dice control goes from the almost perfect—your dice sets, stance, grip, and throw—to the imperfect: once released, gravity acts upon the dice, energy flows from the dice to the table top, where it returns with lesser force and pushes the dice to the back wall. All these reactions cut away at your almost perfect throw. From hand to final decision, the dice lose much of their perfection. But you don't need to be perfect to get an edge at craps, just as you don't need to throw a strike with every pitch to be a great pitcher.

So the things you can do well, you must learn to do them. The time spent on the stance, dice sets, grip, and delivery will ultimately determine how good you'll be. You must learn the physical elements of dice control to have any chance of beating the game. And after that, you must train your mind.

The How of Dice Control

Pick up two dice. The perfect throw—a throw the casinos will not allow you to use very often—is one where the dice land, *don't* hit the back wall, and just die on the numbers that you set—as if Velcro were attached to them. This is a kill shot. It's the shot the Lee Brothers dice team uses, *once* a session.

It is an almost impossible shot to learn—and the casinos are adamant that this shot violates their rules. Indeed, some casino personnel have become salivating lunatics about shooters not hitting the back wall because they think that controlled shooters look to land kill shots. Many casino personnel buy the nonsense. A controlled shot is geared to hitting the back wall. If we miss, the shot is merely random, just like the wingers and the slingers.

The time spent on the stance, dice sets, grip, and delivery will ultimately determine how good you're going to be. You must learn the physical elements of dice control to have any chance of beating the game. And after that, you must control your emotions.

Standing and Scanning

If you were a pitcher in baseball, would you have a better chance of striking out a batter throwing the ball from second base or from the pitcher's mound? Obviously the closer you are to home plate, the more accurate your pitch will be.

This holds true for dice control; the closer to the back wall, the better for your throw. The less energy you impart to the dice, the less energy they have to bounce and randomize when they land on the table and hit the back wall. If you shoot from the back wall to the other back wall, you are maximizing the distance and creating greater problems for your control. You must impart far more energy into the dice to get them up and out and you must put more spin pressure on them to slow them down before they hit the back wall. All this utilization of energy makes it harder to control the outcome.

The best positions for most controlled shooters are stick right one (SR1) and stick left one (SL1)—right next to the stickman, in other words.

Those are the closest points to the back wall. In general, it is better to play at shorter tables than at longer tables because the distance to the back wall is also shorter. Small errors become big errors when distance works on the movement of the dice.

Right-handers stand at stick left (SL), and left-handers stand at stick right (SR). This allows an easy pendulum swing and the release of the dice as close as possible to the back wall. Righties shooting from SR and lefties shooting from SL have much more difficult throws.

You want consistency. Using the baseball analogy again, not too many baseball greats could hit from both sides of the plate. The same goes for dice shooters. Find the position that feels the most comfortable and practice from that position. Master one position before trying to master a second position.

When you are standing at the table, your non-shooting hand should grasp the railing. The preferred stance has the hand on the rail. The arm *resting* on the rail necessitates getting up over your arm as well as the rail to perform your throw, an added difficulty.

In any athletic endeavor—and throwing dice certainly is an athletic endeavor—your stance is important. A baseball player at home plate gets into a stance that will help him generate power through his hitting zone. Your stance should be relaxed, comfortable, and stable; it should give you a feeling of control while giving you free arm movement for your pendulum swing.

If you are right-handed, let's start with the basics from shooting from SL. The basics of this stance would be the same for a left-handed shooter shooting from SR, so if you are left-handed, just apply my instructions to shooting from stick right.

Let's take a look at the preferred stance. Your stomach is up against the rail. Stand with your feet about shoulder length apart. Stabilize yourself by putting your left hand on the rail. Lean over as far as you can. Even Jerry "Stickman," who is 6'4", will get up on his toes.

Next, pick where you want your dice to land. This spot should not be in the corner but about six to seven inches from the straight part of the back wall (at times table conditions will change where you land the dice). Then support yourself, go into your pendulum swing, and hit your spot.

The stances for a right-hander or a left-hander shooting from the non-preferred positions of stick left or stick right are a little different. Let's say a left-hander is at SL or a right-hander is at SR. Instead of standing with your stomach against the rail, you stand with your right or left side/hip against the rail, square with the back wall. This is important to remember, as you need to be square. You must lean over the table so you put more of your weight on your right leg if you are standing SR as a right-handed shooter, and your weight would be mostly on your left foot if you are a left-handed shooter standing SL.

Your backswing will not go back very far because it starts to hurt. The arm cannot do a full pendulum swing from this position. Again you want to lean over the table as far as you can. But even by leaning over, your swing might still be on an angle to the back wall, causing your dice to travel at an angle. Using this non-preferred position makes it harder to control your toss. Through practice, you will be able to gain some control from this stance at the table. But always try to get your preferred position to throw from—make it easy on yourself.

After a year or two, you might decide to practice from both sides of the table, but you must first be successful from one side before you tackle a second side.

Why don't I recommend shooting from the end of the table, especially for novice or intermediate dice controllers? If you were to take the number of home runs that a great home-run slugger hit, how many would be to center field? The closer the fence, the easier to hit a home run. The less power you need. So the closer the back wall, the easier it is to control the dice. If we could just reach out and place the dice, that would be the perfect throw. You would hit whatever number you wanted.

You might have seen dice setters throwing from the end of the table, but they were probably just setting the dice and not throwing with any ability. Deliberately putting yourself in the worst spot from which to throw the dice will just make it that much more difficult to control your throw. Players who claim they can do this (and some few can) would be better off moving closer.

Scanning the Dice

When you are the shooter, you should be in the game at all times. Do not allow anything to disrupt your focus. After you have thrown a number and the dice are in the middle of the table, watch them. Note the sides of the dice. Think in terms of how you are going to arrange them when they come to you. Remember that each side and its opposite form a 7: the 5-pip has the 2-pip opposite it; the 4-pip has the 3-pip opposite it; the 6-pip has the 1-pip opposite it.

Most stickmen will not bring the dice to you with 7s showing. Often they will just bring the dice over to you with the number you just hit or, in the case of really savvy stick people, with the dice set you like to use. Those latter stick people are the best, since you don't have to set the dice at all. You just have to grip them, pick them up, aim, and throw.

If you watch the dice, you will know which spots are where, and making your set will be that much easier.

Dice Sets

Some pitchers have one pitch, maybe a blazing fastball. Some pitchers have a good curve as well. The great pitchers often add a third and fourth pitch. Some might have even more. Each pitch a pitcher throws has a different setup in his hand. A curveball is not set up like a fastball. A knuckleball is not set up like a screwball.

In craps, the set of the dice (also known as the dice set)—that is, the initial configuration of each die to the other—is very important. You set the dice to increase the likelihood that your throw will bring about certain numbers or eliminate other numbers. Since most craps players are Right bettors—they bet with the shooter and against the 7 on the Point Cycle of the game—most of my discussion of dice sets will be about those used by Rightsiders.

To keep things simple, I am only going to recommend three sets in this book. One set will be used to make the 7 more likely, one set will try to reduce the appearance of the 7, and the third set will increase the likelihood of hitting the 6 and the 8.

A word of caution here: do not attempt to learn a multitude of dice sets. That would be overkill. Many good shooters just use one set at all times. This works well for them, as they simply concentrate on the task at hand and don't worry about this or that specific number—other than avoidance of the 7. The 7-avoidance set is called the Hardway set.

Sadly, there is a tendency on the part of some dice controllers to constantly change their sets when their throw is off, thinking that such changes will be beneficial. Indeed, in the short run of a throwing session, a set change might help, but this is like taking an aspirin for a heart attack—it's a temporary solution in a critical situation.

If your throw is off, the problem is probably in your grip, where most of the problems occur. In the long run, it is the excellence of your throw that will determine whether you win at craps or lose. In fact, most sets that are discussed in the dice literature just aren't worth making, as they try to hit numbers with high house edges. The degree of ability you need to accomplish those throws (known as on-axis control) is way too high for most controlled shooters to attain.

Since the appearance of slowness exists with careful shooting, the one thing we don't want to happen is for the box person or floor person to think you're taking too long with your dice sets. So practice your sets at home; let them become second nature to you. When the dice are in the center of the table as bets are being paid off, look at them and begin to visualize how you are going to turn the dice to make your set.

Learn the Hardway set first. Then you can add the All-Sevens set. After that I recommend the 3V. However, many great shooters just stick with the Hardway set. The point about sets is simple—you use them to make money. There is no reward for the shooter who uses the most sets; the only reward that exists in craps is winning money.

Come-Out and Point Cycles

There are two cycles in a craps game: the Come-Out Cycle, which is when the shooter gets the dice and establishes his point number, and the Point

Cycle, where the shooter tries to make his point or, for Darksiders, hit that 7. Many controlled shooters like to set for the 7 on the Come-Out roll. You already have a 2-to-1 edge on the Come-Out with six ways to make the 7 and two ways to make the 11, versus four ways to lose on the 2, 3, and 12. (We aren't counting the point/box numbers in this part of the game.)

Increasing the number of 7s thrown is a great way to increase your edge in this part of the game. You have nothing to lose by trying to increase your edge during these throws, since you can't lose the dice. Setting for the 7 on the Come-Out is a great way to make some money and to see how your throw looks. There are six ways to make a 7. If we have practiced our controlled throw, we can set for the 7 on the Come-Out roll and maybe increase our advantage during this part of the game. The Come-Out use of an All-Sevens set is a good way to try to put some money in your rail before you play the part of the game where a bad throw can eliminate you. The Come-Out roll is also great practice on the table. You can get an idea of the bounce of the table.

The Captain used the same set for the Come-Out Cycle and the Point Cycle and never changed sets during his turn with the dice. This type of play might also be good for you. Changing sets might distract you from the mental job at hand: beating the casinos. So if changing sets disrupts your focus, then use a Point Cycle set throughout your roll.

Come-Out Sets

In the controlled-shooting literature, we read of random rollers being called "chicken feeders," since their form often looks like those old farmers flinging out the grain for their chickens. The only time when a chicken feeder or random shooter has a mathematical advantage over the house is on his Come-Out roll, when he is establishing the point number—that is, if he is betting on the Pass Line.

A Pass Line player will win his bet immediately if a 7 or 11 is thrown. He has eight ways to make these two numbers, six ways on the 7 and two ways on the 11. The player has four ways to lose on this Come-Out roll: once on a 2, once on a 12, and twice on a 3. The other 24 numbers (4, 5, 6, 8, 9, and 10) are point numbers.

So the Come-Out heavily favors the players. By using an All-Sevens set, you try to increase the appearance of the 7 with no risk of sevening out.

As you study these dice sets, think about the axis that the dice rotate on. Imagine a rod through the center of both dice, on which they spin. This axis of rotation has to be the same for the sets that are described, but the number on top or facing you as you set the dice doesn't have to be what is illustrated.

All-Sevens Sets:

T2F4:T5F3   **T3F2:T4F5**

T5F3:T2F4   **T4F5:T3F2**

T5F4:T2F3   **T3F5:T4F2**

T2F3:T5F4   **T4F2:T3F5**

The All-Sevens set has a 7 on each side of the dice, made up of a 4:3 on two sides and a 5:2 on the other two sides. The side faces are also a 7, with 6:1. The axis that this set revolves on is the 6-spot and the 1-spot. You can have any number facing you, either the 4:3 or the 5:2, but you must set the dice with the 6-spot and 1-spot on axis. If you practice throwing and keeping the dice on axis in the air, you will start your turn at the tables by throwing 7s. What better way to begin than by putting money in your rack?

Starting with an All-Sevens set is a wise thing to do. The Come-Out roll is a practice roll because you will get the dice back. So not only can you judge the table, but also you give yourself the opportunity to take more throws if those 7s come up. If you prefer to use the Come betting method on yourself during the Point Cycle of the game, then you would not use the All-Sevens set on subsequent Come-Out rolls because you don't want to knock your Come bets off the numbers.

Hardway Sets:

T5F4:T5F4   **T4F2:T4F2**

T2F3:T2F3   **T3F5:T3F5**

T5F3:T5F3   **T3F2:T3F2**

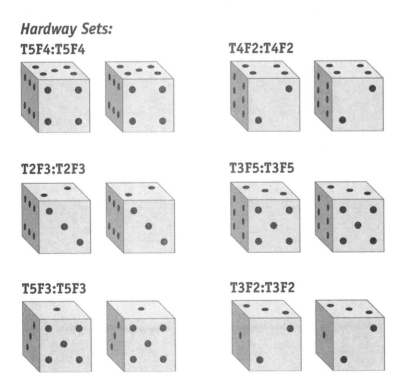

T2F4:T2F4

T4F5:T4F5

This is the best set to begin your dice-control career, as it offers the best protection against the 7. It is the best set to use when you are practicing because you can tell what your dice are doing much more easily than with other sets. It is not, however, a good set to use for specific numbers. The Hardway set is so named because all four sides of the dice have Hardway numbers.

The Hardway set has on its axis the 6-spot and 1-spot.

A simple rule of thumb is to put the 6-spot die to the left and the 1-spot die to the right (or vice versa—but always do it the same way each time). The 6:1 is your axis of the dice. Always do this, and the Hardway Set is easy to make. All you do is make sure you have 3:3, 5:5, 2:2, and 4:4 as the combinations showing. With the 6-spot die on the left and the 1-spot die on the right, you can be confident that your set is the set that keeps that nasty 7 away.

If you take the dice and turn each one a quarter turn, always starting with the Hardway set, you will see that you cannot form a 7. The 7 will only occur when you double pitch, double yaw, or double roll.

The Hardway set is excellent when you start controlled shooting because it protects against the 7 better than any other set. Many great shooters still use the Hardway set exclusively. However, to get that added protection against the 7, you decrease your ability to snipe out other numbers. It's a trade-off but certainly a worthwhile one.

3V Sets:

T3F5:T3F1

T2F3:T6F3

T4F2:T4F6   **T5F4:T1F4**

T3F6:T3F2   **T1F3:T5F3**

T4F1:T4F5   **T6F4:T2F4**

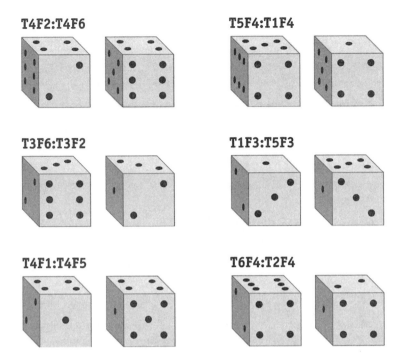

This was the Captain's set and has been my set for more than a quarter century. The 3V set is used to hit the 6 and 8. It requires strong axis control.

The typical way to set the 3V is to have the 2-spot and 5-spot on axis on one die and the 6-spot and 1-spot on axis on the other. Then make sure that the four sides of the dice have 3:3, 4:4, 5:1, or 6:2 all the way around.

Most players have the 3s on top forming a *V* or an inverted *V* (a pyramid). Some shooters prefer to put the two 4s on top. Again, the configuration you use is up to you—as long as all the dice are aligned correctly. Any of the four sides on top will work as long as you have the axis numbers correct.

Using the 3V set is for the more advanced and consistent throwers who keep their dice on axis more often. One word of caution: use the same sides up all the time. You want to get into an unthinking rhythm when you roll. I always have the 3s in a *V* at the top. (If the dice are of the *B* variety, the top will be a pyramid shape with the 3-spots.)

Primary and Secondary Hits

To understand sets completely, you need to understand the difference between primary hits and secondary hits.

A primary hit is when the dice stop after hitting the back wall and the number thrown is one of the four sides of the dice that you set originally. On the Hardway set, if you roll a Hardway number, you have a primary hit. A secondary hit is when one die or both dice land on one of the other sides of the dice a quarter pitch, yawl, or roll, plus or minus, from the original set. An example of this using the Hardway set is when you land with the number 8 composed of a 5:3.

You must document how many secondary hits you get because secondary hits are as good as primary hits. You still haven't thrown a 7 with a secondary hit using the Hardway set, which is why the Hardway set is the best set to avoid the 7.

On the 3V, the primary hits are 5:1, 6:2, 3:3, and 4:4. However a single flip or roll can start bringing up 5s and 9s. The 3V set requires that you be more consistently on axis than does the Hardway set. However, if you are a little off using the 3V, that 7 will tend to materialize because it is not that far away. (You really have to test your on-axis ability with SmartCraps to see if you should use the 3V or any other set.)

Do you have to keep the dice on axis in order to win? No, you don't. The Hardway set is not predicated on keeping the dice on axis as the dice can roll, pitch, or, in my language, flip and flop without that 7 showing. However, the better shooters tend to keep their dice on axis more than randomness indicates. We want to try for those primary numbers, the ones we are setting for, and keeping the dice on axis is the key to achieving that goal.

Grabs, Pickups, and Grips

Random rollers just pick up the dice and throw them down the table. That's fine for players who have no chance to win at the game. But for the dice controller, picking up the dice properly is essential.

If you are using the preferred three-finger grip (discussed shortly), you can put all three fingers on the front of the dice first or, much easier, just grab the dice with your middle finger and thumb, pick them up, come down with the ring and pointer, and proceed.

There are different approaches to grabbing the dice. Your hand can come over the top and/or you can come in from the sides.

Sometimes the dice might split as you are holding them. If this happens, just take your outside fingers and gently close the dice together. Grabbing the dice will become second nature to you with practice. However, if you find that the dice feel uncomfortable in your hand, put them down and start again.

Grips

Your grip is the most important element in the pre-throw. The objective of the grip is to make sure that the dice leave your hand together. You don't want one die lagging and one die leading. We look to make as close to the perfect throw as possible—both dice together, spinning in exactly the same way. The grip is the key to getting those dice to leave your fingers properly.

Most of the problems you encounter with a controlled throw will come down to your grip on the dice. After the dice are released, you don't have any control over them, so the better they are at the point of release, the better chance you'll have of switching the edge from the casino to you. Any little deviation of finger placement will alter the flight of the dice in the air and cause them not to travel on a perfect plane down the table.

Gripping the dice with too much pressure will prevent the dice from rotating freely. With a tight grip the dice will stay on your fingers too long. You should practice so that you can grip the dice without thinking about finger placement or tightness.

A little exercise can help you. Cut a piece of cardboard or ¼" plywood, 12" X 15". Cover this rectangle with felt by gluing or stapling the felt on. You will have a smaller version of a craps tabletop to practice your dice grip. Have it next to you while watching television or at your desk at work.

Which Grip to Use

Your grip will be determined by your finger size, body type, and performance of the dice in the air. Your grip must feel comfortable. The dice should feel as if they belong in your hands.

There are some grips that are better than others in terms of the physics of dice control, but if these premier grips are uncomfortable for you, then you must settle upon a grip that works for you. No two shooters are exactly alike, just as no two baseball batters are exactly alike, so ultimately the grip you choose will be the premier grip for you.

Men and women with big fingers might not be able to keep their fingers straight across the front of the dice without a little overlap on the sides of the dice. If this is the case, you will have to use the two-finger grip. The same holds true for long fingernails. If you have long fingernails and you want to use the three-finger grip, you will have to use the pads of your fingers versus the tips of your fingers to achieve the grip. Again, you might have some overlap on the sides of the dice, so the two-finger or one-finger grip might be for you. (You can also cut your fingernails.)

Pads or Fingertips?

The perfect grip will exhibit each of the following characteristics:

- Very little finger contact with the dice
- Very little force needed to get dice to leave your hand
- Allows the dice to stay together in flight
- You have control and the dice feel comfortable in your hand
- Both dice are perfectly still in your hand during your pickup and swing
- There shouldn't be any splitting of the dice
- All four sides of the dice should be square with the table and walls
- The force to hold the dice should be minimal
- You want the dice to be released from your fingers with little drag
- Your fingertips should be like a fulcrum
- The dice should travel down the table in a perfect arc

If you are at all able, you should strive to use the tips of your fingers on the front of the dice. Using the tips of your fingers gives you the least amount of finger contact. This allows for the smallest amount of drag and friction upon release of the dice. If you grip the dice with the pads of your fingers, you have slightly more finger contact on the dice.

One-Finger Grip

The one-finger grip is so named because it uses your middle finger and your thumb to hold the dice.

Your index finger needs to be perfectly centered between the right and left die with equal pressure, and your thumb needs to be centered in the back with equal pressure. You can use either the tip of your middle finger or the pad of your middle finger, but the important thing is that your middle finger is perfectly centered with equal pressure on both dice.

Some controlled shooters who cannot use the premier three-finger grip use this grip. It can cause some instability in the dice when they are released, because the ends of the dice will sometimes wobble. Wobbling is bad, as it causes the dice to hit on their sides—which tends to randomize the roll. Also, the dice will have more of a tendency to split when released.

Thumb Placement

How should your thumb be positioned on the back of the dice? It really doesn't matter if you use the edge of your thumb, and it also doesn't matter if the thumb is not exactly straight but somewhat slanted. Many shooters' thumbs cannot be placed straight on the back of the dice.

You can also decide whether to use a pad or tip placement for the thumb. The important thing is that the thumb contact should be *equal* on both dice. With all of the grips, how far up or down on the dice your thumb is can change the amount of rotations that you get on the dice after release. As a rule of thumb (pun!), your thumb should be about halfway down the backside of the dice.

Even though the one-finger grip is only recommended as the second grip of choice, it is a very important grip because the No. 1 grip that you should be trying to use, the three-finger grip, uses the one-finger grip to actually hold the dice. So practice gripping the dice with these two fingers and see if you can hold the dice together without them coming apart in your fingers.

Two-Finger Grip

If you have large fingers, you might find that the three-finger grip, the best of all the grips, just isn't for you. Many large-fingered shooters then go to a two-finger grip. Here you use two fingers, usually your ring and middle fingers, to grip the dice. Your index and pinky are off the dice completely.

Three-Finger Grip

The premier grip, and the one that satisfies all the elements shown previously, is the three-finger grip. In the three-finger grip, your index, middle, and ring fingers are on the front of the dice and your thumb is on the backside of the dice. The only finger that is not being used in this grip is your pinky. Do not have your pinky touch the dice at all during the pickup, grip, or delivery of the dice—because that skews your throw.

The holding of the dice is performed with your middle finger and thumb. Your index finger and ring finger are simply placed along the front of the dice and act like wings of a plane and a fulcrum for the dice to rotate on when released.

Your fingers have to be perfectly straight across the front of the dice, and you must make sure there are no splits in the dice at the bottom. A split will cause the dice to move away from each other in the air. The further away they move, the less control you'll have over them. Freedom is good for human beings but bad for dice! Although I say that the middle finger and thumb are holding the dice, the pressure differences between the three fingers on the front are not that great.

Picking up the dice for the three-finger grip can be done in a number of ways. I pick them up with the middle finger and thumb and then, as I aim, I bring in the ring and pointer to their positions. Some dice controllers pick up the dice with all three fingers on them at once. Either pickup is just fine.

The three-finger grip keeps those dice perfectly aligned and allows them to leave the hand together. The spin of the dice is created equally, and they move through the air together. This is not the easiest dice grip to learn, but it is, for most people, the best grip to use. It should be the first one you try to master. Give yourself time to learn it and use it. Do not get discouraged if you find that several days or even weeks are needed to really master this grip.

Four-Finger Grip

Some people just can't get the pinky to stay out of the way with the three-finger grip so they incorporate the pinky in the grip. You slide over the pointer and place the pinky on the dice as well. Obviously your fingers will be wider than the dice, perhaps even a little on the side, but with the proper softness, the dice should be able to leave your hand with equal energy.

Grip Adjustments

You should always carry a set of dice with you. Let your fingers and the dice become friends. Just picture a young person who wishes to develop his or her ability at baseball. What do they do? They always have a ball with them. They throw the ball up and catch it; they throw the ball against the wall and catch it. They play with that ball until its feel, its essence becomes second nature to them. Dice controllers must do the same thing. Your fingers and your dice should become one.

When you are actually at a table and shooting, I don't recommend adjusting your grip too much because to do so causes you to think too much. Too much thinking about your grip will throw you off focus. Shakespeare's Hamlet would not have been a good dice controller—he reflects too much. But there are some adjustments in grip that can be made with very little thinking. Here they are:

1. If you feel the dice slipping out of your fingers during your pickup or your follow-through, you might need a little more contact on the dice.
2. If your dice are not coming out of your fingers with any backspin or are moving flat down the table, then you have to adjust the position of your thumb.
3. Too much backspin is not good because the dice will have more energy to release as they land on the table, and the dice will be random as they land. You want the backspin to almost cancel out the forward movement but not eliminate it because the dice must touch the back wall.
4. Another problem could be that one die may be lagging behind the other or one is traveling higher than the other as they are moving down the table.

Here is a quick checklist that you can go through:

- Make sure that your fingers are parallel with the table and straight across the front of the dice. Some people have problems with either their index finger or their ring finger not being exactly equal to the other two fingers on the dice. You can use a mirror to check for this when you practice at home.
- Make sure that you have equal pressure across the dice and, if you are using the three-finger grip, that your middle finger is perfectly centered on both dice.
- You can put your three fingers on the dice tabletop and make sure they are straight before you put them on the dice. Remember that your fingers will be bent somewhat to stay on the dice in a straight line.
- Last, make sure that your thumb has even pressure on the back. Now you can be holding the dice with the thumb's edge, but you must have the same amount of your thumb's skin contact on both the left and right die.

5. Another problem might be that your dice are ending up in either corner of the table, traveling down the table in a banana-type angle. This problem usually means that your backspin and follow-through are not on a straight line. When your dice land in the corner, known as the mixing bowl, your dice will tumble and roll off axis. The mixing bowl randomizes the best of throws.
6. Perspiration and any oils that you have on your hand can impact the outcome of the roll because of drag or slippage. Always wash your hands before you go to a craps table.

The Throw, Backspin, Bounce, and Back Wall

How you grip and throw the dice, how the dice spin, how they bounce, and how hard they hit the back wall will determine just how close to perfection you can get.

Here are the steps:

- You grab the dice and put your fingers straight across the front so that they are perfectly even.
- In the back, your thumb can be about 40 percent to halfway down the dice, and your thumb must be centered evenly between the two dice.
- The bottom of the dice should be level with the tabletop.
- The front of the dice should be square with the front wall.
- If you start your throw on an angle, it will end on an angle and not give the dice enough surface area to release energy to the tabletop.

You want the dice to be squared to the felt and the walls of the table, then aim and gently bring the dice back and then forward, and release.

Let's go over it again. You grab the dice; grip them properly; pause, making sure that the dice are square; aim; then gently bring them back, then forward with a smooth and continuous pendulum swing; and you release them.

You want your arm to go back enough so that it will have enough forward momentum but not too far back that your arm will bend in. You don't want to push to release the dice; you want the dice to come out of your hands on their own. If your grip is light, a gentle forward motion should release them properly.

The Arc of the Dice

Once the dice are released from your hand, you *usually* want them to attain a 45-degree angle in the air, the perfect angle for a normal dice table. However, on softer tables you have to take the angle down a bit, or the impact will cause the dice to bounce too high.

Backspin the Dice

Once the dice are released, you want a gentle backspin. This backspin will do three important things:

- Keep the dice together in the air
- Act as a break when the dice hit the table
- Help to dissipate the energy of the dice

You do not want the dice hitting that back wall with too much energy. With too much energy, the dice will move more, bounce more, and perhaps become random.

When you release the dice into the air in a smooth, natural manner, a backspin of between two and six revolutions will occur naturally. If your three front fingers and your thumb are properly placed, you should have little trouble achieving a natural backspin. The thumb should be about halfway down the back with the three fingers on the top one-quarter of the dice.

The Bounce

When the dice hit the table, the biggest problem begins. The perfect or almost perfect throw starts to deteriorate rapidly as the dice make their way to the back wall. When they come down, you want the dice to hit solidly on the felt so that first hit takes away a lot of the energy from the dice. In your practice sessions, you will actually hear a loud *smack!* as the dice hit squarely. You want the entire surface area of the dice to hit the tabletop. That is why everything must start with the dice being square to the table and the front wall.

You want to hit the back wall on one bounce. By the time the dice actually arrive at the back wall, you want their energy to be almost completely gone.

Okay, where do you want to hit the back wall? You want to hit where the back wall is straight.

Odds and Angles

You must master the physical elements of the throw to have a chance to win. However, since there is not one standard dice table in terms of length and design and felts vary in their buoyancy, it is important to realize that each table presents you with a unique challenge, just the way each pitcher in baseball presents each batter with a unique challenge.

Tables come in all sizes and shapes. Some are long, aircraft-carrier-sized monsters of 14 to 16 feet. Other tables are 10 to 12 feet. Some tables are wide, some are narrow. You'll note that on some the Pass Line seems quite far from the back wall, and on others it seems very close to it. Some layouts are like trampolines; some are dead, as if they have slate under the felt. When you shoot the dice on a hard table, they will die nicely. Do that same shot on a bouncy table, and the dice could very well sail off the table.

When you shoot at a new casino on a new table, you can do several things to ascertain how the dice react. First and foremost, watch other players shoot the dice. Note the bounce. And during your Come-Out roll, a time when you can't seven out, use however many rolls you can muster at that time to quickly ascertain the table's conductivity.

Exactly Where Should You Land the Dice?

Most accomplished shooters have a normal landing area for their dice on their practice rigs or their at-home craps tables. Their bodies are trained to land the dice that distance, and they do it without thinking or analyzing anything. This landing zone is usually six to ten inches away from the back wall. The dice take one soft bounce and hit the back wall so softly that they die quietly on the felt without bouncing and careening all over the place the way random rolls do.

Regardless of whether the table is wide or narrow; regardless of where the Pass Line is in relation to the back wall, you want to land your dice as far from the back wall as you normally do in your at-home practices. A true-bounce craps table will allow dice landed at six to ten inches from the back wall to bounce almost perfectly, losing most of their energy on that one landing, and gently touch the back wall without much of a rebound. Many tables you will encounter do not have a true bounce.

If you land your dice in your normal area and you immediately notice that they hit the back wall too hard or too high or too lightly or not at all, you might have to change small things in your delivery to get a bounce similar to your practice table.

Bouncy tables might need a landing of the dice farther from the back wall than your normal six to ten inches. Your arc on these tables will also have to be lowered. You will find that with a lowered arc and a longer journey from bounce to back wall, you might be able to come close to a good throw. Usually your throw on these tables will not be as good as your throws on true-bounce tables. However, not changing your throws on bouncy tables can be devastating for your control, so if you are going to play bouncy tables, you must take steps to make that bounce less damaging.

The reverse of a bouncy table is a dead one. You launch your dice in a 45-degree angle with your normal backspin. The dice hit the table—*smack!*—and they die right there or close to it. They never make it to the back wall. The solution for this is rather simple: land the dice closer to the back wall. You keep everything the same, except you add slightly more power, and when the dice land a few inches from the back wall, they will touch down, hit the wall gently, and die. These "dead" tables are good for controlled shooting.

Chips Here, There, Everywhere

Many shooters become bothered when they see all the bets on the opposite side of the table where they have to land the dice. A little logic here can be very helpful. With three or four players at the back of the table, there is still plenty of room available to land those cubes properly. Even if one player has his chips directly where you like to land your dice, just moving your landing area a half inch to the left or right of his chips should be all that is necessary to have your controlled throw working to give you an edge. Letting chips chip away at your throw because you get annoyed or rattled is much worse than having to land your dice a fraction of an inch over one way or the other.

If you are playing with several friends at the table and only two to four of them are shooting, you might want to have the non-shooters take up the positions at the landing zones. When you shoot, they do not use Pass Line bets. Your lane will be totally open for you.

Some controlled shooters like to ask other players to move their chips—a bad idea, as it draws unwanted attention to you. Learn to aim! Once you have been shooting for a long period of time, a year or two, chips should never be much of a problem.

What if the Pit Gets on You?

You can have the most dazzling controlled throw, but if you let your emotions get away from you, you'll find that those seven-outs come like clockwork. Some casinos or casino dealers and pit people have a grudge against careful shooting and will say various things to you to throw you off your game:

"Hurry up with your set!"

"Dice setting can't change the game."

"Look at this, a pro. Ha ha!"

"Make sure you hit the back wall hard."

"You must have read one of those stupid books."

You have two choices when faced with hostility. You can leave the casino and play at another casino that appreciates your action or you can develop a thick skin and deaf ears. Tips often shut up nasty dealers.

Betting Your Edge

Okay, let's repeat for emphasis: in a random game of craps, the casino has the edge. Memorize that sentence. If someone tells you something else, flee that person as if he has the plague because in a sense he does.

The plague of ignorance is manifest in the craps world, and many of the "crapsters" who profess to be experts are the most ignorant of the lot.

Here are the facts: *No* betting system, *no* hedging system, *no* on/off method, *no* right-side or wrong-side strategy can give you an edge over the house in a random game.

Players who think they can outthink the dice are poor thinkers. Authors and self-styled experts who claim that this or that betting or money-management system can overcome a mathematical edge are authoring illusion. Nothing can change the fact that in the long run, you will lose whatever the house edge is on the bets you are making—that is, if you play a strictly random game of craps. Yes, you will win some nights and lose more, but in the end, if you play enough, you will lose the house edge on the money you bet.

Those are indisputable facts.

Casino executives know these facts because they see the bottom line of their craps games, and those bottom lines don't lie. The math of craps is a devastating reality for the players and a delightful fact for the casinos.

Many players have no idea how the casinos actually win money from them in the long run. They have vague inklings that something called "an edge" is working against them, but they don't really know what that means. How you lose money is easy to see. You put a bet up, and the 7 shows, and the dealer takes your chips and adds them to the casino's rack. You can understand you have lost that bet.

However, you also lose bets that you win! Check out the Place bets and the Crazy Crapper bets in the game. All of these are based on short-changing your win. You bet that nutty 11 and the house pays you $15-to-$1 if you win, but the true odds of the bet are $17-to-$1. The house keeps the extra $2.

At craps you lose in two ways: On the Pass, Don't Pass, Come, and Don't Come, the casino wins more decisions than the players. On the Place and Crazy Crapper bets, the casino "shares" in your win by extracting its edge by not paying you at the true odds of the bet.

So you actually lose when you win!

The worse the Crazy Crapper bet, the more the casino takes from you. As a controlled shooter and one who is looking to play with an edge, the worst thing you can do is try to overcome the edges on the Crazy Crapper bets. That's like practicing for a marathon and then jumping off a building to see if you can fly because you are in such good shape. The ground (the house edge) will crush you.

The best bets for most dice controllers are the bets with the least mathematical edge for the casino because they require the least skill to overcome. It is extremely difficult to overcome a 10 percent house edge. It is much easier overcoming a 1 to 2 percent house edge.

Are you a gambler or an advantage player? The more you are an advantage player, the more you make good, not bad bets. Gamblers just can't refrain from making bad bets, and gamblers who pretend to be experts are doing players a grave disservice by recommending the poorest bets in the casino for would-be dice controllers.

Keep this in mind: you can't win money on bets that you can't beat in the long run, and bets with double-digit house edges are losers.

Establishing Your Edge

How you establish your edge not an easy task. The simplest method, and the method I recommend for beginners, is to use the Hardway set and your SRR. The SRR, which stands for Seven-to-Rolls-Ratio, is a simple, handy way to see if you are indeed starting to change the percentages at craps to favor you by reducing the appearance of the 7. It is not the best or the be-all and end-all of craps edge assessing. It is merely a helpful tool as you begin your controlled shooting career. The best way to ascertain your edge is by using the SmartCraps software created by Dan Pronovost.

Remember that the normal SRR for a random roller is 1-to-6, which means one 7 for every six rolls. That is, of course, an average. On a given night, you can see any manner of SRRs from random rollers, but over time the rolls will start to get closer and closer to the average 1-to-6.

Here are the minimum SRRs, rounded somewhat, to overcome the house edges on the various Place bets. It is assumed that all the numbers are equally filled in with the reduction of the 7 (which is not necessarily what happens in the real world of casino play):

Place Bet	*SRR*
6 and 8	1-to-6.2
5 and 9	1-to-6.5
4 and 10	1-to-6.7
Buy 5 and 9 for $30 with $1 vig on win only	1-to-6.2
Buy 4 and 10 for $25 with $1 vig on win only	1-to-6.2

Here is a representative sample of SRRs needed to overcome different Pass/Come bets with odds. The assumption is the Come-Out roll and first placement of Come bets are random and that all numbers are equally filled in while reducing the appearance of the 7 during the Point ycle. The percentages in the boxes are your edges:

SRR	*No Odds*	*1X Odds*	*2X Odds*	*5X Odds*	*10X Odds*
1-to-6.5	1.6%	3.3%	4%	4.8%	5.2%
1-to-7	4.5%	7.1%	8.2%	9.5%	10.1%
1-to-8	9.5%	14%	15.8%	17.9%	19%

It is a *very rare* dice controller who has an SRR of 1-to-7 despite what you may read on the Internet. Keep in mind that the SRR, while an attractive tool for beginners, is not the absolute criteria for a controlled throw. For example, a shooter might have a great ability to hit several of the same numbers on his roll, even though his SRR appears to be a random 1-to-6. There are 3V shooters who hit several 6s and 8s and then seven-out quickly—yet these can be winning rolls for the shooter. So you have to take the SRR as merely an indicator. The best method for ascertaining your edge is SmartCraps software. Using both the SRR and SmartCraps can help even the newest shooter get some idea of what he's doing or not doing with the dice.

Practice, Practice, Practice

Ted Williams summed up his ability as a hitter in three words: "Practice, practice, practice." Your first several hundred or thousand rolls should not be recorded. Just watch your dice at all the stages and make sure your form and how the dice react are proper. When you think you have it down, start recording your numbers. Do 1,000 rolls and record the numbers you hit. At the end of 1,000 rolls, you will then assess your SRR.

Then do another 1,000 rolls and see if you have improved. If you have been throwing correctly, you should see a slight to grand improvement by the time you reach 5,000 rolls. To make figuring your SRR easier and to see which numbers are hitting, shoot in multiples of 36—360, 3,600, 7,200, and so forth.

Do not attempt to do hundreds of rolls in one day. Fatigue can destroy the best shooter's SRR. Keep your initial sessions short, 15 minutes or so. You can do several sessions a day, but you want to make sure that you are on top of your game as you record the throws for your SRR.

Most controlled shooters have recorded about 20,000 rolls. After this number of rolls, which might take up to six months to accomplish, you can then have a good idea of how far you have come.

If your SRR is 1-to-6.5 or better, you are ready to take on the casinos. If your SRR is less than that, you should practice more and also check all the elements of your delivery—the set, grab, grip, finger placement, backswing and forward swing, revolutions of the dice in the air, and how softly they hit the back wall. Any one of these things can cause an SRR to hit the dirt, so you have to be on top of each and every element. Does the above sound hard? It should, because becoming a controlled shooter is not easy.

Famous philosopher Jean-Paul Sartre wrote in his play *No Exit*, "Hell is other people!" For a controlled shooter, losing at craps is definitely other people. There is no way to win in the long run against random rollers, because the casino either wins more bets or takes a cut of the winning bets. My first piece of advice is not to bet on any random rollers. Play alone at the table or play only with fellow dice controllers. But—and I know many of you were already thinking this—it is next to impossible to be alone at a table or to have only controlled shooters at your table. These are luxuries most of us will rarely get. Casinos will most likely become annoyed if you stand at a crowded craps table and only bet on yourself. They want you in the action so they can win your money. They don't want you waiting a half hour to an hour to get the dice. So since you must bet on random rollers, you can utilize three methods:

Method #1 (for controlled shooters): Regulate how much you bet on random rollers in relation to how much you bet on yourself or other controlled shooters.

Method #2 (for all players): Select whom you will bet on by using the Captain's 5-Count.

Method #3 (for controlled shooters): Have separate lines of betting for controlled shooters and for random shooters.

Random Rollers

The section on the 5-Count explains how to select which random rollers you will bet on. But once you know which ones you'll bet on, how much should you wager?

Ideally, a controlled shooter should bet heavily on himself and other good shooters and low on random rollers. Yes, random rollers can sometimes have long rolls. Luck does that. But overall, you will lose whatever the house edge is on the money you bet on random rollers, long rolls or not.

The lower your bets, the lower your losses. Don't think that because some random rollers have good rolls that somehow these rolls are predict-able—they aren't. There are no *ifs*, *ands*, or *buts* about that sentence. In order to be on a given random roller's long roll, you have to go up on *every one* of his rolls, which means...yes, you lose!

Let's take a look at recommended betting levels on random rollers:

Option #1: You bet Come and Pass Line bets at the appropriate time in the 5-Count sequences. These can be table-minimum bets. You can go up on one, two, or three numbers. (I recommend one number.) Taking Odds is your decision. You want to bet about four to 10 times more on yourself than you bet on random rollers.

Option #2: If you do not like the Come betting option but prefer to use Place bets (which have higher house edges), then you only Place the 6 and/or 8 for minimum amounts—trying to get that big differ-ence between betting on yourself and other controlled shooters. In some venues, where you can buy the 4 and 10 for $25 and only pay the vig on a winning bet, you can buy these numbers.

Okay, not everyone can afford to keep the ratio at 4–10-to-1 for betting on random rollers. For you, a drastic realignment of your betting methodology might be in order. If you Place a $12 6 and 8 on yourself ($24 in action) along with a Pass Line bet with Odds, or use Pass and Come betting going up on three or four numbers, then you want to use only one Come bet at $5 (or $10) for a random roller. Indeed, my Five Horseman colleague Jerry "Stickman" and I usually use one Come bet on random rollers. We'd also recommend that you forget the Odds bet on random rollers because you might not have the total bankroll necessary for the variance of such betting.

If you are a low roller, then one Place bet of the 6 or 8 is all you are going to make after a random roller completes the 5-Count. Some readers will say, "But I'm not getting enough action." What that means really is: "I am not losing enough money betting this way!" You must keep your bets low on random rollers. That's the first law of winning money when you play at the tables with random rollers. They lose themselves money and they lose you money.

To really judge how much they are winning on themselves and how much they are losing on random rollers, some controlled shooters use separate betting lines. In your chip rack, the top rack can be the chips you use for betting on yourself and other controlled shooters; the bottom rack can be used for the money you bet on random rollers.

If you are diligent and don't mix up the chips, you will be able to keep long-term records of how much you've won or lost on controlled shooters and random rollers. The longer you play the game of craps as a controlled shooter, the more stunning the difference between what you make on controlled shooting and what you lose on random rollers will become.

CHAPTER 6

The 38 Steps

Follow the traditions and practices of the craps tables:
1. Do not hang your hands over the table when someone is shooting
2. Do not say the word "seven" when at a craps table. Say "the devil" or "that number" or some such phrase.
3. If you are shooting and a die or both dice leave the table, ask for "same dice."
4. Do not make bets when the shooter has the dice in his hand. Make all bets when the dice are in the middle of the table.
5. Do not buy in until a shooter has made a point or sevened out.

Practice good manners at the craps tables:
6. Do not yell or scold someone who has sevened out. Everyone sevens out sooner or later.
7. Do not shout your number into the shooter's ear or whisper it up his nose so he can smell your breath.
8. Do not take it personally that a Darkside (Don't) player wants the 7 to show.
9. If the dealer makes a mistake, be polite as you state your case. Do not engage in arguments. An angry player makes other players uncomfortable.
10. Make sure you know what bets you've made so that you do not interrupt the game.
11. Do not be lascivious at the craps tables. Since the game is mostly a male domain, be a gentleman. Most women don't want to be flirted

with, sexually badgered, or made to feel uncomfortable at a table surrounded by salivating males.

12. Do not whine about your losses. Do not brag about your wins.

13. Always use the 5-Count on other shooters. It will eliminate approximately 57 percent of the random rolls.

Here are the rules for dice controllers:

14. Do not take longer than 10 seconds to set the dice, grab, grip, aim, and throw the dice.

15. Always hit the back wall, but when you don't, please give an indication that you have screwed up. Don't wait for casino personnel to yell at you. Apologize even before anyone can say anything to you.

16. Do not discuss dice sets, dice throws, bounces, backspins, or anything of any depth at the craps table. Stay away from any and all dice-control talk.

17. Act as if you are a regular player at the tables. Don't be snooty. If someone has a good roll—be he a random roller, the best dice controller, or anyone in between—cheer when he hits his point.

18. Do not give advice to anyone while the game is progressing. If a random roller asks you a question, refer him to the dealer with, "Ask the dealers, they're the experts."

19. You might try to get in the line that your spouse or significant other or best friend is a slot nut who plays long hours when the two of you come together. It's good to be looked at as one of a gambling couple, the second of which (your wife, friend, son, daughter, etc.) is a big loser.

20. When you are having a good roll, do not become an egomaniac. Even if your dice are so perfect that you can call your number, don't do it.

21. The dealers live on tips. Be generous with your tipping. If you're on their side, they'll most likely be on your side.

22. Be friendly to the box persons and the pit personnel.

23. If you happen to like the casino you're playing at, let the dealers, the box, and the pit know that you like them.

24. Do not do the fire drill at the table and fully switch positions back and forth.

25. Do not ask other players to move their chips from your landing zone.
26. Know how much you are going to get paid for a bet.
27. Make your presses at the right time and not out of order. Make sure you have won enough to make the added risk worthwhile.
28. Keep the game moving. Make your bets all at once; don't wait until the last second to throw out a new bet.
29. Don't constantly keep calling your bets on and off. On random rollers, it doesn't matter what numbers they hit—it's random!
30. Make sure you do not shortchange yourself when playing. You need a proper bankroll to play your *A* game. Never borrow money from friends in order to play. Bet small in relation to your total bankroll.
31. Realize that a dice controller will have plenty of losing hands and losing sessions. Even the Arm sevened out.
32. Never play when you are tired.
33. Take the dice three or four times, and if you are not hitting, then take a break.

Betting rules for all craps players:

34. Craps is a controlled riot. Get caught up in the emotions of the players who are hitting outrageous Crazy Crapper bets and you will find major losses over time.
35. Remember this: the more you play random games the better the chance that you will be a loser.

General rules to play long and prosper:

36. Ignore all systems that have as their underlying basis any kind of trend betting as advantage play.
37. Don't fall for new-age gobbledygook about sensing the energy at a table or psychically feeling when a hot roll will occur. There are no such things as hot tables or cold tables. What happened in the past of a random game cannot predict what will happen coming up. A table is just a table.
38. Even if you become a highly skilled dice controller, keep your perspective. You are playing a game.

PART III:
Today's Dice Controllers

CHAPTER 1

Today's Dice Controllers

The day of the dice controller is now in full swing—a new age ushered in by the Captain.

The casinos know that some players have the skills necessary to beat them at craps. Luckily so many players "set" the dice that casinos are not always sure who has the skill and who doesn't based on short-term results. In my career I have made major mistakes in this regard, playing too many days, weeks, months, and years in select casinos where the bosses have nailed me. I did that big-time in Mississippi and I have done it big-time in Vegas and Atlantic City.

Today there are many individuals and schools that teach dice control. Some of these schools are ludicrous, those pushing trend-betting and charting random shooters.

I was one of the founders of Golden Touch Craps along with Bob "Mr. Finesse," the late Bill "Ace-10" Burton, and Dom "the Dominator." Golden Touch recruited many fine controlled shooters to be instructors: Daryl "No Field Five," Billy "the Kid," Arman "Pit Boss," Howard "Rock 'n' Roller," Randy "Tenor," Jake "from Pitt," Chris "Sharpshooter" Pawlicki, Fred "Chip," "Doc Holliday," and best-selling author Jerry "Stickman." Most of these instructors came from PARR.

Once the classes got rolling, we recruited our best students to become instructors: Mark "Dice Pilot," Raf "Rafter," Lee "Section Eight," author John "Skinny," Randy "Randman," Nick@Night, "Missouri" Rick, John "Glue Factory," Tommy "Two-Names," Tim "Timmer," Boxcar "Boris," Dave "Satch" (yes, of the Captain's Crew), Pat "Dr. Crapology," and John "the Rolling Rooster."

On our instructional staff were two excellent female dice controllers, Marilyn "the Goddess" and Janis "Alligator Rose." Women make up fewer than 5 percent of craps players, and these two are at the top of the dice-control pyramid, right up there with the best of the men. Both have had rolls of more than 50 before sevening out, with the Goddess being the first woman to do it in front of witnesses, according to Golden Touch's official records. She and her husband Charlie "Sandtrap" (who rolled the fifth-longest recorded roll—an amazing 90!) are a devastating husband-wife team. Alligator Rose and her husband, Dr. Crapology, regularly beat the casinos across the country.

In my decade with Golden Touch, we successfully taught just about all of our students to control the dice, yet I am guessing that maybe only 10 to 15 percent ever made money from the skill,.

Why is that?

Most craps players are gamblers, even the ones who evince a desire to control the dice, and being gamblers causes them not to want to bet the conservative bets that they can actually beat, but to continue to go crazy with all manner of poor betting choices. Most gamblers just can't control themselves. As the Captain always said to me, "The contest is not between you and the casino; it's between you and yourself."

CHAPTER 2

The Five Horsemen

I had the good fortune to play alongside the Captain, Jimmy P., and the Arm (in retrospect I think of them as "the Trinity"). But I also had the good fortune to play with the Five Horsemen from 2007 to 2012. I gave us the name; it sounded special. Just as the Four Horsemen of the Apocalypse heralded the end of the world, the Five Horsemen would herald the end of the casinos—though we never ended any casino's existence.

Our team consisted of Dom "the Dominator"; author John "Skinny"; comp wizard Nick@Night; the man with the perfect throw, best-selling author and columnist Jerry "Stickman"; and me.

Since Golden Touch did five or six classes a year, we would spend time before and after those classes playing craps. We'd also make separate trips to Vegas, Atlantic City, and Tunica just to play—no teaching, no students, nobody knowing where we were. Yes, that was the idea of those private trips—*privacy*—but somehow word would get out that the Five Horsemen were playing in any one of a host of casinos we enjoyed frequenting. Often there would be mob scenes when we arrived.

The Five Horsemen preferred to play in the early mornings, just after the drunks staggered to their rooms and before the yawning morning crowd arrived. Often we'd have a table all to ourselves.

Our favorite casinos treated us with great favor—at least in the beginning. We were big bettors—with Skinny and Nick@Night being megaplayers. Until the casinos realized that we were all doing well, we had little trouble. Some of that had to do with our propensity to tip the dealers, give gifts to our hosts, and play the game calmly and properly. We also didn't spend long hours at the tables.

Each of my fellow Horsemen was a great shooter, and some were also great advantage players at other games. Check them out:

The Dominator

The Dominator came to the fore on the exciting History Channel special *The Dice Dominator*. I served as a consultant and shaped that show. I was able to convince the History Channel that Dom was at the center of the new dice-control revolution, that he was "the man."

Dominator was becoming quite well known during this time period. I requested and received permission from two of my publishers to use Dom's picture on the covers of two dice-control books. I gave him coauthor status on two of my books that I alone authored. I made a point of getting Dom on television as often as possible. Nothing helps business like television, and nothing works better than someone with a dynamic personality. Dom was charismatic. He was an excellent speaker with an exciting dice-control style. He was the perfect point man for the skill.

Dom began his dice-control career in the late 1990s after reading *Beat the Craps Out of the Casinos*. Dom has one of the top 10 longest rolls of all time, according to the Golden Touch world records page—a 79, which means 79 rolls before sevening out.

Dom has the perfect hand for dice control—with flat fingers and a thumb that can sit perfectly square between the two dice. Most people do not have the ability to set that thumb flat against the dice and must cock it at a slight angle, as I must. Dom credits his piano playing for allowing him such finger dexterity.

From the earliest age, Dom was a gambler; in fact he still is. "I think I got my gambler's instinct from pitching pennies as a kid. I'd pitch pennies every day and I usually won. But I knew I needed more than luck to beat casino games," he said.

Before dice control Dom was a card counter, driving to Atlantic City every weekend from his home in Yonkers.

Dom discovered craps indirectly. He said, "I had no interest in the game. I just felt it was a random game and I didn't want to waste my time or money. But one day I just stopped and watched, and it dawned on me that I might be able to control those dice or, at least, I thought that such a thing would be possible.

"So I started to read about the game. I read [Frank's] books, and they convinced me that such a thing could be done. I began practicing at home, and then took the PARR 'rhythm rolling' course with Jerry Patterson and Sharpshooter. I seemed to have a natural talent for throwing in a controlled way. Of course, I did practice a lot, but it just felt natural to me. There was no strain at all.

"I met Frank at Treasure Island in Vegas when he was researching his book *The Craps Underground* [Note: I dedicated the book to him], and we became partners. We've had a lot of interesting times and adventures together."

Dom has a fiery temper, and some of his confrontations with casino management are legendary—well, they are legendary for me because I was there for many of them.

He told me, "I have to admit that sometimes I violate a fundamental rule of the Captain's: I let my emotions take over. That is a mistake, and it costs me because sometimes it affects my rolls. I also have a tendency to gamble a little, which is a mistake for an advantage player."

However, sometimes Dom's anger affects his rolls in a positive way. He said, "There are times when I just want to shove it into the casino's face. I hate it when a snotty dealer or a box man will sneer and say, 'You know what you are doing doesn't work.' Okay, so why don't they tell shooters who obviously can't win that what *they* are doing doesn't work? Of course it works, and that's why they tell me it doesn't work. They just want to rattle me."

During one Treasure Island visit Dom and one of the suits had several set-tos. Some of the dealers were, as Dom said, "dicks." They razzed him. The more Dom's face got red, the more they insulted him. The box man ripped Dom, as did the floor person. Dom exploded in anger several times.

Finally, Dom's point was a 4, and he angrily said he'd hit it as a Hardway. The box man snorted, giving a look of scorn, and said, "I doubt that!" Dom then threw out a $100 on the Hard 4, set the dice, announced to anyone within earshot that the Hard 4 was coming, and then threw the dice—and damn it, a Hard 4! The suit slunk away.

Dom, Sharpshooter, and I participated in an unedited contest filmed by the A&E network against three casinos in Las Vegas in 2002—the Gold Coast, Sam's Town, and Sunset Station. "Unedited" meant no shots would be edited to make us look good. No ending other than the real ending would be shown. This was in the early days of Golden Touch Craps. There were two teams competing—not against each other, but against the house.

Our Golden Touch team played a disciplined game—using the 5-Count on the members of Team 2, even though every shooter on that team was supposedly a controlled shooter because we figured the pressure might get to them. It did. Indeed one of their team members dropped out after the first session at Gold Coast—he had lost all his money with his poor shooting and terrible wagers. The guy was a Crazy Crapper. The other two players on Team 2 practiced controlled shooting but also believed in mystical energy and charting and intuition—the exact nonsense you read about previously. Those beliefs did not help them in that contest.

Our team only made the lowest-house-edge bets while Team 2 made some of the worst bets at the table, thinking a hit or two would give them a win. Maybe they were also applying their mystical energy—call that "mistake-al energy"—which also sunk them. Their betting was gambling, not advantage betting. They shot from every spot on the table—close to the stickman, at the end of the table, and everywhere in between. They kept changing their dice sets. Our team stuck to our best shooting spots and we used our normal dice sets. They played frenetically; we played calmly.

What Team 2 showed is what causes most dice controllers to lose or to do far worse than their skills warrant. They never settled down, never focused on the goal. They were all over the place.

We all lost during our first session at Gold Coast, though the Golden Touch losses were far less than Team 2's, owing to our use of the 5-Count.

At Sam's Town, Dom and I had monster rolls. Our team made quite a lot of money. While Team 2 also made some money, it was much less because they bet on themselves from the get-go while we 5-Counted them and saved our money when they sevened out early—which they did quite often.

Finally, at Sunset Station Sharpshooter went on a tear; we all won money, and the final score was Golden Touch 2, Casinos 1. Sadly, Team

2 lost money overall in the contests because of their poor betting and shooting performances. Both remaining members of Team 2 are now teaching classes in dice control—the female believes in mystical and intuitive applications to craps play (utter nonsense); the male is hawking an expensive trend-betting system (more utter nonsense). The male actually has a good controlled throw when he shoots from the proper areas of the table—stick left or right, positions one or two.

Over the years the story of the A&E challenge has taken on mythical properties, both good and bad. Some dishonest Internet "gurus" have attempted to explain our success away by saying that what actually happened before the camera actually didn't, or that there were no actual witnesses to the events—just the camera crew, the casino crew, and the players. More nonsense. There were many non-production witnesses, all of whom came forward to testify to the truth of the show. I guess it doesn't really matter; the A&E show was the only time that dice controllers actually got to take on the casinos in a filmed real-life, real-money contest. Golden Touch won; Team 2 and the casinos lost.

Skinny

Author John "Skinny" (he wrote the Pai Gow section of *Everything Casino Poker*) was a student in Golden Touch Craps, one of the best. His acumen in betting, and his ability to shoot from stick left and stick right made him a perfect Horseman. He often wagered in the orange chip category, and when one of the Horsemen got hot, he raked in the big bucks.

Skinny was an aggressive presser. Before you knew it, he'd be up on every number, and if the roll was touching 40 or 50, he'd be up with Come bets with full Odds *and* Place bets on those same numbers.

But Skinny's claim to fame other than his authorship, his dice control ability, and his betting heroics came at the very same Claridge in Atlantic City where I first met the Captain.

Normally a session would see us taking the dice three or four times, and if nothing happened, we'd call it a night (or day). That particular evening we started play around 9:00. It wasn't just the Five Horsemen at the table, but several other Golden Touch players as well—the Goddess, Sandtrap, Randy "Randman," and Jack "the Raging Baritone."

We were all hot. And we were playing the fire drill method—meaning only shooters from SL1, SL2, SR1, and SR2 would shoot—but we'd rotate everyone into those spots

Just about every shooter had winning hands—even if those hands were short, they were composed of repeating numbers. At 3:00 AM—yes, 3:00 AM!—Skinny took the dice again. By that time there were several suits in the pit anxiously watching the game, which had *big* money involved. Even the $5 bettors were in the black. Skinny's bets were through the roof!

Skinny shot 23 numbers, and then his dice curved around the pyramids of the back wall with one landing in the casino's chips. It was a box number, and the dealer called it. Then a suit leaned over the table.

"You missed the back wall!" screamed the man, whose name was Francis; I could read that on his name tag, and he was the casino manager or shift or pit boss. "You do that again, I'll take the dice away from you!"

"Both dice hit the back wall," Skinny said. "One just went around that way." Skinny pointed to the casino's chip stack. "And you lost track of it because it was out of your sight."

The wild-eyed Francis bellowed, "I saw *everything!* I saw everything! Your dice didn't hit the back wall!" Francis was leaning over the table, his eyes bulging, with spit flying out of his mouth as he screamed.

Skinny, an eminently reasonable man, looked at the dealers, who were standing straight as if they were at attention in the army. None of the dealers looked at any of the players. "The dealers saw it," Skinny said. He looked to the dealers for confirmation, and it was as if the dealers were statues. They just stared straight ahead. They didn't want to dispute their angry boss.

Skinny got the dice again and, with Francis hanging over the table glaring at him, shot another eight times before his dice did the exact same thing—both hit the back wall and one scooted around to land in the casino's chips.

Francis bellowed, "You did it again! You did it again!" And then in a moment of lunacy, Francis leaped across the table—yes, right over the layout so that his head was in Skinny's chip rack and his legs were right next to the box man's head, screaming, "You can't fool me! You can't fool me! There! There! You see?"

Then Francis slid slowly onto the table off Skinny's chip rack with many of Skinny's orange chips falling onto the layout along with Francis' face. The dealers stood stiff. The box man looked in chagrin at Francis sprawled on the craps table.

The box man and the dealer to the right of the box man helped Francis get off the table and stand up. Francis looked menacingly at Skinny. Skinny didn't say anything; obviously he realized that Francis was a half inch away from being institutionalized or murdering someone, probably Skinny.

Francis walked to the back of the pit, where other suits seemed to try to calm him down. The box man indicated that Skinny could continue to roll. The box man said under his breath, "You hit the back wall both times."

Skinny rolled another six numbers and then sevened out. We called it a night after that. The confrontation with Francis had drained all of us—that plus playing more than six hours.

I went back to the Claridge a few times after the Skinny incident, but when Francis was there he stalked me. I stopped going, and that was that for the Claridge.

It is rare that you can flat-out say, "So-and-so destroyed the casinos for the last four days!" I am happy to say that Skinny destroyed Atlantic City four straight days in an exhibition of shooting that was truly amazing. Dom and I were there. We saw it, applauded it, and profited from it.

We had been invited to bring the Five Horsemen to Atlantic City to shoot a television show for a Netherlands station. It would be a two-day shoot. Only three of the Horsemen could make it.

The show's host, a tall, slim blonde who also emceed *Holland's Got Talent* and *X-Factor* shows—had just finished running the New York City marathon. He also once swam the English Channel. Dom and Beau had something in common—they were both heavy smokers!

The worst way to start a trip is to dig a deep hole and spend most of your remaining time shoveling out. Not so this trip. The very first time Skinny got the dice he rolled a 41. We weren't in a hole; we were starting our climb up the mountainside. His next two hands were both in the mid-20s.

We each took the dice six times that first day over two different sessions. Skinny went six-for-six.

I had a decent four-day run of repeating numbers, but only twice did I have rolls that went more than 20. I remember one stretch where I hit four 6s and three 8s in 10 rolls before sevening out with one critic at the end of the table pronouncing, "That guy sucks!" Evidently he wasn't on the 6 or 8.

Skinny repeated his Monday on Tuesday with another 40+ roll, two 30s, and three teens—all handsome winners for the three of us.

Skinny then repeated his Monday and Tuesday performances on Wednesday during the morning and afternoon sessions (six straight winning turns with the dice), but, not truly being a god, he sucked on Wednesday evening. So did I. So did Dom. We did a series of point sevens, and after three turns with the dice Skinny and I called it a night. Not so Dom, who decided to continue. That's when he had his monster, while Skinny and I slept.

We didn't get to the craps tables on Thursday morning because our spots were taken.

We had one session left to play Thursday evening. And that is when lightning struck. We had three other players at the table that took care with their rolls after setting the dice in either the Hardway set or the 3V. One of them came over to me after he had a damn good roll and said, "Frank, I've read your books, and I have to say you have helped me so much. Thanks!"

Skinny, Dom, and I had winning rolls on our first two turns with the dice as did the other three shooters. What a great session it was. Then it was Skinny's turn. At that point I was guaranteed a nice big win to bring home no matter what Skinny did.

And then he did it.

He rolled and rolled and rolled. Black chips were spread out on the table. Then purple chips. Then orange chips appeared. Skinny rarely rolled a bad number. The man was on fire.

When he sevened out, the table exploded with applause. I leaned over to him and said, "Sixty-three, sixty-three."

"Great rolling, sir," said the dealer on our side of the table.

"Great rolling," said the stickman.

"I'm just glad that's not my money you won," laughed the floor person.

We quit right then, colored up, and had a delicious dinner, where we toasted our great week and Skinny's demolition of Atlantic City.

It is wonderful to see someone put on such a show. For those four days, Skinny was the man of all men.

I never did get to see that Netherlands television show.

Nick@Night

Nick@Night is a lefty—a rare commodity in dice-control circles. If you have a team shooting from SL1/SL2 and SR1/SR2, you either need right-handed shooters capable of shooting the awkward SR shot or you need a lefty. Of course, for us, not any lefty would do. We wanted our team to be perfect or as close to perfect as we could get.

Originally we had Rock 'n' Roller as our lefty shooter. At one time he was the best modern shooter. I once called him the Babe Ruth of dice control. What happened to him was sad—a great dice controller became, well, not so great. I'll have more to say about him later in the book.

We weren't looking for just any left-handed shooter once Rock 'n' Roller was gone, since Dom and Skinny could shoot from SR1 and SR2. Still, Skinny was a better shooter from stick left, so "drafting" an accomplished lefty was our goal.

Nick@Night filled the bill. A high roller, Nick was very much like Dom; he found it hard to drag himself away from the tables—that's the gambler in him. But he was a truly calm shooter and a major asset to us. Nick was an aggressive player and rarely used the 5-Count on any of us. That was probably a mistake, because there were times when all five of us stunk up the joint. Still, in some sessions I didn't use the 5-Count either, but that had to do with one or more Horsemen being hot.

Of course, when any of the Horsemen got hot or even made several repeating numbers, Nick@Night made a fortune. He tended to be a Come bettor, so he would be on the repeating numbers. Yet his ups and downs were gigantic, far more than mine or Stickman's.

Nick milked the comp systems of the casinos. Indeed, he was able to spread his comps around so other players could enjoy them. Think of being a $5 or $10 player and having the casino pick everything up for you, thanks to Nick. Skinny was also like that. Those two spread the wealth around. Unfortunately some individuals took advantage of their generosity.

Still Nick@Night was a terrific shooter, certainly a better shooter than what ultimately became of Rock 'n' Roller, and Nick was integral in helping the Five Horsemen beat the casinos. He was also one great guy whose company I enjoyed.

Stickman

Finally, meet the shooter with the perfect throw, author and columnist for *Casino Player*, *casinocitytimes.com*, and *BJ Insider Newsletter*, Jerry "Stickman." Jerry wrote the video poker section of my book *Everything Casino Poker*, where he explains the video poker games that can actually be beaten and the strategies to use in order to do just that.

Anyone who knows anything about a controlled throw marvels at the beauty and near perfection of Stickman's form. Stickman stands 6'4" and uses his height to great advantage, getting all the way out over the table so his dice go down in a perfectly straight line to the back wall, where they bounce gently, hit the pyramids softly, and die. If you want to see the model throw, then look no further than Stickman's.

I have played with Stickman as a part of the Five Horsemen and as a tag team. I am in awe of how he throws and the results he gets. He is poetry in motion.

Jerry is not limited to craps. He was a part of our Tunica blackjack team. I have the full story in *I Am a Card Counter*! He is a video poker expert and he also scouted and found slot machines that at times favor players. These can be found in my book *Slots Conquest*.

Jerry is a great advantage-player. It is truly rare that an advantage-player can perform at such high levels at craps, blackjack, slots, and video poker—in addition Jerry "Stickman" has contributed a wealth of knowledge writing about these games.

Jerry has had many great rolls—two of his best occurred back-to-back, a 44 and then a 77. That 77 saw him roll no sevens until he rolled a seven-out. That is also a world record!

Jerry wears hearing aids in both ears, and when he shoots the dice he removes them and puts them in his shirt pocket. According to him, he hears almost nothing. That allows him to get into his "stick zone." The casino almost ceases to exist; his world becomes internal. If a dealer or suit says something to him, he just smiles and nods.

Stickman is the most consistent of all the modern-day dice controllers. Many players believe that he is the best shooter in the world. It is rare that he goes on any long losing streaks. He has a great ability to hit those repeating numbers. In Tunica he started the week where I was banned from the whole state by having a roll at the Grand that is—for those who know about it—legendary.

I have the ultimate respect for Stickman. When I was teaching I would be the one to introduce Jerry to our students when it came time for the instructors to show their throws. Naturally, I told the students exactly what you just read—how perfect, how great, how beautiful his throw was. I'd even ask other instructors what they thought of his throw. Invariably the word "perfect" would be used.

During one class in Atlantic City, I went through my routine— "Stickman is great. Stickman is terrific. Stickman has the perfect throw. You are all in for a treat to be able to watch him." As always, the students were riveted to Stickman.

"Okay, kid, here are the dice," I said, and pushed the two dice to him with a flourish. He took the dice, set them, bent over the table—way out over the table—aimed, and threw them. They didn't make it even three-fourths of the way down the table. "Ha! Ha!" I laughed. "Very funny."

Jerry had this weird look on his face. I pushed the dice to him, again with a flourish. He took them, set them, leaned over the table, aimed, and threw them. They didn't even make it halfway down the table. "All right, all right," I said. "Very funny. Now show them the great Stickman throw."

"That *was* the great Stickman throw," he said.

The students looked confused. I am certain that I looked confused.

"What are you talking about?" I asked.

"I hurt my shoulder and I can't lift it. My backswing is more or less gone. I can't get the proper propulsion."

"Are you serious?" I asked. He nodded. "Why didn't you tell me?"

"I did."

"I don't remember that."

"You might have been thinking of something else," he said.

Yes, I was thinking about something else. Dom is a heavy smoker, and he would light up even in nonsmoking areas, such as the banquet rooms where we held our classes. The supervisor in charge of the banquet rooms had come to me to ask who had been smoking in the room. I lied and said no one had. Dom ignored her.

"Someone passed by who had a cigarette, and the smoke must have floated in here," I lied.

Sadly, the students in that class never got to see the perfect Stickman throw. I guess you can't have it all. I wish we could have used some kind of smoke and mirrors during that non-demonstration instead of just the smoke.

Stickman; his wife, the Sainted Tres; the Beautiful AP; and I have become fast friends outside the casino world. All of us have traveled together many times. (Jerry was away from home 240 days in a single year!) And Jerry and I are making that grand tour of the baseball stadiums throughout America I mentioned earlier. The story of our adventures can be found at my website, frankscoblete.com.

The Five Horsemen had great times together for many years because "veni, vidi, vici" (We came, we saw, we conquered).

CHAPTER 3
Other Dice Control Teams

Men and women often look across a gulf at each other. It is amazing that any relationship between the sexes can last. Yet some husbands and wives not only have found the secret to a great marriage, but they have found an avocation that gives them joy, teamwork, and a strong sense of accomplishment—beating the casinos. Some do this at craps, and some do this at blackjack.

I already recounted my experiences as a teammate with my beautiful wife in *I Am a Card Counter*, but other husband-wife teams also exist. I know of three—two I found wonderful and one I found weird.

Among the Golden Touch instructors, our first married team was Marilyn "the Goddess" and Charlie "Sandtrap." The second team, which came several years later, was Janis "Alligator Rose" and Pat "Dr. Crapology."

The Goddess, Alligator Rose, and Dr. Crapology were all excellent instructors at Golden Touch. The Goddess became the first woman to roll 50 numbers before sevening out. She did it in Canada with many witnesses. That weekend I was doing a Frank Scoblete's Gamblers Jamboree at what is now Caesars Windsor. The Goddess put on a show that evening. She has now had many rolls greater than 50. Perhaps her greatest achievement is her record of having 34, 30, 34, 30, and 32 rolls in five consecutive turns with the dice.

Not to be outdone, her husband, Sandtrap, rolled 90 numbers in succession before sevening out. He did this in Atlantic City—the fifth-longest witnessed roll in the Golden Touch world records. One thing that truly sets the Goddess apart is her awareness of the little things that can go wrong in another dice controller's form. Let me quote Sandtrap: "She's driving me crazy!" Her driving him "crazy" probably resulted in the almost perfect performance he had when he rolled 90 numbers.

Alligator Rose and her husband, Dr. Crapology, have made playing craps a way of life, and they can be found in casinos all across America putting their skills to the test. Each has had rolls in the 50s and 60s, and Dr. Crapology even went more than 70! Both have beautiful throws, and with their calm demeanors they are a devastating team.

Janis and Pat are excellent teachers, and they use their extensive casino experience to help players who just can't seem to stop playing like gamblers, which means betting foolishly and letting the casinos dictate their pace and the bets they make. To beat the house as Alligator Rose and Dr. Crapology have done requires total discipline, and those two have it in spades.

Then there are Heavenly Kitten and Star Shine, a married couple (I think) who love craps, and they play it all over the country because they live in a trailer. When they are not being abducted by space aliens, they think of craps as a way to get away from the world. Seems they spend a lot of time "out of it," if you will.

They also use certain psychic vibrations to find the casinos where they can win money. Sometimes they will travel hundreds of miles if "the universe" tells them where to go. Star Shine will often go outside the trailer in the dark of night, smoke from a bong, raise his hands to the heavens, and if the aliens do not come down to abduct him for his regular anal probing (that's what space aliens do when they abduct you—they give you a colonoscopy), he will hear the "spirits of the night" telling him when to go to the casino to play craps, even if they recommend a casino far, far away.

Of course, I can only state for the record that they took several Golden Touch classes, but as for their other adventures, I leave that up to you to decide if the "spirits of the night" and space aliens messing around with bottoms are worth meeting. Have they won? I doubt it.

Not all teams are composed of husbands and wives. Teams of friends dominate the dice-control landscape. There are plenty of multimember groups playing as teams—sometimes as casual teams, sometimes as serious teams. I know a team made up of priests—the Holy Rollers. (Some blackjack team also blessed themselves with the same name.)

I only know one professional team—*professional* meaning that they make their sole living from craps. That team is the Lee Brothers. Their story was written about in *The Craps Underground*, but theirs is a story worth retelling.

As a prelude, I am not an advocate of becoming a professional craps player—it is nerve-wracking. The pressure to win is overwhelming. My advice? Use dice control as an avocation. Playing as a pro—or even playing 130 days a year as the Beautiful AP and I did—can be a grind, a chore.

The Lee Brothers

It was in 2002 when I met them—at the very beginning of Golden Touch Craps. They are not brothers, and their names aren't Lee. They are Korean or Vietnamese, or maybe they aren't; maybe they are Japanese or Chinese. Or German. "We all look alike," laughed Tony Lee, "except to us, and so make us what you will."

"You don't make us be recognized," cautioned Larry Lee, whose name isn't Larry or anything close to Larry.

Larry Lee doesn't talk much; English isn't his first language or his second. He was born "over there" in a poor village and came to America in the 1980s. He got his citizenship in 1995 and of *that* he is proud, saying, "America is great. Casinos suck."

For a man of few words, Larry Lee sees the world in black-and-white. He also sees the world through a cloud of cigarette smoke, as I have yet to see him without one—unfiltered no less—dangling from his mouth, except for the times when it was in his nicotine-stained hands.

I met the Lee brothers strictly by chance. I was playing craps at Sunset Station in Henderson, which is just outside of Las Vegas, when these two came to the table. I was all alone at the table and doing quite well, thank you, so I wasn't too thrilled to have players buying in. Tony bought in at SL1 for $500. I was on SR1, and Larry moved right in next to me, smoke billowing out of his mouth and nostrils. He crowded me and threw down $1,000. "Hey, man, I'm shooting," I said.

Larry didn't give an inch. The box man laid out his bills—$5s, $10s,

$20s, $50s, and a few $100s—counted them out, and passed him his chips. He didn't put down a Pass Line bet. He just smoked. Tony didn't put out a Pass Line bet either. "Just move over a few inches," I said to him, "we're the only ones at the table."

He didn't budge. The dice were passed to me. I had a choice. I could stop the game and complain to the pit that this idiot was crowding me or I could concentrate on what I was doing and continue what, until then, had been a 15-minute roll with only me at the table. I decided to continue my roll.

I took a breath, cleared my mind, concentrated on my breathing, and then picked up the dice and set them. When Larry saw me set the dice in the 3V, he suddenly stepped all the way back and gave me plenty of room. I then lofted them to the back wall.

Tony placed the inside numbers (5, 6, 8, and 9) for $110, and Larry bought the 4 and 10 for $25 each. I rolled again. And again. And for another 20 minutes.

I totally forgot about Larry standing next to me. He had moved not only out of my way, but also out of my vision; the only reason I knew he was still there, aside from his bets, was the smoke that wafted over every so often, but even that wasn't all that much. (I learned later that Larry purposely blew the smoke as far from me as possible during my roll. Usually he blows it right at people to get them to leave the table.)

When I sevened out, Tony gave a big round of applause. I looked over at his chip rack and noticed that he had a hell of a lot more than $500 in chips after my roll. I didn't look in Larry's direction, and he didn't say anything. Other people started coming to the table. Controlled shooters often like to play alone, whereas random rollers love the crowds and don't want to be the only player at the table. Unfortunately, more often than not, when a controlled shooter is playing alone, it doesn't last for long. Others gravitate to the table.

In a real way, we act as shills for the casinos—since we open tables and get the action going. Two of the other people bought in. One was a woman of indeterminate age, wearing sunglasses; the other was a whale of a man. The woman stood next to Larry and cashed in for $100. The whale cashed in for $2,000 and he stood at the end of the table on Larry's side.

It was Tony's turn to shoot. I played the 5-Count on him. Larry had gone right up on him with $440 inside (that's $100 each on the 5 and 9, $120 each on the 6 and 8).

I felt a nudge on my arm. Larry was nudging me. I looked at him. "Bet," he said softly, "good shooter," and he nodded toward Tony and blew smoke out of his nose. He looked kind of like a dragon, I thought at the time. "I will," I said, "when he gets warmed up."

Tony set the dice—in the 3V! He gripped the dice in a very similar fashion to the Captain and had an incredibly smooth delivery and throw. The dice arched up and landed, just touching the back wall. "Good shooter," whispered Larry in my ear, "bet, bet."

Tony bought the 4 and 10 for $100 each, then he turned to Larry and said, "Leave him alone, he's playing the 5-Count."

Bowl me over with a feather! I looked over at Tony, but he was busy setting the dice. His first point was a 6, and he made it right back. Then a beautiful young woman came to the table and stood about one person away from Tony. She bought in for $20. She placed a Hard 6 and 8 for $10 each.

"Working on the Come-Out," said the stickman. In Vegas proposition bets work on the Come-Out roll, unless you say they don't; in Atlantic City they do not work on the Come-Out, unless you say they do. Go figure.

Tony set the dice in the 3V and threw an 8. It was the 3-count, and I still had to wait before going up on him. Tony's next number was a 4, then he came back with another 8, his second point. The 4-count was completed. Since he couldn't possibly seven-out before the 5-Count, since he was on the Come-Out roll, I placed a Pass Line bet and placed the 6 and 8. Tony then rolled an 11, then a Hard 6—the beautiful young woman had won her bet. "Parlay," she said.

She had $100 riding on the Hard 6, and Tony had just completed the 5-Count. I was in the action too. Tony then hit a string of outside numbers, 4s and 10s, then he hit some 9s, some 8s, if memory serves me right about three 5s in a row, and then: "Six! Hard 6! Winner! Winner! Six, came the hard way!"

The young woman collected her $900 and said, "Take me down." She then left the table as the box man said to Tony, "You have to hit the back wall." On his last throw both dice had just, well, died, *without a single bounce*, about three inches from the back wall. I was later to learn that once a session Tony Lee does his trick shot (also known as the "kill shot") Hard 6 or Hard 8—a move he has perfected and is successful with about a third of the time. The dice go up in the air and, with the backspin and trajectory just right, they land and stick to the table as if they have Velcro on them. He is the only—I repeat *only*—player I have ever known who could actually do this on purpose. Once in a while you see someone do it accidentally.

The young lady, known as Vixen (I kid you not), who had placed the Hard 6 was not all that young and, if Tony is to be believed, was not even a woman, but "she" was a member of their team, composed of Tony, Larry, the indeterminate woman named Lola, and the human whale. (By the way, I am not being insensitive by calling the large man "the human whale," because his nickname was Whale. He's a whale in stature, but he's also the bankroll behind this very effective dice control team.)

Tony rolled several more times before sevening out. The dice made their way to Whale, who passed them to Lola, who also passed, and then they went to Larry, the smokestack. With a cigarette dangling from his mouth [he smokes even more than Dom], Larry made his Pass Line bet. I moved out of his way so that he could get as close to the stickman as possible. I had an inkling that Larry and Tony were somehow a "team," but I had no idea about the other three.

Larry set the dice, also in a 3V, only he inverted it, like a pyramid. He, too, had a nice soft delivery, but he sevened out rather quickly. Then it was my turn to roll. I took the dice, set the 3V, and...

"You guys all set the dice the same way," said the tall dealer. "Look, all three set them with the 3-spots up." He indicated Larry, Tony, and me.

"They copied me," I said, hoping this would ease the light the dealer was shining on such a remarkable coincidence.

"He's right," Tony said, "we copied him."

The box man waved his arm twice: "Come on, come on, get the game moving."

I set the dice and tossed and had another great roll, about 20 minutes. Then Tony rolled and he had an epic roll, about 40 minutes. When he sevened out, I walked behind the stickman and whispered to him, "You are damn good."

"I know who you are," he said. "I've read all your books."

"I'm finished," I said. "When you're finished, meet me for a drink in the center lounge."

Tony looked over at Whale and did some kind of gesture I didn't catch. Whale, Lola, and Larry all colored up and went their separate ways.

About a half hour later, Tony showed up in the center bar at Sunset Station. He ordered a beer, I ordered a cabernet. "You have some nice roll," I said.

"Oh, yes, I have worked on this ever since I read your two books on the Captain. Is the Captain..." he paused.

"Real?"

"Yes, I sometimes think you made him up to get out your ideas."

"No, he's real. I would have taken full credit for everything if he weren't. I wish I had come up with all these ideas, but I didn't. I would have named them after myself."

"Well, he has made me a lot of money. Me and Larry."

"Who's Larry?" I asked, but I could guess.

"The other Korean at the table, my brother."

"That other guy is your brother?"

"No, but I call him my brother because we are in the brotherhood of craps players."

Then Tony told me their story.

Larry Lee came over from Korea in 1980 as a 10-year-old with his mother and her brother. They settled in Brooklyn, in what is euphemistically called "a bad neighborhood." His father remained behind in their village, along with his sister, who had just gotten married, and his grandparents on his father's side, one of whom, Grand Pops, was dying of lung cancer. Larry's father joined them in 1983 upon the death of his own father.

At first Larry Lee and his mother worked for several greengrocers, all relatives, and lived over the store, saving as much money as they could and working seven days a week. Larry attended school but was an unremarkable student. When Mr. Lee arrived with the family "fortune," and having amassed enough capital from several years of nonstop work, the Lee family opened their own store in New York in, as Larry said, "a good neighborhood, where everyone complain all the time. They drive you crazy complaining."

The Lee family built up the business, and when Larry graduated high school in 1988, they sold it, again to relatives, and moved to California. Larry started college but then found that he enjoyed working more than school, so he quit after his first year. He held a series of jobs, mostly with family, and in 1997 ran into Tony Lee in Las Vegas. It seems Larry had gotten the gambling bug, played with his paychecks, and was always broke. "I didn't know what I do," he said. "I play blackjack, but I don't know strategy."

Tony Lee was different. A fourth-generation American who was fluent in several languages, Tony was 35 years old, held a master's degree in engineering, and worked for a small firm that designed shopping malls, but his real passion was gambling. However, unlike Larry, who was just throwing his money down a rat hole, Tony counted cards at blackjack, was very cautious with money, and was practicing with a rhythmic roll at craps. "I had read *Beat the Craps Out of the Casinos* and *The Captain's Craps Revolution*, and I knew that the Captain was on to something. I set up a half craps table in my small office, and analyzing those books, I was able to perfect my roll. It took me a year to have enough confidence to play craps in the casino and use my roll. But right away I saw that it worked, and I've been doing it ever since. But in 1997, I was still a small player."

Larry was watching Tony roll the dice. Tony was in the midst of a blistering roll that would last one hour; Larry was smoking incessantly and inching closer and closer to Tony to see his form and exactly what he was doing, when Tony asked him to move back. Larry said something in Korean, Tony's second language, and when Tony finally sevened out, Larry asked him how he, Larry, could learn to roll like that.

Tony took Larry aside and scolded him about smoking so much. ("That was the first and only time I ever said anything about Larry's smoking," Tony said. "Everyone in his family smokes, and all of them have died from lung cancer, and the ones still alive still smoke.") Then Tony explained what he was doing.

Larry saw the possibilities immediately. Tony laughed when he remembered this: "He just said, 'We make a good living!' I don't know if he knew that I was having real problems on the job. I hated the boss; the boss hated me. I made okay money, but I wasn't happy. I was only happy when I was playing craps. Once I had my roll down, I stopped playing blackjack. Craps was everything."

Larry and Tony hooked up. Since they lived some 50 miles apart, it was not hard for them to get together. Tony taught Larry his rolling technique. "Larry was very motivated. He also had great dexterity. He was a little crazy in the betting department, so I had to tone him down there, but he was a natural roller. And he loved it. He was now able to make money when we went to Vegas on weekends."

It was on a trip to Vegas in 1998 that Tony and Larry, who played their own bankrolls rather than pooling their money, met Whale. Tony and Larry would use the 5-Count on the other shooters, and this particular table had been cold. In fact, when Tony looked up, it was just Larry and him at the table. Then Whale came. A huge man, standing maybe 6'6" and weighing close to 400 pounds, the Whale spread his $6,400 across all the numbers and threw out about $300 worth of proposition bets, as Tony picked up the dice. "I was thinking that maybe if I had a good roll this big bettor would tip me. It had happened in the past. You have a good roll, and a big player puts out some Hardways for you. You never know."

As luck would have it, Tony had one of his famous blistering rolls that lasted about 50 minutes. At one point, Whale put up a Hard 6 for $500. "Come on, kid, hit that and I'll split it with you," Whale said.

Tony set the 3V and then, "I don't know, just by luck or fate or something, I lofted the dice just a little too high and I thought, Oh, shit, here comes the 7,' but instead the dice landed like they had a magnet on them right on the Hard 6. It was incredible. But that's when I realized that hitting that Hard 6 [or its opposite side, the Hard 8] would be possible if I didn't hit the back wall and got that trajectory and spin just right. So after that day, I went home, and that's all I practiced. So now I do it once a session, not too much, and we try to get a parlay on a Hard 6 or 8, and then I do my trick shot to nail the parlay."

Whale was impressed with Tony and did indeed share his Hard 6 win with the young man. Then it was Whale's turn to roll. He established his point, hit a couple of numbers, and then sevened out. Larry was up.

Larry's set, grip, and delivery are mirror images of Tony's. He rolled for a half hour. Whale was impressed and asked to speak with them away from the table.

Whale told them that he was a small-time porn producer. He asked them if they were used to having such good rolls. "I noticed how you throw the dice. You seem to have some kind of control, right?"

At first Tony was hesitant to say anything to the big man; after all, he might be a casino spy. But finally Larry said, "Yeah, so what?"

"Here's so what," Whale said. He took out $20,000 in $100 bills. "I'm prepared to bankroll you guys right now. I've lost millions of dollars playing craps. I love the game, but I hate those fuckers"—he indicated the casino and by extension the casino world—"and I want revenge. You double this $20,000, and I'll give you each $5,000 of it. What do you say?"

Larry held out his hand. "Give money," he said.

They went to the table and for two days played high-stakes craps, and not only did they double Whale's $20,000, they tripled it! Whale was delighted. Then he had another plan.

"I want to form a team. I'll bankroll the whole thing. You guys get 20 percent each of what we win. I have two other people I want involved, because I want us to be able to take up at least half the table so we don't have to worry about betting on these other fuckers [meaning other players]. You guys work for a living?"

Tony and Larry gave the details of their jobs.

"Quit them. They suck. The first six months, not only will I bankroll you, I'll pay all your living expenses and transportation."

Neither Tony nor Larry was married; they figured they had nothing to lose in accepting Whale's offer.

And that's how I found them, a five-member team—Whale; two of his "actresses," Vixen and Lola; Tony; Larry; and a boatload of money.

The battle plan for the team is interesting. They never play the same casino more than once on the same trip. Says Tony: "We hit about 25 Vegas casinos in a month. Then we go to Reno for a few days. Then Tahoe, then to the South, then Atlantic City, then the Midwest, then back to Vegas. We play all the time—sometimes with Whale, some-times without Whale."

They always have the two "actresses" with them. "We are all friends. They take up space at the table, pass the dice to us, and make the Hardways bets for the team," said Tony. "They also distract people when we're really putting out big money. Today they weren't dressed up, but they can be very sexy when they want to be, especially the guy." He laughed. Then he explained that one of the "actresses" was really a guy— "prettiest guy you'll ever see."

Their bets range from $640 to $3,200 across the numbers, between the two of them, but only when they roll. "We play the 5-Count on everyone else. We don't bet very much on the ones that get to the 5-Count—$100, $200—but it makes us look like regular players."

Because they play at least six of every seven days, they know that their rolls are fine-tuned. "This not luck what we do," Larry explained. "This skill."

I wanted to know if they had ever met any other controlled shooters or teams on their travels. Tony shook his head, "No, no teams. I haven't seen any other teams. They may be out there, but I haven't met them. We have seen some good shooters like you, but not many. This is not easy, and not many people can do this; you know, you don't win every day."

"What's the longest losing streak you've had?" I asked.

"I didn't have a winning roll for four straight days; Larry went about a week once without a single winning roll. But usually one or the other of us is on even if the other one isn't."

"So what do you make?" I asked. "If you don't mind?"

"Okay," said Tony, "but you must swear that when you write about us we cannot be recognized at all."

"Make us Germans," said Larry.

"No," said Tony, "Oriental."

"Chinese? Japanese? What?" I asked.

"Everything," said Larry.

"No one can know what we look like."

"Okay," I said. "No one will be able to figure out who you guys are."

"I only talked to you because you are Frank Scoobleet..."

"Sco-bleet-tee."

"Scoblete, the great author. You are the man."

"Well," I said, "I don't think of myself as the man; the Captain is the man."

"We are making a little over $1,000 a day each, the actresses make half that, and the Whale gets the rest. The Whale books our flights, pays the expenses, even now because he likes us, and we play. That's all we do is play. I never get tired of playing. And we make sure that we aren't too well-known. We won't be coming back to this casino for at least a year."

I did some quick calculations: six days a week equals $6,000 a week; 50 weeks a year would be $300,000. Not bad! All expenses paid, so that made their $300,000 each pure profit, minus taxes. (Uncle Sam is the other member of the team.)

Of course, the Lee brothers are extreme examples of what a dice controller can do in a casino. The Lee brothers are the only team I have ever met in the casinos and the only full-time professional team I've encountered. True, I have read on Internet craps sites that this or that team or this or that individual is a huge long-run winner, but so much self-serving hyperbole is written on the Internet that I am skeptical of anything so publicly proclaimed. In truth, even if *all* the Internet's self-proclaimed great players and teams are actually real, they still make up fewer than 1 in 40,000 casino craps players based on my calculations.

The Lee brothers were staying at MGM but playing mostly at the downtown and off-Strip casinos that trip. "We are giving only three Strip casinos a look," Tony said. "Bellagio, Paris, and Bally's. We are playing very early in the morning."

By early he meant 4:00 AM, when the tables started to clear. I had a choice. I could stay up late and try to join them or I could go to bed and try to get up to meet them.

"Where will you be at 4:00 AM?" I asked.

"Paris," Tony said.

"See you then," I said. It was around 11:00. If I went right to bed, I could get four hours of sleep, shower, and be ready to play with the inimitable Lees. I put in an alarm call for 3:00 AM and went to sleep.

My adrenaline was pumping, and it took me time to fall into a slumber. I was charged up in anticipation of playing with the Lees.

After showering, I dressed, ate a banana, and then walked the Strip from Flamingo to Paris. When I arrived at Paris, there was still a crowd at the tables. The Lees were just standing around, waiting for their spots to open. "Hey," I said.

"Hey, the man is here," Tony said.

"What happened to your eye? And your cheek?" Tony had a slight shiner and a small scratch on his cheek.

"Vixen in love with him," laughed Larry.

"Really?"

"She...he had a little too much to drink and..." Tony started.

"He fight her off," Larry said.

"She doesn't look it, but she is strong," Tony said.

"I helped or he be raped," Larry said.

"She's not with you guys anymore?" I asked.

"No, no, they *kiss* and make up," Larry said.

"We didn't kiss and make up. We shook hands. You know, things got a little out of hand. We've been traveling together for a very long time."

"He irresistible," Larry said.

Just then an entire table suddenly became available. This happens every so often. A table is crowded, there are a few awful rolls, and people flee. Larry immediately took SR1, Tony SL1, and I took SL2. A moment later Vixen arrived, smiling, and cashed in for $100. She stood next to me. I took a quick look at her face. She had a slight shiner under her eye as well. Then Lola appeared and stood next to Larry. The only one missing was Whale.

"He's making a movie," Tony said. "I think it's called *Saving Ryan's Privates*." Tony laughed at his own joke.

Then the game began.

And we got killed. It was a rare performance by the Lees, a rare *awful* performance. I did much better, which is to say that I made money on my rolls, but none were extraordinary. I started the session by going right up on the Lees, but they sevened out early so many times that I started to use the 5-Count on them. It helped, but only a little. We ended the session at 6:00 AM. I was down some money but happy as always to watch such a skillful team in action.

The Lees decided to take a break and go back downtown around 10:00 AM. The fatigue of the week was beginning to get to me. I was worn out. I told the Lees that I wasn't going to hook up with them downtown that day. I was bushed.

I wanted to get home to the Beautiful AP and resume a somewhat normal life.

It's funny, but when I'm in Vegas I usually think, *I don't ever want to leave this place*, but sometime toward the end of my trip, I begin to get homesick and also tired of my gambling high-wire act.

Playing as I had been for almost two straight months, I was hot, I was on; my throw was just about as good as I've ever seen it. Practice makes perfect, and playing daily makes it "perfecter."

But it was time to go home.

In the years since I first wrote about the Lee brothers, I have lost contact with them. I have no idea if they are still playing. But they were an incredible team, and Tony Lee is the only shooter I ever saw who could successfully do the kill shot. Many of us have spent hours attempting to develop that skill, and we've all failed.

CHAPTER 4

Golden Touch Craps: The Good, the Bad, the Sad

I will never forget my 10 years (2003–2012) with Golden Touch Craps. I made some friends among the instructors and with some of the students. I had many adventures with them too—some good, some not so good. Those people all meant something important to me in the last years of my advantage-play craps experiences. I also had some major disappointments and one truly *devastating* betrayal.

You have read already that one of the founders of Golden Touch was Bob "Mr. Finesse." Self-described as "short and fat," old eagle-eyes Mr. Finesse patiently taught both new players and highly skilled players the ins and outs of the controlled throw. He was excellent with one-on-one instruction.

He did have "eagle eyes" because he could see the slightest mistakes in even the best dice controllers' throws. He helped me once when I was landing dice in a way that constantly saw them scooting together around the curved part of the back wall, thus randomizing the results. It turned out my dice were not level when I released them and I was not aiming—two important ingredients in having decent influence. Even excellent dice controllers need other eyes on their throws. Like batting coaches for major league players, other dice controllers have a better eye to see what you're doing wrong.

Bob had an unusual throw. He was quite short, and he could not lift himself high enough to face the back wall. He'd have to face the area where the box person sat and throw in a kind of twirling motion. It took him a while to get his throw down, but he certainly had it down by the time I met him.

Mr. Finesse was usually calm when he played, but he did have something of a temper, though nowhere near as volcanic as Dom's.

Once in Tunica I was at the end of the table protecting the landing zone of Rock 'n' Roller, who shot from SR2. He had a decent roll. Bob was shooting from SL1 and he was not having the best of nights. I was talking with another player. Bob suddenly became enraged. He stormed right behind Dominator, who was at SL2, passed behind "Stickman," who was at SL3, and came over to me. "Shut up; just shut up, you are making me lose my concentration!" he raged. I looked over at Dom as Bob stormed back to his shooting spot.

"He's getting like you," I said.

Bob took the dice, carefully aimed, and sevened out.

The Goddess used to make arrangements to get us a private table at the Taj Mahal's high-roller room—in fact it was a private *room* within the high roller room. We'd bring in eight to 10 GTC teachers and enjoy a leisurely game with a casino that did not care we were using dice control to beat them. Often high rollers who were not dice controllers would join us.

Once Skinny and I had 40-plus back-to-back rolls and a high roller at the table (not one of our guys) made $250,000, having been down about $75,000—that was a turnaround of $325,000! This did not faze the bosses at the Taj because they knew that player—a wild player who reminded me of some of the Captain's Crew—would quickly lose all of it back during his upcoming visits. Sadly, Taj Mahal went to new layouts that were quite bouncy, and we went to other casinos with more welcoming tables.

We were playing there one afternoon, and Mr. Finesse was shooting the dice. I was at the end of the table next to Randman, who was telling me a story. He was moving his hands as he talked. Suddenly the dice went whipping by Randy's head like two bullets. Luckily Bob's aim was not eagle-eyed at that moment, and the dice missed entering Randy's skull by about an inch. "You don't think he did that on purpose?" Randy asked.

"No, no," I said. "No, he just lost control." I wanted to say, "He lost control of his emotions."

Then Bob yelled, "Stop waving your hands!" So much for me covering for him.

Usually GTC shooters do not worry about anything happening at the tables. If you are focused and doing your roll as you have practiced day after day, what happens at the table is rarely or barely noticeable. But on those two occasions, Mr. Finesse lost his finesse. I remember so clearly because that rarely happened with him; Finesse was a great guy.

The guy who drove many of us crazy was Rock 'n' Roller. During the start of Golden Touch, he was a major investor. He also had perhaps the best throw in the world at that time. He was (as I've said many times) the Babe Ruth of dice control.

Unfortunately, when he rolled he would ask players to move their chips from his landing zone—a no-no. Craps players never ask other players to move their chips—only a dice controller would do that. Besides, you should have enough control of the dice to land them next to or behind the chips.

I remember once at Bellagio two guys were at the landing end of the table when I was shooting. They both had a stack of red chips on the Pass Line with a stack of chips in Odds. Not only that, they each had Pass Line bets for the dealers with Odds. It looked very crowded down at that end of the table. In truth, there was plenty of room. You just look for the best spot to land the dice and land them there. The chips are irrelevant.

I'd talk to Rock 'n' Roller about it, and he would always say he'd stop doing it. But he never stopped. Dom would *yell* at him, and again he would say he'd stop it. And again he never stopped.

That was Rock 'n' Roller.

He'd tell you what you wanted to hear and then do whatever he wanted to do. The irritation with the landing zone made me uncomfortable playing at the same tables with him, but he was such a good shooter, how could I not want to make money on his rolls? So I played craps with him—*a lot*—all over the country.

He was a hell of a nice guy and a great artist. As I write this I can see one of the two paintings of his that I have in my house. The other is a huge painting over my mantle in the living room. I considered him a very good friend.

Then something happened to him at craps.

Then something happened to our friendship.

The first had to do with his shot. Not satisfied with being the home-run king of dice control, he figured he'd try other shots from various areas of the table. Some shooters can do that—the Captain, Dom, and Daryl "No Field Five" to name three offhand. Since Rock 'n' Roller almost always had his spot open, it was silly for him to give that up to shoot from the end of the table. I mean the guy was great at SR1 or SR2—capital *G great*. Why use an inferior shot? It was nuts.

Some GTCers think he wanted to be like Dom and Daryl, who taught the end-of-the-table throw to our advanced students. Our general mantra was that it wasn't good to shoot from the end of the table—excellent advice for almost all dice controllers.

So now in casinos with students watching us play, suddenly Rock 'n' Roller shot from the end of the table and told players to move their chips from his landing zone. Then he started screwing around with his shot from SR1 and SR2. He was getting fancy and, sadly, becoming a less-than-proficient dice controller. Indeed, one weekend in Tunica No Field Five spent two days giving Rock 'n' Roller one-on-one help to retrieve his old throw. It worked, as Daryl is an excellent teacher and an elite player.

The old Rock 'n' Roller was back! My Lord, his shot looked magnificent.

Then we all went to the casino, and the old Rock 'n' Roller disappeared and the new one reemerged. One of the best dice controllers ever had become merely ordinary. Dice control's Babe Ruth, the home-run king, had become a bunter.

In addition to some petty Internet bickering about the end-of-the-table-throw business, Rock 'n' Roller had another problem with Dom. He always thought Dom cheated him. After every class, he'd call me (or he'd talk to the Beautiful AP, who got roped into these talks) and say Dom wasn't paying him properly. His salary was the most of any instructor—four figures for three days' work. He worked for GTC from 2003 through part of 2008, when Dom and I bought his shares. Rock 'n' Roller just had a bad feeling about Dom.

So why did I drop him as a friend? Because one time as we were discussing Dom, he said I was a part of cheating him. He quickly took it back, but the damage was done. I didn't handle the money or business end of GTC—I never even saw the books—so obviously his attack on me was uncalled for. Work the math out for yourself. He had a $10,000 investment. Dom and I bought that back. In addition we did six classes a year, and he was with us for five years. GTC was the best advantage play he ever made.

So I was done with him. I do not make friends easily and I do expect loyalty from my friends. I thought his was the greatest betrayal I would ever experience. I would be proven wrong in that. The greatest betrayal had yet to come.

A good friend of mine was the late best-selling author Bill "Ace-10" Burton, who died much too young. I'm proud that I helped Bill start his writing career because I saw in him an expertise that was rare among casino gamblers. He knew the games perfectly and he could write interesting copy about them.

There were some writers I took a great interest in, and he was at the top of the list. Bill never let me down. He wrote two masterful books— *Get the Edge at Low-Limit Texas Hold'em* and *1,000 Best Casino Gambling Secrets*—and contributed the Texas Hold'em and Omaha Hi-Lo sections to my book *Everything Casino Poker*. He wrote for many of the best gambling magazines too.

Ace-10 was an advantage player at craps, blackjack, poker, and video poker. He also had a great sense of humor and was fully aware that we gambling writers were not writing tomes that would cure cancer or change the world; we were writing about games people enjoyed playing. Bill said to me, "I'm giving a little help in a little way to people playing games. That's still a good thing." He was right.

Bill was largely responsible for bringing me into the world of the modern-day dice controllers. I didn't know any of the current greats. Bill opened those doors for me.

Bill had a pivotal role in Golden Touch. He was in charge of making sure the classes ran properly and that all the throwing and receiving stations were being used to assure students they were getting intense hands-on lessons. I can also see his beautiful throw on the DVD I wrote and directed, *Beat Craps by Controlling the Dice*. His throw looked wonderful on that DVD. Bill was also an excellent speaker and was at home doing radio shows and interviews. He was the total gambling package.

He was quite a guy.

He was quite a friend.

Parkinson's did him in.

I miss him.

One of the best and most versatile shooters in Golden Touch was Daryl "No Field Five." Daryl could effectively shoot the dice from stick right, stick left, and from straight out. As mentioned, the end-of-the-table throw is very difficult because it is a long shot that requires more energy. Daryl could make that throw almost as soft as the throws from next to the stickman.

In addition to being a dentist, Daryl was a musician, playing fiddle and mandolin in the Third Coast Band. Added to that he was also a referee in both football and hockey. The guy was multitalented.

No Field Five was the perfect bettor too, except for one otherwise poor bet that he could hit like magic: the Place bet of the 5, for which he got his number-specific nickname. He was one of the few shooters that I would often bet on right away. On many occasions (don't tell anyone this) I'd even Place the 5! The 5 is a Place bet with a 4 percent house edge, a bet never to be made on a random shooter and almost never to be made even on a dice controller. My placing of the 5 was my compliment to a great shooter. His personality was even better than his shooting—a classy guy all the way.

Daryl and his best buddy, the loquacious Billy "the Kid," were casino hoppers. They'd show up at Bellagio, take the dice once or twice, leave, and head over to another casino. They did that most of the day. Their travel from one casino to another was their rest period.

Another fun-loving and humorous player was "Boxcar" Boris, a man who could mimic many sounds as he played. Casino suits looked for the various birds and rodents who sounded as if they were crawling around under the table. Boris also did a tremendous amount of publicity for the fledgling Golden Touch. He was a quality guy.

Randy "Randman" was exasperating to Dom, but I enjoyed his company and his nervous energy—although, yes, at times he was exasperating to me.

Randman had an excellent though unique throw, a Randmanesque throw. Randman fell into disfavor at times with Dom because he tended to teach his own particular throw with a lifted leg and a low arc. He was a man who always seemed to find himself in the thick of things—which means he had many run-ins with Dom. During almost every class, Randman would take me aside and ask, "Is Dom angry at me?" I would talk Randman down from the ledge and talk Dom out of throwing Randman off that ledge.

Strangely enough, while Dom had that fierce temper and many instructors and students were fearful of setting him off, the dirty work of Golden Touch—meaning the guy who fired people and spoke to people privately about whatever had to be spoken about—was done by yours truly. I was the mediator, and when all else failed, I was usually the guy who did the deeds that had to be done. I was also the guy who spoke to Randman when Dom was fuming about him.

I will never forget Randman's first attempts at dice control that saw him davening when he'd take the dice. [If you aren't Jewish, davening is bowing as one prays; you see this at the Wailing Wall in Israel.] That was when he first started playing in the casinos. He told me he had been nervous and davened without even knowing it. I guess you can always use God on your side in the casinos.

A big disappointment was Chris Pawlicki. I had a lot of respect for Sharpshooter and I was instrumental in helping him get a big book deal with Bonus Books in Chicago. I started a line of books called Frank Scoblete's *Get the Edge* Guides and I signed Sharpshooter to write two of them, *Get the Edge at Craps* and *Get the Edge at Roulette*. Both were excellent.

Was he an expert in dice control? Absolutely. He had carefully read about the Captain, and the roll Chris developed was remarkably similar to the Captain's roll. Sharpshooter did even more because he figured out exactly why and how a controlled throw worked. Even the Captain had not really figured out the physics and mechanics of controlled shooting.

Could Sharpshooter control the dice? Yes. He could also successfully shoot from SL1, SL2, SR1, and SR2. He was a small-stakes player, but that's fine. Not everyone is comfortable betting big money. It's not really how much you bet, it is whether you win or lose. Sometimes big money (or what the shooter thinks is big money) can hurt one's throw. Thinking about money when you are shooting means you are thinking—and thinking is bad in controlled shooting. The Captain was right about that.

In a one-on-one teaching situation, Sharpshooter was quite good. Unfortunately, when teaching a class, he put his students into altered states of consciousness or fast asleep. Dominator, Stickman, Pit Boss, Ace-10, and "the Kid" had excellent presence. Sharpshooter didn't.

Sharpshooter had been the star at PARR and had been treated as such. But in Golden Touch, he was not the star. There were many stars. That's the way to make a company robust. You want everyone to be seen as a star, so the potential students know they are going to be in the presence of great shooters and teachers. You highlight *all* of your instructors so everyone knows about them. You create excitement when the teachers are known public personalities.

Sharpshooter was not in charge of the classes and he did not do any of the lectures. He taught at the tables, as did almost all of the instructors.

The deal we all agreed to clearly stated that no one would work any other dice-control schools, including PARR, or give private lessons that were not a part of Golden Touch. Sharpshooter had agreed to this, but still he did not seem happy with his station. Several instructors/partners such as Dom, Mr. Finesse, and Ace-10 told me Sharpshooter wanted to be the only star of Golden Touch. It was easy for me to herald *all* of our great teachers and dice controllers, and that did not seem to sit well with Sharpshooter.

So Sharpshooter decided to work with PARR again, even though he had committed himself to Golden Touch. Sharpshooter denied he was working with PARR again, which was not true. So we finally told him to go away, and he went away.

I did feel bad (and sad) about that because I thought the guy would have some loyalty to a person who had helped create his writing career. His two books made him a national figure, not the PARR classes. I am guessing that most students wanted to be taught by Sharpshooter *the author*, not the guy who made grand entrances during a PARR class. It was oil and water with Sharpshooter and Golden Touch.

The Six Seven-Outs

In any company you have winners and losers, good seeds and bad. Almost all of our instructors were good seeds. But we had some bad seeds—from a serial womanizer to a phony doctor and porn producer to a brilliant scammer.

In my 10 years with Golden Touch, we hired 36 instructors, of which six had to be let go—16.67 percent. Other instructors/partners left for other reasons, such as the rigors of traveling or work commitments. These would be welcomed back at any time, such folks as Randy "Tenor" and Doc Holliday.

I don't know if a 16.67 percent firing percentage is big or little—but that was the number. When I was a teacher in high school, I thought about 20 percent of the faculty should never have gotten tenure. The same held true for this 16.67 percent. As a slight aside, a seven has a 16.67 percent appearance rate in a random craps game, so we can say these six instructors sevened out of Golden Touch.

The six seven-outs were former students we hired based on their dice-control abilities and their ability to communicate the methods being taught. Dom and I and/or other instructors went to the tables with them to see how they performed in the casinos. But a person's personality is not necessarily showcased under such scrutiny. People become who they are once you start to see them working with you, relating to you, engaging with other people and with students.

Golden Touch had a four-level instructional staff: interns, assistant instructors, full instructors, and instructor/partners. The interns would work about six to eight classes, mostly working with the instructors to see our methods. We also got to judge their ability to notice how throws could be improved. They were not to give any instruction during their internship.

The assistant instructors could teach, but they were closely monitored and often were assigned to co-teach with full instructors for six to eight classes.

One of the seven-outs, a married man with children, couldn't stop chasing the women in the class or the women who showed up to my Frank Scoblete's Gamblers Jamboree weekends. He even went after my wife's girlfriend by telling her that if she went to bed with him she'd be "sleeping with a celebrity." When I warned him to stop, his defense was always that the women were adults. Nonsense. As a teacher he had a certain stature in the eyes of the students—hitting on them was not in the playbook, at least not in my playbook.

After enough time to see that he wouldn't change, I took him aside and told him to hunt for his harem elsewhere. In fact, he did just that. He still teaches dice control, he has a little circle of fellow teachers, and I assume he is still stalking his prey.

Another individual was handicapped, living on $2,000 a month in Social Security disability benefits. This guy had all of us fooled—all but Satch, a detective, and Stickman. Instructors would pay for this individual's airfares, his hotel rooms, and his meals. Pit Boss was a major sap, as was I. When we played at the tables with him, we constantly made bets for him as if we were tipping him.

At that time two of our instructors were dentists, Doc Holliday and the great No Field Five. Doc was a surgeon who removed this guy's decayed teeth, and Daryl fixed him up with false teeth—all *free*. He was flown to Seattle for surgery and comped to a hotel room and his meals. Then he was flown to Texas, again comped to a hotel room and his meals. Think of how much money was spent on this guy—overall it had to be more than $100,000.

Satch was quite suspicious. "How come this guy doesn't work? He has skills. Why doesn't he get a job? Why is he sitting on his fat ass collecting Social Security? Look at all the money GTC is giving him. There's something wrong here," he insisted.

There was something wrong. We had a professional scammer in our midst. He lamented to students about his awful poverty and his handicapping condition. He then took money from them on class weekends. Many of our students were in the top 1 percent of income and quite generous.

Indeed, phone calls from students went out to other students after the classes, and thankfully to instructors (that's how Dom and I heard about it), soliciting monetary donations for him. Tens of thousands of dollars were pledged in just several days after one such class. I pulled the plug on the guy and called everyone who was suckered into pledging donations. Dom and I told our students they had been conned.

Our "destitute" scammer would even go to tables with students, and they would give him money to play. Just about every instructor had dumped money into this guy's coffers. When someone takes advantage of you like that, you feel foolish, angry, and hurt.

Like our first seven-out, who wanted to screw some of our students, this particular seven-out wanted to screw them too, just in a different way.

We had a "doctor" who claimed to possess all sorts of degrees and expertise in everything from meditation to sexual "problems" (he had "materials" he would sell) to investment marketing. His wife, a pretty young woman, wanted him to become really famous and asked me to write glowingly about the "doctor" in an upcoming book. She even sent me the exact copy she wanted.

I told her I did not use other people's copy. Then she made me an offer she thought I couldn't refuse. She emailed me that she would be happy to give me a "world-class blowjob" if I helped push her husband's career.

The toughest part wasn't telling her that I didn't need or want her to give me a world-class blowjob. The toughest part was showing my wife the email. I was a little concerned when I first read it—that is after I said "Holy shit!"—because what if the Beautiful AP thought I had led this woman on? That thought was only in my mind for a moment. Of course I showed AP the email.

"Holy shit!" she said.

I then called Dom and read him the email. "Holy shit!" he said.

At that point we terminated the relationship with the instructor. I haven't seen him in more than a dozen years.

The self-described Top Banana was someone I did not want on our staff. Prior to his joining our teaching group, Golden Touch held the World Craps Championships at the Atrium, a non-casino hotel in Las Vegas. We had small cash prizes and trophies for the winners of the various competitions—I think there were some 27 different awards given. This was not gambling, just tournament-style play—such things as who could hit the most box numbers in 10 throws, that type of thing.

The Top Banana competed in the tournament. However, he was unhappy with the monetary prizes and started a movement with some other disgruntled competitors to challenge those cash prizes as too low. For some reason we felt the need to uphold our honesty, and Dom and I sent him every bill for the event and showed him the total number of people who had actually paid for the tournaments. We did everything we said we would do in our publicity of the event. Since this was not a class, I handled the money.

This individual and his cronies thought we should be giving out cash awards similar to what casinos awarded. As stated, we showed him all the books and hard copies of the bills. Every penny was accounted for. (Again, I really don't know why we did this. I should have followed Dom's advice and said "Fuck him.")

And then Billy "the Kid" got the idea of making the Top Banana an intern, and Dom went along with it. Dom and Billy are fast friends. I was against it. Why would we want that guy to be one of us?

Dom and I had an arrangement about making decisions when we disagreed. Whoever felt strongest about his side of the disagreement would get his way. Dom felt stronger about bringing the Top Banana into the teaching fold than I felt about not bringing him in. Billy the Kid's vote counted as well.

So the Top Banana, who had not taken an advanced course or been fully screened in the casinos, was offered an internship. This carping troglodyte would become one of us. Stranger things have happened in the world...I guess.

"I thought I was going to be an assistant instructor," the Top Banana insisted. "Frank, you told me I would be an assistant instructor."

I didn't remember telling him that, but it was possible. So I said, "Okay, you're an assistant instructor." I figured he'd go through the intern program anyway, but we would call him an assistant instructor.

"Assistant instructors make more than interns," he then said.

That's true. So we scheduled him for a class in Vegas, and I agreed to pay him the assistant instructor's salary. For that class we had no interns working, so there wouldn't be that awkward moment when the Top Banana strutted and bragged about the money he was making. I had a solution for that, if it came up: we would give everyone the assistant instructor salary for as long as the Top Banana worked the classes.

That wouldn't be long.

The whole weekend the Top Banana complained to everyone (students and instructors), saying, "Frank is not using my expertise properly," "Frank is wasting my time since I am only observing," and, "This is not what I expected. I expected to teach people."

I took him aside after I got wind of his whining. I explained that he would not be teaching for at least a year or two, something I had already told him. His early time with us would be to learn the ropes. That obviously didn't make him happy. He then complained that he didn't want or need to wait to fully take part in the classes. He believed he was ready right then.

In the weeks that followed the class, the Top Banana called various students and potential students. He also wanted to have a permanent column on our website because he had a lot of important lessons to teach people. He thought he should be a major writer in the official Golden Touch pages. He also offered silly recommendations to improve our offerings—hinting he should be in charge of the Golden Touch improvement program. Dom gently reflected on this, saying, "He's fucking nuts."

I talked with the crestfallen Dom and Billy the Kid—actually I said, "That was the stupidest thing we did hiring him." I also took what was happening with the Top Banana to our instructors/partners and asked for their input. "Fire him," was their input. Naturally I was the one who did the firing. I told the Top Banana that he and Golden Touch weren't a good fit. In short, good-bye, Mr. Banana.

I had hoped that would be the last we'd ever hear from the Top Banana, but that was not to be. I had two friends, the late Walter Thomason and my Five Horsemen teammate Skinny, who would send me (I think they *delighted* in sending me) Internet postings by my critics—almost all them from the lunatic fringe. Suddenly into this bedlam strutted the Top Banana.

He started writing vicious posts on a minor message board about how awful and evil I was, how fat I was, how crooked I was, what a sham Golden Touch was. He stated that we cheated people at the World Craps Championships (yes, he resurrected that lie), that everything we taught in our classes was nonsense. His animus toward me was overwhelming.

Still, here is the amazing thing: whenever he offered craps advice he was basically paraphrasing from my books.

He also seemed insanely jealous of the fact that the Five Horsemen and other GTC instructors enjoyed eating at the best gourmet rooms in Las Vegas. To him we were snobs, even though we had (stupidly) invited him to come to dinner with us any time he wanted. We had open invitations for any member of our staff to join us at various restaurants. Top Banana railed about this quite a bit.

I think he did his Internet rampage for a couple of years and then faded into the ether, as such people invariably do.

This kind of crazed and deliberately misleading behavior on the part of Internet "experts" seems to be typical. One "historian" created a colorful history of dice control where he and some of his "no-buddies" were at the center of it all, totally dismissing the Captain. This same guy decided he had found the secret of my writing success, that I'd write about losses in the first part of my trip reports and then I'd come roaring back to win. If you've read my books and articles, you know this is not so. Sometimes I win right off the bat; sometimes I don't.

Other Internuts said I lied about my rolls, that I only write about my good hands, never about my bad hands. Certainly not true. I related in painful detail 72 straight turns with the dice where I lost on every one of them. Those rolls occurred in front of students!

One guy started hammering me after I turned down his invitation to team up with him. He begged me, but I told him very politely that I wasn't interested. He went berserk attacking me, stating that I only write books but refuse to play the game. Why didn't I come to Vegas and join him? "Because Scoblete does not know how to play," he answered himself. On and on such madness went. One online attacker said that I was a "blood clot," while another said that if he ever woke up, looked in the mirror, and saw that he was me, he'd kill himself.

The attacks on the Captain reached the lowest levels. The Captain was attacked for wearing a diaper because he was "an old wet fart." And someone else said he caught rabies from "engaging in bestiality." Still others said that the Captain didn't exist but that if he did, he was stupid. The madness seemed to know no end.

As for the Top Banana, we all slipped on that banana peel in a big way.

Dom suffered his share of personal attacks as well. At first they upset him quite a bit. "These fucking people don't even know me," he fumed. But at times it *was* people he knew. After all, the vitriol of acquaintances can be immense, especially from those acquaintances who think of themselves as competitors.

One night at the Il Fornaio restaurant in the New York, New York casino in Las Vegas, just a few months after Dom was starting to be known throughout the country, he happened to look up a craps website. "That dirty fuck!" he shouted.

"What?" I asked.

"That no-good, dirty little fucking liar!" screamed Dom.

"What?" asked the Beautiful AP.

"Lassieman, that fuck! He said he saw me roll at Golden Nugget and that I stunk. He said Blubberbutt had the best roll. That fucking liar! Blubberbutt sevened out right away four times! He didn't have a winning roll all fucking night. I had the best roll of the night—about 35 numbers. All my rolls were winners except one! That fucking fuck!" and Dom threw his napkin on the table and stood up.

"What are you doing?" I asked as he got up.

"I'm flying to San Francisco and beating his fucking head in!"

"Whoa, Dom, you're going to get on a plane to San Francisco so you can beat that guy up?" I asked. "That's not the way to handle criticism."

"I'm gonna kill him," he said.

"Dom," said the Beautiful AP, "this isn't the way to handle criticism."

"No," I said.

"Yeah, really, how?" said Dom.

"Ignore it," said the Beautiful AP. "You're becoming well-known, so you better get used to criticism."

"But he's lying," said Dom.

"It takes a while to laugh when they go after you, but they are just jealous of you. Scobe [me] had to just put these people in perspective. They are just jealous of the top guys. You are now a top guy. Get used to it."

I laughed. "Welcome to the club. You can't kill everyone who lies about you or criticizes you, no matter how nasty they are. You just gotta take it."

"After a while you'll laugh at these jerks," said the Beautiful AP. Dom picked up his napkin, sighed, and sat down.

Perhaps the worst attack on Dom came from some anonymous Internet posters who claimed to know "for a fact" that Dom owed so much money to the casinos that he had to borrow more than $100,000 from his friends to pay them off but that he also had to sneak out of Las Vegas for fear of being arrested by the casinos from which he had taken other markers.

They pictured him as a thieving scoundrel, as if to say, "Would you take a dice-control course from someone who steals money?" They labeled him a crook and a person not to be trusted. This reminded me of Jerry Patterson's warnings.

Finally, Dom had a stalker who constantly called him in the middle of the night from a pay phone in Atlantic City. This stalker would threaten Dom with all manner of sexual abuse. How did Dom find out where the calls were coming from? He called the Atlantic City police, and they traced where the calls originated—different pay phones. Thankfully the calls stopped after about two years.

As bad as the Top Banana had been with his "back channels" silliness, I don't think he took payment for his advice; I think he just got some much-needed ego satisfaction. But one of our seven-outs parlayed his assistant instructor status into holding secret classes in his home.

That was the redoubtable Tie Clip, who was quite a good teacher. Sadly, he created his own "back channels" list of students who preferred to pay substantially less than Golden Touch charged. He did this for a couple of years, until he made a phone call to the wrong person—a student who immediately informed us. Tie Clip did not lie by saying he never did it—he just said he wanted the money. I guess there is honesty in some crooks. I fired him.

Finally we had Drugman. He was a happy guy; he was happy all the time when he wasn't sleeping. He was a good shooter too, when he wasn't sleeping. Unfortunately he would miss too many classes when he *was* sleeping. I think he actually vanished into the ether because he disappeared—perhaps into dreamland. After he floated away, we found out that the major source of his income was selling drugs—that is, when he wasn't sleeping.

Stars of Golden Touch

I do miss our instructors, I really do. You've already met many of them, but I would be remiss if I left out the rest of our stars.

Arman "Pit Boss" was an elite teacher and speaker with a great skill working on the physical techniques of a controlled throw. I remember a time when he played a prominent role at Bally's in Las Vegas when 17 of us at two tables were told to leave the casino.

A herd of suits came from wherever suited herds congregate and told us we couldn't play there anymore. Dom leveled a string of invectives against them, and then I saw a pit boss and Arman "Pit Boss" squaring off. They were nose-to-nose. If they fought, I knew that our Pit Boss, who was an athletic and extremely strong man, would kill the casino pit boss. The casino pit boss backed down—still 17 of us got the boot.

There was Mark "Dice Pilot," who was a class act all the way, a true innovator in creating methods for checking on a controlled throw. You will never believe what he could do with toothpicks! Just as important, he had a great throw and he could teach up a storm. He was a natural with students, and they really responded to him. In fact, students loved him.

Dice Pilot was—you guessed it—a pilot, and he did stunt flying at various air shows. He was also one of the diners at Fiamma at the Grand in Vegas when we discovered on the bill that we had been charged extra money for drinks that had ice in them—four dollars extra per drink! Then we discovered we were charged two dollars extra if a drink *did not* have ice in it.

Then there was Lee "Section Eight," an intense shooter who played constantly in Vegas and made some casinos his own private ATM machines. A former CIA agent and a talented man in the arts with a truly great sense of humor, Section Eight did the PowerPoint slides for our 10th anniversary dinner at Treasure Island. Section Eight was an excellent graphic artist and he had a beautiful eye for copy and, more important, for shooting.

And Raf "Rafter" comes from that new generation of dice controllers who can handle the bounciest of tables with élan. He was an excellent teacher who knew how to prod the minds of even the most stubborn gamblers to teach them how to do things correctly. I remember 10 of us went to the M Casino for the first time and we were having trouble shooting on their layout. Our shots were completely off. Then Raf said, "I can beat this table," and he took over a spot from Stickman and proceeded to have a monster roll. We were then comped to breakfast. We had food to fill our bellies and money to fill our pockets, thanks to Raf. Another great guy.

There was "Missouri" Rick, a former ranger, our man of steel, the Superman of GTC who served many years in our wars in Iraq and Afghanistan. And Tommy "Two Names," an excellent shooter who was comfortable using both his left and right hands. How about John "Glue Factory," the only player I know who was a partner with his mother in a mother-son craps team!

And, of course, there was Tim "Timmer," an inspirational mentor to students. He wrote extensive notes on his students' performances, which he gave students at the end of the weekend classes. He kept in touch with students long after they had taken the class. He has played in casinos all over America and has a beautiful, winning throw. He was a dedicated teacher who really understood all the elements of what made a dice throw a controlled throw. He was also loved by his students.

And there was John "the Rolling Rooster," the man whose family probably first coined the phrase "a chicken in every pot."

There are many people I came to admire who were not members of the GTC staff, Jack "the Raging Baritone" and his wife, Betty; the devastating Lee Brothers; and Sam "Dice Doctor" Grafstein among them. I'd love to list and reflect on all the students I liked, but that list would be much too long.

CHAPTER 5
The Beginning of the End

G TC instructor Billy "the Kid" was a great advantage player, especially at Spanish 21 and traditional blackjack. He was an excellent dice controller as well. Sit down with him, and he would expound about his many and varied adventures. At a craps table he was truly funny. He told so many jokes and had so many quick-witted comments that he had the dealers and the pit people uproariously laughing. His idea of "the moron factor" has helped many craps players play properly for fear of being termed, yes, a moron. Readers enjoyed his writing.

Billy the Kid was an excellent teacher, a good writer, and along with his best buddy, Daryl "No Field Five," was in charge of teaching the advanced classes and our Video Elite courses. I had respect for Billy's abilities.

But Billy also caused me concern. He gave a bad example.

Prior to the classes on Saturdays, Dom and I held meetings where we reviewed how the weekend should go. Yes, the instructors were pros, but our Saturday morning meetings consisted of a pep talk mixed with a reiteration of what we wanted to achieve with the new students and the refreshers who were taking their second course with us. At times instructors strayed from the course material and started to teach their own eccentric ideas. That was the ongoing situation that Dom saw with Randman. Dom and I wanted uniformity of instruction

Our class would be split up into teams with usually four or five players per team. They had a mentor who stayed with them the whole weekend. During lectures, all students stayed together, but the most important part was the hands-on instruction from the instructors.

Through the course of the weekend each team would go around the room to various instructors' tables and be taught by that instructor. The mentor made sure that each instructor was aware of what the previous instructor(s) had said to the students. In this way, there was continuity. The mentor also made sure the students took notes. So you always had an instructor and a mentor with the students at all times.

Why go to different instructors? Each instructor had areas of expertise. For example, Pit Boss was an expert at body movements—his analysis of a student's physical posture was the best of any GTC instructor—Skinny was an expert on aiming, and so forth.

I had no problem with Billy's teaching ability. He knew his stuff, or we never would have allowed him to teach the advanced classes and the Video Elite classes. However, his attitude rubbed me the wrong way and annoyed me more and more over the years.

Billy arrived late for the majority of our Saturday morning meetings, and when he sat down he'd take out his laptop and ignore everyone and everything. There were even times at our Friday night meet-and-greet presentations (given to our entire student body, their spouses and friends, and all of our instructors) that Billy would be sitting up front and ignoring the speakers onstage. Often he'd be tooling on his laptop so everyone could see he didn't give a damn about the speakers—at least that's how I translated his actions. I saw this as an amazing show of disrespect to me, to Dom, to the Goddess, to Randman, and to any others who spoke at the meet and greets. In addition, students were asked to give a few sentences of introduction about themselves. Billy would noticeably ignore them, too.

And then the weekend from hell happened, involving Dom, Billy, the supervisor of the hotel's banquet rooms, the catering manager, Randman, Mark "the Dice Pilot," and Tim "Timmer"; and a thought jumped up in my head that maybe I had had enough of Golden Touch.

Here's how that weekend from hell went down: I arrived at the Alexis Park All Suite Resort, a non-casino hotel in Las Vegas, on Thursday at noon, just before we would set up our classroom and practice room. I went to registration to get my room and gave my credit card. I had just gotten two calls from customers saying Dom owed them money and that he wouldn't return their calls. This happened other times during the years as well. I told Dom about it, and he said, "No problem. I'll take care of it."

Dom always said he would "take care of it," and I assumed he always did—I now realize that I *needed* to assume that. Still there were other unsettling things that started to churn in my consciousness about Dom. He rarely brought much money to play with during our trips. He was always underfinanced. He didn't take markers. Luckily it was only on very rare occasions that we got so clobbered that he ran out of his cash. But there were plenty of sessions where Dom lowered his bet to that of a low roller to be able to continue play.

Every so often I would get letters from the New York State Tax Department telling me that Dom owed them back taxes and penalties for more than 20 years and that since I was a person known to associate with him, they informed me that any money I owed or would pay Dom had to go to the New York State Tax Department.

Dom said that issue had been resolved by his cousin "the lawyer" long ago. It hadn't. I continued to get those letters. After a while I simply scrawled over the letter that I do not pay Dom any money and I do not owe him any money for anything. But those notices just kept coming. Dom would keep telling me that he "took care of it." In 2014, long after I left Golden Touch, Dom told me his debt to New York State was $106,000. But he also said that he "took care of it" through "the lawyer."

Yes, when these things occurred Dom always said he "took care of it" or that he would "take care of it." And I—kind of—put the incidents out of my mind.

The receptionist at Alexis Park handed back my credit card. "I'm sorry, sir, your credit card has been rejected." I immediately knew why because it had happened before. As the primary on the American Express business card, if the bills were not paid, my *personal* American Express card would be frozen. Of course, I never received the Golden Touch American Express bills or had anything to do with the money. The money was in Dom's domain. If he were lax in paying the bills, my credit card got frozen. Also, my credit rating took a hit. I used to have a perfect credit score. No more.

Dom was behind me checking in. I told him that my card had been rejected. *"Again*, Dom," I said, truly annoyed. He said, "I'll take care of it." I gave the receptionist a different card. Dom never apologized for screwing up my credit rating. That surprised me. But I pushed it to the back of my mind, where it could churn with the other stuff on which I didn't want to dwell.

The setup started at 1:00 PM. It would take about three hours to get the practice room finished, as we had three full craps tables and about a dozen other tables along with filming equipment to set up.

The woman in charge of the banquet rooms was an uptight, by-the-book type, and any new requests we made had to be paid for. I understood that; I didn't like it, but I understood it. In short, she was the boss—a stiff-necked boss.

Dom hated her attitude, and he let her know it. He told her she was the worst supervisor we'd dealt with at any of the hotels where we did classes. He was right. She was the worst. Of course, Dom loudly scolding her did not make her any more malleable. If anything, her neck became stiffer.

We needed to change our evening's meet and greet to another room because the original room was just too damn hot and way too small. We would have far more than a hundred people, plus instructors, crammed into the original room, and in the hot Las Vegas summers, in a room not properly air-conditioned, it would be quite uncomfortable. She wanted to charge us $200 to move the tables and chairs. We said we'd handle that ourselves, no problem. She wouldn't hear of it. Dom stormed out of the room at that point. I negotiated with Lady Stiff Neck, and we wound up paying $100 to the hotel to move everything to a rather large double banquet room across the hall that could seat 400 people.

My most emotionally draining job during Golden Touch weekends occurred in private. I ran interference for Dom with the supervisors. Aside from his continued smoking in the nonsmoking banquet rooms, he was often in conflict with the supervisors. I would then step in and take over the person-to-person discussions. I was often the Golden Touch mediator between Dom and the hotel supervisors and between Dom and the instructors—even well-established instructors/partners who to this day have no idea that they were angering Dom.

Dom's temper often ignited not just at our classes, but at the tables. My father had a hair-trigger temper that came on him—*snap!*—just like that. I was used to dealing with such a person—but sometimes Dom's temper got the best of him, and bad things happened. There was a two-day period after a class weekend where Dom had a number of explosions at the craps and Pai Gow Poker tables in Bellagio. He had been foolishly using a martingale betting system (a double-up as you lose—a truly bad system) at Pai Gow and getting his ass kicked. He was constantly in a rage. I finally thought, *I'm not having fun this trip. I'm tense all the time going to the tables.* So I checked out of the hotel and went home early. Originally I was scheduled to stay another week.

The night of the weekend from hell's meet and greet, Dom had it out with another supervisor, the individual in charge of the refreshments. We had a whole spread, enough to feed an army, but for some reason we had to pay for the drinks individually—these being soda and water. We had known we would have to pay for alcohol separately, but we were under the impression that the soft drinks came with the fee for the food and service.

That dispute went on for about a half hour, and we compromised. Everyone could have two sodas and/or waters, and on the third, we would be charged. (We had X number of participants, and when we went over $2X$ we would start paying for individual drinks.) Dom tipped the staff generously, so the workers, waiters, and bartenders liked him and tended to be in our corner, meaning we never reached $2X$.

A huge crowd showed up for the meet and greet, and our staff circulated, talking to students and the students' friends and spouses. Our mentors gathered their student groups to introduce everyone to everyone else. After an hour of this, the presentations began.

I gave my talk. Dom and I had a whole routine we did to relax everyone with laughter while giving important information about craps and dice control. Dom was excellent in front of an audience, a natural. Then I introduced the students, who told us about themselves, and then I introduced our staff. At that point I was really tired—not just from speaking, but from the problems with Lady Stiff Neck and with the catering service supervisor.

Randman got up to give his talk. Randman kept track of all the craps games in the country—a monumental task. And Billy ignored him. Then the Goddess gave a wonderful talk about her experiences going from newbie to veteran. She specifically thanked Billy, and Billy ignored her. Everyone saw that. He sat at a table facing the audience, right in front, using his laptop. So the lights were illuminating the Goddess onstage, and the light from Billy's laptop was illuminating his face for all to see. He sat ignoring everything taking place on the stage—he sat right in front of the stage, *right in front!*

What were students to think if one of our main instructors, a name everyone knew before they ever attended a class, the famous Billy "the Kid," blatantly showed his disdain for Dom, Randman, Marilyn, me, the mentors, the students, and the other instructors?

After the meet and greet, we would have a private party with the instructors. At this party I took Dom aside and said, "I'm firing Billy."

"What is it?" he asked.

"Everyone is giving their talks, and he's sitting there using his laptop in plain view."

"You really want to do this?" Dom asked. Dom and Billy were close friends, but in my partnership with Dom, as I've stated, if one of us felt more strongly than the other about an issue, the one with the strongest feelings got his way. That worked well for us.

Dom was fully aware that Billy often came late to the meetings and that he often ignored what was going on at meet and greets. Dom and I talked about it many times. But this particular meet and greet was by far the worst.

When I went back to the party, Billy and Daryl "No Field Five" had left. "I'm telling him tomorrow morning," I said. "He can finish out the weekend, but that's it."

"Okay," Dom said. "I'll be with you." I thought Dom's willingness to be there when I spoke to Billy showed great support for me. As I've stated I put great stock in loyalty from my friends.

We had one final argument that night with Lady Stiff Neck. We had plenty of food left over and we wanted the hotel staff to wrap it so we could take it with us. She would not allow this, citing a Las Vegas health law. Instead, she said we could wrap our own food, but the staff couldn't touch anything.

Dom exploded in a rant about this stupid law and how idiotic Lady Stiff Neck was being. That law happens to be on the books. I got between Dom and Lady Stiff Neck again. Dom stormed off.

That night I had a restless sleep.

Billy was late for the Saturday morning meeting, so I wasn't able to take him aside. Then I was even more annoyed than I had been the night before. So the class began.

In Golden Touch the sequence of lessons generally went this way:

- Alert students to poor gambling ideas pushed by people who knew nothing about the math's impact on the games
- Explain exactly how often to practice and how long it takes to gain proficiency
- Discuss where to stand and how to set the dice in the Hardway set
- Teach the elements of the throw, including a proper grip, backswing, dice spin, landing, bounce, hitting of the back wall, and stopping on the felt
- Show students how to establish what their edges are by using the Seven-to-Rolls Ratio and SmartCraps results
- Explain to students how to bet into their edges
- Instruct students about how to keep their cool at the tables when they are being harassed

These lessons were interspersed with hands-on instruction, starting with the instructors demonstrating their throws.

Then the students began their hands-on experiences with their mentors and instructors. Later in the day we talked about proper betting on random rollers (don't bet on them or use the 5-Count and make one bet). At the end of class that day, we told students not to play craps that night but to get a good night's rest so they were refreshed for Sunday.

On Sunday Dom and I could usually identify the students who would probably not get an edge at craps—the ones who had gone to the casinos the previous night and stayed up all night playing, most of whom were hungover and continued to make idiotic bets.

At the end of Saturday's class, I decided not to speak to Billy. I'd speak to him on Sunday during lunch. I didn't want to fire him and then not have him show up to teach on Sunday. I mean, the guy came late when he was in good favor; it was quite possible he wouldn't show up at all if he were in bad favor.

I never played on the weekends of the class. I learned from experience that it was too tiring to teach a class and then play. So I went to dinner with the Five Horsemen and a couple of other instructors. After a leisurely meal, I headed back to Alexis Park and went to bed. Again I had a fitful sleep. Sunday would be a tough day—it isn't easy to fire someone.

Around 3:00 AM I fell asleep. At 6:00 my phone rang. It was Mark "Dice Pilot." "I'm sure you heard what happened," he said.

"No," I said.

"It's about Timmer. Dom went after him in class yesterday afternoon. He really went after him. He kept screaming at Timmer. He shook Timmer up really bad right in front of all the students. Timmer won't be teaching today. He's too upset."

"Shit."

"According to Timmer, Dom went into a rage when Timmer explained something to a student during Dom's talk."

"Give me Timmer's cell; I'll call him."

"You can't treat people who work for you that way," Dice Pilot said. "I've had plenty of people work for me. You have to control yourself if you're the boss." Indeed, Dice Pilot was a very successful businessman who was able to retire in his early 40s to enjoy his hobby of stunt flying.

I called Timmer.

Timmer was indeed shaken. His voice kept cracking during our conversation. According to Timmer, several of his students had not understood what Dom had just said, so Timmer quietly explained it to them. That's when Dom went off on Timmer and didn't let up. I don't recall if Timmer left the class or was thrown out of the class by Dom. The end result was Timmer calling Dice Pilot and talking to him through the night.

I came to Sunday's class a little early. There were instructors already in the practice room and some students practicing what they had been taught the previous day. Dom was there as well. "Dom, I have to talk to you," I said.

"I'll stand with you on Billy, you know that," he said.

"No, no, not that, something else."

"What?" he asked.

"In private." I indicated the classroom.

Once in the classroom, I shut the doors. "It's about Timmer," I said.

"What the fuck, that little fuck! What did he say?"

I recounted Timmer's story.

"What instructor called you to tell you about that fuck?"

"Not important," I said.

"Dice Pilot, I'll bet it was Dice Pilot. I don't need Timmer. I don't need Dice Pilot. I don't need any of the instructors. I can replace all of them. I just need you. The two of us are the big draws in this company."

"Let me hear what happened, okay?" I said.

"Timmer just got up, walked across the aisle, and started a conversation with some of his group. Right in the middle of my lesson. That fuck! And he's complaining? Right in the middle of my lesson!"

I taught high school for more than three decades, and a student or students talking during a lesson was not unheard of—in fact it was standard for just about all teachers. Of course, it upset some teachers quite a lot, and they lost their composure and started yelling, screaming, and some even threw students out of class. Dom had never experienced such a thing, and he reacted as he usually reacted—by exploding.

Dom and I talked about Timmer. I said that the guy was a great mentor and would become a great instructor. Dom totally agreed. "You know me, Frank, I get angry, but I get over it." Dom paused to think. "You can tell the little fuck that he's welcome to come back for the next class and teach."

Dom went back into the practice room. I sat down in the classroom, doors closed, alone with my thoughts, and who should walk in but Lady Stiff Neck. What the hell was she doing there on an early Sunday morning?

"I want to speak to Dom," she said, waving several pieces of paper in my face. Oh, great, this is what I needed, a confrontation between Lady Stiff Neck and Dom.

"He's busy. I can handle it."

"Well, Frank, nothing against you personally, you've been easy to deal with, but Dom has not been, and he signed the catering form." She thrust a paper at me, saying, "He signed off on the type of payment for nonalcoholic drinks."

Her tone clearly expressed her strong dislike of Dom. This was not the first time I saw such strong feelings against Dom. Once Dom told me, "I got a call from my favorite uncle yesterday, and he said that everyone in my family hates me. He said *he* hated me." Dom also told me that his estranged wife's family disdained him.

I chalked this up to his temper as opposed to anything else. It wasn't until later that I began to think maybe *something else* might have played a role.

So I read the contract Lady Stiff Neck handed me. It was unclear to me, as it obviously had been for Dom. "Uh, it isn't just Dom. This is unclear for me too. I agree with Dom. Can't we just stick to the compromise we made Friday night?"

She pursed her lips. "I will let you get away with this on this one occasion," she snapped. "But from now on, you tell Dom he better live up to his commitments." She then stormed out of the room. By the time our next class took place at Alexis Park, she had been fired.

A few moments later, Dom entered. "You still plan on talking to Billy at lunch?"

"Yes, yes, I am," I said.

When Billy arrived, I told him I wanted to talk to him at lunch. And class began.

Just before I went to the podium to begin our Sunday class, Randman came up to me and whispered. "Is Dom mad at me?"

"Not that I know of," I said.

"He just walked right past me without saying hello."

"He's got a lot on his mind," I said.

The students who had played the previous night—against our advice—talked about their evenings. Some shot well; some did not shoot well. The ones who did well claimed it was their dice control ability that made the difference. Those who had shot poorly claimed dice control didn't seem to work. None of them—not a single, stinking one of them—used the 5-Count. None of them had absorbed the idea that it might take months to get competent.

I mentioned to them in strong terms that if they dismissed what we had said the day before and continued to ignore what we were teaching, they would be long-term losers. Some faces turned red; some faces hardened.

We still had a chance with the ones whose faces turned red. The hardened faces? Little chance of them becoming advantage players. They would probably drift over to the Internet's dice gurus who sold trend-betting, hedging, and intuitive/psychic methods.

None of the previous day's "good shooters" had any dice-control ability from attending one day of class. Nor did the bad shooters. These folks had just played random games. Too many would-be dice controllers confuse good random luck with dice-control skill.

I kept looking at Billy during the class. The advanced students liked him as a teacher. Did I really want to fire him? Maybe I should say my piece and leave it up to him whether he wanted to stay with Golden Touch. Perhaps that was the way to go. After all, Billy was a good teacher and he was a minor partner. Being a partner had nothing to do with whether you taught a class, but maybe a talk with him would change his attitude. I actually did not want to lose Billy. I also didn't want to lose Timmer. I figured Timmer would quit GTC after being tongue-lashed so severely by Dom. That would be a true shame. The Timmers of the world are often irreplaceable.

Before lunch the Goddess took me aside and said, "You should speak to Dom about what he did to Timmer. Everyone has been talking about it."

"Yes," I said.

Still more instructors talked to me. The general opinion—actually the *unanimous* opinion—was that Dom had gone too far in how he handled the situation. Everyone wanted me to talk to him, which I had already done.

Lunch couldn't come quickly enough.

"You know, we were all wondering, is Timmer okay? Dom really got angry," said one of Timmer's students.

Obviously everyone knew about the day before. It appeared that I had been the last to know about it.

I had told Timmer's group first thing that Timmer would not be mentoring on Sunday. I put Marilyn in charge of his group. They had been there, they saw, they heard—as had *all* the students—what Dom said when he went ballistic. They knew the situation better than I.

Billy and Dom were waiting outside the hotel, talking and smoking. I think they were the only two instructors who smoked. They stopped abruptly when they saw me.

After saying a quick hello, I went through all the things Billy did that I felt were disrespectful to his fellow GTCers—his lateness to meetings, his missing meetings, his ignoring the speakers and letting the students see it, his use of the laptop at the meet and greet and during our private meetings. These things had not just happened once or twice. They had happened for years. "Do you want to continue to be a part of the teaching staff? Do you want us to buy back your shares of the company so you are no longer a part of it? We did that with Howard."

Billy's face turned red. He then explained he hadn't done any of those things on purpose. He was sorry and he did not want to leave the company. That surprised me. I thought he was going to tell me to go to hell.

"Billy, let me speak to Frank privately for a second," Dom said.

Billy went inside.

"I think he's sincere," Dom said. "It's your call."

I took a moment. "Okay," I said. "Okay, he stays, but he has to change his behavior."

And that was that. Billy did change his behavior—at least while I was still with the company.

Still...with...the...company.

I was not enjoying the classes anymore. I didn't enjoy being a constant mediator. I was also losing my interest in playing as often as I did. When the Beautiful AP and I were a card-counting team I needed to play upward of 130 days a year. But now? Did I really want to devote five or six weeks to Golden Touch, plus my other playing dates? Did I really want to be away from my wife that long?

My good friend Satch had also left the company. He was starting his career as a professional voice-over artist.

And what about travel? Essentially I had seen the casinos of America for 25 years, but I hadn't really gone anywhere else. There was a whole world out there to explore. I didn't need to do the casino thing to make money. Unless we took a big hit, the Beautiful AP and I were set.

If I didn't enjoy doing GTC anymore, if I didn't enjoy actually playing in casinos for an extended number of days a year, what then?

And those were my first coherent thoughts about leaving GTC. Even though I just thought them, I knew that soon I would leave the company.

CHAPTER 6

The Media, the Madness, and the Stalkers

As a writer I am always looking for opportunities to plug my books. Television and radio are two great avenues for getting the word out about my books and, of course, about me.

Most of my television work generally revolved around a given topic such as blackjack, card counting, craps, dice control, slot machines, casino rules, and general gambling advice. Radio was also similar, except the return from radio shows was nowhere near as good as the return from television.

I wrote and/or consulted for many television shows for such stations as A&E (I developed the idea for the contest between the dice controllers and the casinos), the Travel Channel (I wrote and consulted on many shows for that channel, including the show *What Would You Do If?*),; also CNN, the History Channel (where I constructed *The Dice Dominator*), TBS, the National Geographic Channel, the Discovery Channel, and the Learning Channel.

My strangest "partnership" with a show had to do with the History Channel's *Breaking Vegas* episode titled *The Dice Dominator*. This was to be the story of dice control. I worked with the writer closely. I explained the tremendous impact the Captain's ideas had on dice control; I explained how Dom and I met at the Treasure Island Casino and how we started Golden Touch. I pumped up Dom as almost the "second coming." Naturally I gave full credit to Sharpshooter's impact on dice control.

Jerry Patterson was interviewed, as was Sharpshooter and Stanford Wong. My idea for the show was simple: Go from the Captain to Sharpshooter and Patterson with PARR to Dom and me as partners and players. I thought that show would be interesting. The public could see the evolution of this prized skill.

The show wound up being somewhat of a fabrication concerning the origins of dice control and how Dom and I met. In real life, as you now know, we met at Treasure Island, became partners and friends, and helped to create Golden Touch. In the course of everything, we had many great adventures in the casinos.

The show presents it this way:

- There is no mention of the Captain at all
- Dom meets Sharpshooter in a garage (didn't happen)
- Barely a mention of the impact of PARR
- Dom joins Sharpshooter and Jerry Patterson's low-stakes dice control team Rosebud (didn't happen)
- I then arrive at this garage sometime later as a guest (didn't happen)
- Dom dumps Rosebud because they don't play high enough stakes (Dom wasn't on the team)
- Dom and I team up (happened) and play together, where I am portrayed as something of a skinny, low-life jerk (no way)
- I threaten the life of a stickman in the show by saying if he bothers us again, "You're a dead man." (I've never spoken that way to anyone in my life)
- The actor playing Dom is this tall, good-looking matinee idol type; the guy playing me looks like a crack addict
- Much of our adventures are accurate (thankfully)

While this show had a tremendous impact on gamblers' views of dice control, it gave many misimpressions. The fact that the Captain was not even mentioned was the worst thing. Without him there would have been no Sharpshooter, no Jerry Patterson, no Dominator, no Stickman, no Frank Scoblete, and no dice controllers out there right now. He was the creator, the inspiration. Leaving him out is like leaving God out of the bible.

Dracula

Perhaps the strangest interview I ever did for television had to do with slot machines, but this anecdote will give you an idea of what can happen when you go on TV.

Here's an excerpt from a letter I received from a television viewer: "I was watching *Hit the Jackpot* on the Discovery Channel and I noticed that you were wearing an earring. I thought you were a conservative kind of fellow. That doesn't go with earrings."

I have nothing against men or women who wear earrings, but I do not now, nor have I ever, worn an earring. What the viewer actually saw on that television show was a bead of sweat hanging off my ear. That's right, on a national television show, on a channel that seems well financed, that shiny thing hanging off my ear was my own sweat.

You see, that show—though about slot machines and slot jackpots—was not filmed in the airy precincts of a casino. It was filmed in the low-ceilinged basement of the producer's home. Yes, the show looks really good on television, and I did a commendable job (in my unbiased opinion) of appearing to be comfortable and relaxed.

But here's the inside story. The producer needed to finish this project quickly. Since she lives in New York and I live in New York, it seemed stupid to fly out to Vegas to film my segment, which was one-half of the hour-long show. She decided to film at her house, which was in a ritzy part of upstate New York.

I arrived on time, and the producer and I talked a little bit about what I would talk about on the television show. She had been impressed with my book *Break the One-Armed Bandits!* (now superseded by *Slots Conquest: How to Beat the Slot Machines!*) and wanted to focus on many of the ideas about which I wrote.

That was fine with me. That would give my book some good publicity.

"Where are we filming?" I asked, noticing that it was just she and I in the house.

"Downstairs, the basement. We've decorated it to look like a casino backdrop," she said.

Her dog ambled over—a smelly thing holding a disgustingly ratty yellowish tennis ball in his wet mouth.

"That's Dracula," said the producer. "He's friendly."

Dracula rubbed up against my leg, leaving some shiny spit on my suit pants.

We went downstairs to the basement. A cameraman and a sound technician were down there already, putting the finishing touches on the "set."

"We're just about ready," said the cameraman.

The producer made the introductions.

"Okay, we're ready," said the soundman.

The lights came on. With about a seven-foot ceiling, the basement heated up to frying proportions in about a third of a second, maybe less.

"Are you hot?" asked the producer.

"Yes," I said.

"Here's some water," she said. "I have a wet towel, and we'll wipe you off when we see you sweating."

I couldn't tell her that my underarms were already sweating, as were other parts of me.

"Now, Frank, just to get a sound test, state your name, spell it, and state the name of the book we're basing this interview on," she said.

"My name is Frank Scoblete. F-R-A-N-K S-C-O..."

From upstairs came the loudest howling I ever heard. "Roooffawwwww-yeooooow! Roooffawwwwyeooooow!"

"B-L-E-T-E."

"Roooffawwwwyeooooow! Roooffawwwwyeooooow!"

"Hold up," said the producer, "I was afraid this would happen. Dracula doesn't like to be alone. We'll have to bring him down here. You don't have any problem with the dog being here do you, Frank?"

"No," I said.

"Roooffawwwwyeooooow! Roooffawwwwyeooooow!"

"I'm coming, Dracula!" yelled the producer.

She zipped up the stairs. I heard her open the door, and I heard the dog scramble down the stairs, and then he appeared, the drool-soaked tennis ball still in his mouth. I wondered how he was able to do that terrible howling with that thing in his mouth.

Dracula ran around the basement like a madman...mad dog, actually.

"He has to calm down; he gets so excited," said the producer.

Finally Dracula quieted.

"Okay, Frank, give us the title of the book," said the producer.

"The title of the book..."

I noticed Dracula walking right toward me into the hot lights.

"Sorry, the title of the book is..."

Dracula shoved his head into my crotch.

"Owwww!" I yelled.

Dracula dug in even deeper.

The producer got up and dragged him back to her chair.

"He likes you," she said.

The basement was a thousand degrees.

"Frank's head is sweating a little. Where's the towel?" asked the cameraman.

We all looked around. Dracula's tennis ball was on the floor by the producer's chair, and Dracula was a little ways from it with the towel in his wet mouth.

"Dracula, we need that towel," said the producer.

It looked to me like Dracula made the towel go into his wet mouth another few inches. The producer grabbed the towel, and Dracula started shaking his head like a mad dog again.

"I'm fine," I said, "I don't need the towel." Inside my suit I was soaking wet. The dog still shook his head like a maniac with the towel in his mouth.

"I'm fine," I repeated.

The producer stopped grabbing the towel, and Dracula stopped shaking his head. When Dracula saw that we were not interested in the towel anymore, he dropped it on the basement floor and sauntered over to get his tennis ball.

"Okay, Frank, I'll ask you the questions. You kind of repeat the questions and then answer them," said the producer. "I'm sure you've done this a lot."

"Yes, no problem, I'm ready," I said, and thought, *Let's do this before I melt away!*

The producer asked me a question, and I rephrased the question and answered it. I could see that Dracula was eyeing me.

"Frank, in your book Beat the One-Armed Bandits..." said the producer.

"It's *Break the One-Armed Bandits*," I said.

Dracula moved toward me.

"What?" asked the producer, distracted by Dracula.

"I...uh!" and the dog dug his head, with gooey tennis ball in his dripping mouth, into my crotch again.

There was absolute silence in the basement.

"You know," said the producer, "He might just stay quiet if we let him stay there. He's under the camera's range."

"Let him stay, or we'll never finish this interview," said the cameraman.

"Do you mind, Frank?"

Now, my gentle readers, please hear me out and understand. It is important for writers to be on television. Book sales usually soar after a television appearance, especially when they print the title of your book under you as you are answering questions; your publishers and editors are happy to see one of "theirs" on the tube, which allows you to ask for more money for your next book; it makes you appear important. You understand all this, I hope.

Because I said to the producer, "No, I don't mind."

And I did the interview with Dracula digging into me as if he were attempting to reach China.

But I looked okay when they broadcast the show, even with my "earring," although the book sales for *Break the One-Armed Bandits!* did not go up because the book was titled *Beat the Bandits!* when it appeared on-screen under my sweaty head.

You can't win them all.

But one thing I know for sure—Dracula had a great time during that television interview. My testicles didn't.

Magic Mike and Mr. White Vine

I enjoy speaking in public, and I enjoy teaching classes. Usually my lessons go smoothly. I'm funny; I get my points across.

The biggest problem a person can have when performing before or teaching a group is if one (or more) people in that group thinks he should either compete with your humor or debate your ideas by jumping in when you haven't even finished a sentence.

Magic Mike, the nickname he had given himself, thought he was a comedian. I don't mind if someone gets off a funny line, even if it is at my expense. A small amount of give and take is fine. I can handle myself in front of a class or onstage.

But Magic Mike only *imagined* he was funny. He'd throw in his zingers—or what he *imagined* were zingers—and the other students' eyes would roll. Some would mumble under their breath after a while. Not one thing Magic Mike said was funny. There weren't even the funny puns intended to make you groan. There was only one person who laughed at Magic Mike's constant "zingers," and that person was Magic Mike.

Finally on Sunday morning some of the students came up to me and basically said, "Why don't you throw that idiot out of class?" What could I do? I could talk to Magic Mike, but he really didn't seem to be the type of guy who would recognize that he was a royal pain in the ass. So I found a second eraser at the dealer school where we were holding the class. I put it in my back pocket. I then started the lesson. Within two minutes Magic Mike lofted a "zinger," and eyes rolled in just about everyone's heads. The time had come.

I opened the window to the classroom. I stood there silently. We were on the second floor. I took the eraser out of my pocket and showed it to the class.

"Magic Mike," I said, and then I threw the eraser out the window. "Go fetch!" The classroom erupted in applause, and that shut up Magic Mike.

The guy I had the most fun with—actually the guy every instructor in GTC had fun with—was Mr. White Vine. He was about 70 years old and a little hunched and feverish looking. He was the type of student who would never allow you to finish a thought before he'd jump in and disagree with you.

"We know that in a random game, following trends..." I started.

"Is the only way to play the game of craps," said Mr. White Vine, who was seated directly in front of me.

"No, no," I corrected. "In a random game you cannot make predictions..."

"Yes, you can. I've been on many rolls where a certain number got hot and I made money on that number."

"We have to take a look at the math behind what you are saying..."

"Math, poof," he said. "If math boys knew anything, they would be rich." He then turned to the class and asked, "Isn't that so? Aren't I right?"

It didn't matter what the topic, old Mr. White Vine disagreed with what I said or what any of the other teachers said. Students' heads would shake when he jumped in. Unlike Magic Mike, Mr. White Vine never tried to be funny; he just succeeded in being irritating, a human diaper rash.

Dom tried gentle persuasion: "Mr. White Vine, would you shut the fuck up?"

During breaks we all wondered why a guy like that would take our dice-control class since he seemed to disagree with everything we said. He was wasting a lot of money to learn nothing.

By Saturday as the class ended, the instructors sat in the classroom. "What are we going to do with that idiot?" was the universal question.

"I got it," Dom said. "I bought this to have some fun at dinner tonight, but I think we now have a better use for it."

"What's that?" I asked.

"It's a fart machine," Dom said. He held it up. There were two parts: a remote and a loudspeaker part. "We tape the loudspeaker under Mr. White Vine's chair. Then when he opens his big fucking mouth, we let loose a fart."

"Great," everyone chorused.

So we went about fixing up Mr. White Vine's chair with the speaker. It was small, and we taped it under the seat. We put the remote in the podium. Of course, we all enjoyed practicing with the fart machine. Nothing can get middle-aged men, older men, or boys of almost any age into a state of hysterical laughter quicker than farts. Women do not understand this type of subtle humor. My wife threatened to divorce me because of a chapter about farts I wrote for my book *Confessions of a Wayward Catholic*.

"The plan is this," I said. "We go with small farts, almost inaudible, at first as he talks. He probably won't hear them with those hearing aids, but all the students behind him will."

So we worked out the sequence of the farts. The first few would be low and slow, then a little louder, then the wet variety, then louder, then soaking wet and really drawn out. We all knew at some point Mr. White

Vine would start to hear the farts, but who cared? The instructors and the students would get a laugh, and maybe, just maybe, it would shut Mr. White Vine's big mouth.

Sunday's class began with a review of the major elements we had practiced on Saturday.

"We now want to make sure we all remember the sequence of the throw..." I started.

"I don't want to pay money for refreshing me," Mr. White Vine said. "I learned all that yesterday."

I was at the podium, and as he finished his sentence I pressed the low-and-slow fart, *Pluurp.*

"This will only take a few minutes," I said.

"This is a waste of time." *Pluurp.*

"Okay, now, Stickman will go through the motions," I said. "Each element has to be done perfectly."

"No human can be perfect," huffed Mr. White Vine. *Pluurp, Pluurp.* Some of the students behind Mr. White Vine smiled. There is a good chance that, at that point, the students thought the farts were real.

"Take your position at the table like this," Stickman said. "Remember you want to be square."

"Everything's square. You're square, the dice are square," interjected an annoyed Mr. White Vine. "We know all this. Come on!" *Pluurp, Pluurp,* and a little louder *Pluurp.*

A little while later, Mr. White Vine said, "Okay, we wasted all this time. Can we..." (louder) *PluUUrp.* "Uhmmm." I think he heard that one. "What was I saying?" *PluUUrp!* Half the students let out giggles that they tried to suppress.

"Thanks, Stickman," I said. "We are going to talk about betting styles..."

"It's about time," Mr. White Vine said. Louder and wet: *PluUURp poo!*

"With dice control, you must make the bets you can overcome with your skill. It is no use to have the ability to change the nature of the game only to make bets that you can't overcome," I said.

"I think we have to realize that hedging is a good way to play," Mr. White Vine said forcefully. *Okay, I'll forceful that!* I pressed the loudest button—a long, ridiculously wet fart—*BA-BOOM-POO-POO-PLOP!*

The class, the instructors, and, yes, believe it or not, Mr. White Vine laughed. "I thought I was hearing farts," he said. Everyone applauded.

So did that stop him from continuing to be a pain in the ass? Nope.

The Stalkers

Even though I am what you'd call a very, very minor celebrity, I have had a few somewhat weird (maybe a little scary) stalkers. I don't count those players who emailed me or left messages on my business phone asking if and when I would be playing in the casinos and whether they could join me. Those folks seemed normal (mostly).

But the ones who dropped by my house—with the exception of a New York City police detective—have been strange. There was a rabbi in the town next to mine who showed up at my door several times asking if he could have dinner with the Beautiful AP and me to talk about craps. Obviously I didn't invite him in. Thankfully, he got the message.

The Beautiful AP and I would go to dinner with my in-laws once a week at a local restaurant, at the same time, and on the same night of each week. There were two fans invariably there. One was a local volunteer firefighter who was a pleasant fellow, and we'd talk a while. The other was out of his damn mind. He came to the restaurant to talk to me. He'd order a drink, stand over our table, and regale me with his gambling knowledge. Even when the food came, he wouldn't leave our table. Finally, the owner of the restaurant explained to him that I was to be left alone when I ate there. I would have changed the night of our weekly meal, but my in-laws couldn't make it any other night.

Thankfully, that got rid of him at my weekly dinners. Instead he started to show up at my house. Finally I had to tell him to go away. Then he started writing these awful posts on some message boards. How did I know it was him? He used his own name!

I did have a few female stalkers. One called me up and invited me to her suite at the Claridge, where she said she would "show me the best time of my life." I told her I was happily married, and she said, "Bring her too!"

Several women sent me suggestive photos of themselves—in their underwear, and one was nude. These women would never win beauty contests. I ripped the pictures up and threw them out. I guess they got tired of not hearing from me and moved on to someone else.

My latest stalker is a totally shorn monk convinced that he has been the inspiration for my books "through the province of our Lord, Jesus Christ." He sent a picture and he is the weirdest-looking guy I've ever seen. I guess God *does* work in mysterious ways.

PART IV:
Adventures

CHAPTER 1

The Greatest Rolls

Craps players dream about the monster rolls, the Godzillas, where number after number comes up one after another as chips pile into one's chip rack as if a gambling tsunami has washed such chips ashore. Most veteran craps players will experience rolls that last 45 minutes or maybe even one hour. Translated, these lucky players might have seen 40 to about 60 rolls in such cases.

Lucky long rolls do happen all over the country and the craps-playing world. The greatest roll, 154 numbers by Pat DeMauro, was a strictly random event—an event that overcame about 5.59 billion–to-1 odds against it, according to mathematician Stewart Ethier.

Pat was indeed a lucky roller, taking the dice for the second time in her playing career. Still, a random roll is a random roll, no matter how spectacular, and the fact that Pat did this remarkable feat does not indicate that she has suddenly gained any control of the dice. What does it mean? Simply, it's best not to bet on her rolls, or if you must, then use a minimum bet on her after the 5-Count as you would on any other random shooter.

Then there are dice controllers who can (over time) be counted on to have not only winning records, but often epic rolls far and away more often than random rollers.

I have been extremely fortunate to be on some terrific rolls, including my own 89-number roll, which has made the top 20 list that follows. Many of these epic rolls have been done by Golden Touch teachers and students, all of whom are excellent dice controllers, and, of course, by the Captain, who had two wonderful rolls—one of 100 and one of 147. I did

189

not see the 100 roll, but I was there for the 147 roll, as you have read. Dom has also had numerous monster rolls, as has Stickman.

Here are the top 20 rolls that have been recorded at the Golden Touch all-time world records pages. All of these rolls had witnesses that have confirmed them.

Standing	Shooter	Number of Rolls
1.	Pat DeMauro	154
2.	The Captain	147
3.	Stanley Fujitake	118
4.	The Captain	100
5.	Charlie "Sandtrap"	90
6.	Frank Scoblete	89
7.	Timmy	88
8.	Charlie F.	86
9.	Charlie F.	84
10. (tie)	Dominator	79
10. (tie)	Metafast	79
11.	Ronin	78
12. (tie)	Jerry "Stickman"	77
12. (tie)	Back-in-Black	77
12. (tie)	Johnny Carson	77
12. (tie)	Chaz Taverna	77
12. (tie)	The2ArmKing	77
13.	The Captain	76
14. (tie)	Dominator	75
14. (tie)	A.P. Black	75
15.	Gunslinger	74
16. (tie)	Pistol Pete	73
16. (tie)	Stanford Wong	73
17. (tie)	Big Baby 4353	72
17. (tie)	Dr. Crapology	72
18.	ACPA	71
19.	Skinny	70
20.	Various	50–69

CHAPTER 2

Dominator and Me

It was a glorious afternoon in May in an off-Strip Las Vegas casino. After three happy days of Dom and me hammering the casino in blackjack, with our betting spreads going from one unit in low counts (house-favorable counts) up to 10 units in high counts (player-favorable counts). There was no heat, either; none of the pit personnel had even bothered us. They laughed and joked with us, as did the dealers.

Also Dom and I had been the only ones who ever tipped the blackjack and craps dealers, so our action was great for them too. I didn't think anyone at the casino knew who we were, even though we were handing in our player's cards and getting RFB (full comp) for everything—gourmet meals, beautiful suites, limo rides wherever we wished to go, shows, and even airfare; in short, the casino gave us the real life of Riley.

Our good fortune was the same in craps. While neither of us had had any monster rolls, that fact really didn't matter. We had consistently won on our rolls in the teens, hitting repeating number after repeating number. Indeed, we had won on even shorter rolls in the single digits. On-axis shooters don't need monster rolls to bring home the bacon; we just need to consistently hit the same numbers.

Still, monster rolls are fun and the stuff of bragging in voice and print, which is fun if what you have to brag about actually happened, preferably in front of witnesses. When lightning strikes, it's remarkable.

And that afternoon lightning struck. Dom and I got so hot at the craps table that we could have burned down Chicago had Mrs. O'Leary's cow not done it before us. Two of our students happened to come to the table at the start of Dom's first turn with the dice. That was strange, since we had rarely met anyone we knew at that particular casino—one of the reasons we went there, in addition to its great games. I nodded to them; they nodded to me and bought in. Each took a position at the end of the table to my left as I was on SL1.

With the addition of the two students, the table had seven of us altogether—us, the two students, and three others who were obviously locals. Dom was on SR1, and when he got the dice, he proceeded to roll a masterful 23. I rolled an eight hand, with four 6s and one 8, before I sevened out.

The dice went around the table. The two students were out of their shooting positions since Dom and I each had one of the locals next to us at SR2 and SL2. So the students did not shoot that afternoon but passed the dice when it was their turn. The locals did shoot. The local next to me went next and had a nice hand of 18, winging the dice down the table as if he wanted them to go through the back wall. I got on his roll after the 5-Count and bet one Come bet on him. I won several of these, and when he sevened out I had a profit from his roll. The man clapped for himself after his roll, and so did the rest of us. He was a slender, good-looking man of about 70, with wispy white hair, who was neatly dressed as if he were going to play golf later that afternoon. So I thought of him as the Golfer.

"Nice roll," I said to him.

"Thanks," he said.

Our two students passed the dice. The local at the end of the table on Dom's side went next. He was a tall, strapping, beer-bellied man of about 50, who had seen far, *far* better days. He was unshaven with several days' growth on his face, and he was already a little tipsy at that point (he would get far more tipsy as the session progressed). He wore a stained, faded T-shirt, his fingernails were dirty, and his nose and ears had tufts of hair sprouting out of them. I thought of him as the Pig.

The Pig got the dice, and he was one of those players who liked to bounce the dice off the wall under him until the faces he wanted appeared. When these faces finally appeared (sometimes after several months), he set the dice, which also took about half a year, and then he threw those dice high into the air. Several times the stick person had to tell him to lower his arc because the dice were going above the stick person's eye level, which is a no-no in craps, since the stick person has to watch the dice and the bets in the center of the table as the dice are in the air. He can't do that if the dice are over his head.

The Pig sevened out just after establishing his point. He snorted and ordered a beer from the cocktail waitress. Since the casino was not crowded, the cocktail server, a pretty young lady whose weathered face had hosted too many tans and inhaled too many cigarettes, always hovered nearby. The Pig never tipped. He would just take his beer, gulp some, ignore the server, put the beer in the drink rack under the chip rack, and continue playing.

The local standing next to Dom on his right shot next. He was a young man, really skinny, timid, mousy-eyed, seemingly muscle-less, displaying a somewhat puffy hairdo with a trace of slow balding, and he was quite pale. He really didn't look very healthy, and his mannerisms also seemed a little fussy. Dom had whispered to me when the young man was buying in that he thought the guy was gay. The guy also looked as if he were several minutes away from dying, and so I called him the Dying One. The Pig constantly looked at him with a combination of disdain and disgust.

The Dying One took the dice and gently threw them down the table. His throw actually looked pretty good, very soft, though he was not a controlled shooter. On the Dying One's very first throw, the Pig slobbered, "You throw like a girl. Be manly. Christ almighty."

"I *am* a *girl*," said the Dying One, her voice dripping with sarcasm, shooting the Pig a look that could turn him into bacon, extra crispy. The Pig's eyes bulged a little, and his face turned pinkish under his whiskers; he snorted, looked down, grabbed his crotch, then his beer, and gulped the rest of it down his throat. "Another beer, sister," he said to the cocktail waitress, in an overly manly voice.

The Dying One made it past the 5-Count, then immediately sevened out. I made money because she sevened out just as I put down a Come bet.

It was Dom's second turn with the dice. His eyes had that fiery look. The Pig had irritated him. The Pig was classless. Saying something like "Be manly" to someone Dom had originally thought was gay, only to find out the young man was in fact a young woman, on top of the Pig's not apologizing, not tipping, and rampant snorting, scratching, and belching had gotten under Dom's skin. It's not too hard to get under Dom's skin, as you know. He can be volatile.

Also the Pig dressed like a pig. Dom is a meticulous dresser, with a clothes closet in his house as big as some people's living rooms. I think the only person Dom has ever been able to tolerate who doesn't dress up and looks to be somewhat ratty is me. I've never been a clotheshorse. My clothes closet is about four feet by two feet and is half full of clothes I rarely wear. Give me sweats or give me death.

Dom's eyes were burning, and he had a slight scowl on his face. As discussed, that look often heralds a great roll.

And so it went. Dom took the dice, and off we went to the races for a spectacular hourlong roll of 63 numbers. He was almost perfect in his throw, totally on axis on a healthy majority of them. He was making his usual array of bets, including hopping some doubles such as 3:3. Dom really likes to hop his numbers on the Come-Out roll, where the only thing in his mind is that Hop bet.

Naturally I could see those two students of ours quizzically looking at him when he put his money on those Hop bets. They looked at me too. I whispered, "I'll explain later." This scenario happens almost all the time when students are at the table with Dom.

The Pig was happily wallowing in his slop, too, cheering and drinking and burping, spewing beer-soaked saliva over the layout as he roared his approval while Dom hit number after number. I think the Pig's disgusting antics spurred Dom on even more. The whites of Dom's eyes were actually red, the way Christopher Lee's eyes were blood red when he played Dracula in various horror movies such as *Horror of Dracula*.

I don't actually remember Dom's roll moment by moment because I was fascinated by the Pig's spit sailing up and then falling down on the layout. On occasion some droplets of his spew would hit the Dying One, who threw him looks that she probably hoped would kill him. Unfortunately, he lived.

Dom was in the rolling zone and forgot that the Pig even existed. He was hitting a decent proportion of his Hop bets and he seemed to be truly honed in. He was in his zone, and the money poured in.

Every time he made his point, I would clap and cheer and say, "Keep it going, baby! Keep it going!" He kept it going, too.

The Golfer was having fun. "Man, this guy is a great shooter!" The students were nodding their heads. Its was the first time those two had ever been at a table with us, and they were seeing Dominator put on a show.

Interesting enough, except for Dom and me, the other players were basically red-chip players, though the Dying One and the Pig did begin to increase their bets as Dom's roll continued.

When Dom sevened out, the table exploded with applause. Dom walked away, ignoring the applause, found a slot machine nearby, and kicked it. The Pig, with drool on his chin, said, "Whas the fucks wrung wit das jer-p...?" He couldn't quite finish his sentence because he burped on the last word, which I believe he wanted to be "jerk" but instead came out "jer-p." We all looked at the Pig. How could he criticize a guy who had just rolled a 63?

"What a roll," said the Golfer.

"He rolled 63 numbers," I said.

"Wow!" said the Golfer.

Dom returned to the table. As he tells the story, he said to me, "Okay, Frank, do me better. I know you will do me better."

Well, yes, he did say that, but on my turn, I didn't have the roll of a lifetime. I rolled a 12 and sevened out. The Golfer passed the dice, and so did the two students. Everyone wanted Dominator to shoot again, except for the Pig, who took the dice and did his thing. But he was wrecked by then and couldn't quite remember what faces of the dice were appearing as he banged them against the wall under him. Finally the box person said, "Sir, just pick the dice up and throw them. We don't have all day."

The Pig started to argue, and I walked to the bathroom. When I got back, the Pig was arguing about something else. I looked down at the table, and it was wet. This disgusting "jer-p" had spilled his beer on the table. The cocktail waitress came over and soaked a towel with the guy's beer.

"Suster giip ee anotter wahn," slurred the Pig.

"Is he still rolling?" I asked the Golfer.

"No, he sevened out and then dumped the remains of his beer on the table. He's sloshed."

After the Pig's place was cleaned up, Dominator got the dice as the Dying One had also passed up her turn. He had a good roll of 18 with a lot of 6s and 8s. Then it was my turn again.

"Go, Frank, go for it!" shouted Dominator. The Pig snorted and rasped, "I ga piss nah. Dis eye cont shoo." He weaved his way toward the bathroom.

"What a fucking dick," Dom said.

You know in some turns with the dice totally disparate thoughts come into your head. Usually when this happens they whip by your consciousness and disappear into the blackness of thoughts past and never to be remembered. But I often tend to catch these and remember them. A passing thought crossed my mind: *Dom had a 63 roll and no one came to the table to join us. This place is really dead.*

I had $25 on the Pass Line. I set the dice in the All-Sevens set, established a point of 9 and took the full 4X Odds. I placed the 6 and 8 for $150 each.

I set the dice in the 3V. I gripped carefully, aimed the dice, and threw them softly into the air, where they backspun their way to the back wall.

Passing thought: *There are plenty of slot machines being played, just no table-game players.*

The stick person called out, "Six the hard way!"

Dominator: "Keep hitting those Hard 6s!" He collected a stack of chips.

I set the dice.

Passing thought: *This is definitely a slot place during the week.*

I threw.

One of the students: "Yes! Another!"

I set the dice. The Dying One had just bet the 6 for $30. I threw.

The Golfer: "Three Hard 6s in a row!"

I set the dice.

Passing thought: *The Pig's area is dry. I don't feel wetness on the dice when I get them back.*

I threw.

"Just 6s and 8s," shouted Dom.

I set the dice and threw them.

"Nine, nina nine!" shouts the dealer. I made my point.

Passing thought: *I like this casino. I like the table crew. The stick person steps back to give me a clear view to the back wall. Why not? Dom and I both have money on the table for the dealers. They are in the game too. We always keep the dealers in the game.*

I set the dice and threw. Point of 6 established.

I set the dice and threw again.

"Six, right back with it, a repeater, easy 6!" shouted the stick person.

"Hop the Hard 6," said Dom, throwing out a green chip.

Passing thought: *Don't look at the students. I'm sure Dom has stunned them again.*

I set the dice. I threw. "Eight is the point!" shouted the stick person. The Dying One placed the 8 for $30 and clapped her hands.

I bought the 4 and 10 for $50 each. The vig is paid on a win only so this is a good bet with a 1.3 percent house edge.

Passing thought: *She's actually not a bad-looking girl. I guess early 20s. Wound up, though.*

I set. I threw.

One of the students: "He owns the Hard 6!"

I set and threw a garbage number.

Passing thought: *Any number I'm not on is a garbage number.*

I set. I threw a good number.

Passing thought: *Good numbers are any numbers I am on.*

I set. I threw an 8 and made my point again.

"Same good shooter," said the stick person passing the dice to me.

Passing thought: *Oh, shit.*

The Pig was staggering back to the table. He took off the towel the crew had put over his chips, blew his nose in it, and flung it to the dealer on his right. The dealer jumped out of its way, and the towel fell to the floor.

"What a fucking pig," Dominator snarled.

I got the dice and established a new point of 5.

"We think you have had enough, sir," said the floor person, who had been closely watching the game.

"Ah wahn bee," said the Pig. "Ah wahn bee."

I was distracted. Should I set and throw? I was not in my zone. It would be strictly random. I paused and thought of my mantra. No good. My mind was on the Pig.

Passing thought: *Hit him with the dice.*

I set the dice.

Passing thought: *He might come at you.*

I gripped the dice.

Passing thought: *He can hardly walk.*

I aimed the dice.

Passing thought: *For God and Country!*

I winged the dice at the Pig's chest. They zoomed through the air like two bullets. One die skimmed off his shoulder and went zooming off under the closed craps table behind us. He didn't even notice it. The other die hit him square in that shoulder. He didn't notice that one either.

"Same dice," I said. The dealers were grinning. The floor person scurried off to get the die that had sailed off the Pig's shoulder and was resting under the table behind us.

"Gif ee a cig rat," he said to Dom, who was taking a cigarette out of his full pack.

"I ran out," Dom said coolly.

I got the dice back. I was far more relaxed as I set the dice. I aimed and started my backswing. The Pig dropped a handful of chips all over the layout and reached over to pick them up, dropping still more from his hand onto the layout and knocking chips off his chip rack, which fall to the floor as he pulled back his arm. I put the dice down. I'd seen this happen before—both with drunks and people who are nervous. The chips spurt.

The floor person walked around the table to the Pig. "I think you should take a break, sir," he said. The Pig was having trouble picking up his chips. His hands didn't seem to be obeying him. The floor person nodded to the dealer, and the dealer helped the Pig pick his chips off the layout. The floor person picked the chips up off the floor. A really big stony-faced heavily muscled security guard came up and stood next to the Pig.

The floor person said, "Let's cash in your chips at the cage, sir, and you take a break for a while." The floor person was quite professional.

The Pig seemed about to object, and then he saw the Hulk next to him and chose instead to allow himself to be escorted to the cage by the floor person and the Hulk. "Thank God he's gone," said the Dying One.

Dom blew out a stream of smoke and said, "It would have been fun to put my cigarette out in his eye." Everyone stared at Dom. A pause. Then he laughed, and we all laughed. The tension created by the Pig had dissipated.

"Okay, let's get back to the game," said the box person.

And we got back to the game.

"Come on, Frank, roll for a month," said Dom, taking a long drag from his cigarette and blowing the smoke into the air. I really wish Dom would quit smoking.

I set. I threw. And *eternity* happened. Well, actually, the craps equivalent of eternity. I had my best roll to that point in my career—89 numbers before I sevened out.

When you have long rolls, there comes a time when you are in a dream world, an alternate universe. Your body is doing what you have trained it to do. It is operating automatically. Everything feels removed from everything else. Yes, you are there at the craps table, but you are also somewhere else, far, far away. Time expands. Passing thoughts just pass through, leaving little memory of them.

I remember bits and pieces of thoughts—nothing really solid, just shimmers of what must have passed through my mind during that roll. I heard the numbers being called out by the stick person. I saw several stick changes. I was on every number by the end of the roll. I know that. The money didn't even seem real. I didn't even think anything of the money. There were just piles of chips on the numbers.

I had some very big bets out there. Dom had been hopping bets like crazy, and I knew he was winning many of those because he whooped it up when he did. But all of those things were in the distance just beyond concrete reality, which was also in some distant place. It was all ephemeral, and then...

"Seven! Seven out!" shouted the stick person. "What a great roll, Frank, great roll!"

I was back in the world. The other players were clapping and cheering.

Dom walked behind the stick person to me and started patting me on the back.

"Not bad," I said.

Dom laughed and hugged me, "Not bad at all! But couldn't you have gotten to a hundred?"

We colored up. The Hulk walked us to the cage. I asked for a check. I don't like carrying around a lot of cash.

One of the students came up to me and said, "Great roll."

"Thanks," I said.

"I just wanted to ask you a question," he said.

"Dom makes those bets because he still has a little gambler left inside him. Nobody's perfect," I said.

It was late afternoon by then, and I was tired and happy.

"Let's go to the pool," I said to Dom.

"No, no, I'm hot," he said. "I'm going to play some blackjack."

"Dom," I said, "you never want to quit."

"I'll play a little and then I'll meet you at the pool in an hour or so. We're having dinner at 7:00. We have plenty of time."

At the pool, I swam a little, took a comfortable chair, and stretched out in the shade. I enjoy lounging by the pool and I really liked that pool. There was almost no one there, ever. The property was quite nice, but it seemed to be underused during the week.

I feel a nudge on my arm. "Frank, Frank, wake up," Dom said.

"Oh, man, I fell asleep. I was gone."

"All that excitement," Dom said.

He wasn't happy.

"You don't look happy," I said. "You lose in blackjack?"

"I won," he said.

"Great, what a great day."

"And I've been banned," he added.

"What?"

"Yeah, can you believe it? Those fucks banned me." (My wife, the beautiful AP, tells me to get rid of the *fucks* in my books when Dom speaks— except Dom owns a franchise in that word. It's how he speaks. You want to hear Dom's voice? Then *fuck* is the word! Sorry if that offends you.)

"You were banned at blackjack?"

"No, they told me I couldn't play craps or blackjack in their casino again, and if I tried I'd be trespassed."

Being trespassed is a serious thing, because that means the casino will consider your very appearance on their property to be an illegal act of trespassing. They can't have you arrested for controlling the dice or counting cards, since neither is illegal—though they can stop you from playing—but if they tell you that they no longer will allow you on their property, then the next time you show up, they can have you arrested... for trespassing, not for skill in gambling. It is immoral, I agree, but it is the law. Casinos are private businesses, and in Nevada and most other states, they can ban you and/or trespass you, and that is all there is to it. Sadly, Dom and I have been trespassed in some casinos.

"They've been so nice," I said. "It's hard to believe they banned you."

"And you," he said.

"Me? I was here sleeping."

"They told me that when you came back into the casino they would tell you the same thing."

"Today was too much for them," I said.

"What are we supposed to do? Give them some of their money back?"

"You know what we won is really only a tiny drop in the bucket. But they want every drop in the bucket."

"Greedy fucks," said Dom, taking out his cigarettes.

"Dom, I really wish you'd stop smoking."

"I'll stop smoking when the casinos stop being greedy fucks," he said, and lit up.

I guess Dom will never stop smoking.

CHAPTER 3
Bye-Bye, Mississippi

an a casino gambling venue go from being the best in the country to the worst almost overnight? Yes—Tunica, Mississippi. I used to laud this venue as having the best craps games, best dealers and pit personnel, best executives, and some of the best blackjack games and comps in the country. Sadly, none of this is true any longer. Yet even as Tunica started to go downhill, I was treated with respect...until:

Friday, February 17
I was at LaGuardia Airport in New York for my 11:15 AM flight to Memphis, Tennessee, on the bankrupt Northwest Airlines. I was already missing the Beautiful AP, who would not be with me. She retired from playing in the casinos as soon as our son Michael graduated college in 2001.

The day was dreary with rain and light winds. I was scheduled to get to Memphis at about 1:15 PM Central Time, and then gambling author and blackjack guru Henry Tamburin, along with Dominator, Stickman, and I, would set up for the (now-defunct) Golden Touch Blackjack class.

As a writer I write about all the games—even the ones that can't be beaten—but my casino play tends to center on the games I can beat. And my advantage-play teams strictly concentrate on taking from the casinos what the regular patrons have given them—money.

In the upcoming two weekends in Tunica during that trip, we were doing our advantage-play seminars at blackjack, where we taught the revolutionary Speed Count and the Optimum Basic Strategy, both created by Dan Pronovost, a skinny Canadian. The following weekend we were doing our dice-control seminar. The blackjack method was easy to learn and execute in the casino and could gain a competent player between a .5 and 1 percent edge over the game. That meant for every $100 wagered, your expectation was to win 50¢ to $1. That might not sound like a lot, but that is the edge the casino usually has over the players—and over time that edge can win a lot of money. Our Golden Touch Blackjack methods were simplicity themselves. Not so with dice control. Dice control was harder to master.

A couple of years before that weekend, we had scheduled a dice-control class at Tunica's Grand Casino-Hotel—in fact, the Grand had asked for us to do one of our classes—but when we showed up, all hell broke loose. It seemed that a month prior, an executive at the Grand had phoned the Mississippi Gaming Control Board and asked if it was okay if we taught students how to play the games.

"The person this executive spoke to," Dom explained, "was an assistant to an assistant. She wasn't even a lawyer for the board, but she started to cause trouble. I think she wanted to make a name for herself. We had to send faxes of our gaming tables so the board could see that they weren't regulation craps tables because the Grand could not have such tables other than on their gaming floor."

Dom continued, "When we showed up on the Friday before class, the control board announced that Golden Touch couldn't teach anyone the games in Mississippi, and our class was summarily cancelled—the day before we were scheduled to hold it! The control board went even further and said we would all be arrested if we tried to teach anyone about casino games in Mississippi. We discovered that agents of the control board were stationed at all the casinos to make sure we didn't switch properties. There was security everywhere. Our instructors were even followed by security."

Think about it. Here we were about to teach students from all over the country, who had flown down to out-of-the-way Tunica, Mississippi, about dice control—a *legal activity*—and a government agency was stopping us. We had 50 students, 15 highly paid advantage-play dice-control instructors, and no place to go in the land of cotton.

Luckily Dom set up a phone chain on that Friday night, and after dozens of calls, we found a hotel at the Memphis Airport, and the next day we bused everyone to the class. Then we hired an excellent attorney to petition the Mississippi Gaming Board that our civil right to free speech was being violated.

After months and months of hearings and meetings *and fees*, we won our case. The assistant to the assistant had misread the Mississippi regulations, and we were free to hold classes in Mississippi. The good citizens of Mississippi or elsewhere had the right to accurate knowledge of the casino games, and we had a right to teach them that knowledge.

I looked forward to getting back down there. At that time Tunica had great games, though there were rumblings that the Harrah's takeover of the Grand, Sheraton, and the Horseshoe was ruining those previously great properties by making their games far less player-friendly. The rumors held that the pits, which had been universally friendly to me in the past, had undergone a change, and suddenly suits were sweating the money for fear of losing their jobs in the Harrah's takeover.

I'd have to see that for myself. That is, if I could see. I'd just had a laser procedure on my left eye after my mother had a serious illness. "This eye thing," said my retina specialist, "is caused by stress." I was not allowed to have daylight touch my skin for 72 hours, so I was completely covered when I entered LaGuardia Airport—the drug they used during the procedure affects the skin's ability to deal with daylight and halogen light. I was wearing an Indiana Jones hat and white gloves, so I had almost no skin exposed. People looked at me and then quickly looked away.

I had some real trouble with my vision for several days after that procedure.

The winds in New York that day, what there were of them, delayed the flight for more than an hour, but once in the air, the flight to Memphis was smooth. I was supposed to meet Dom at the Memphis Airport, but since I was going to be so late, he rented another vehicle and headed to Tunica on his own.

I rented an SUV from Avis. The trip to the Tunica casinos is about a half hour from the Memphis Airport. It's an interesting drive—cotton fields, shacks, soybean fields, shacks, a strip joint, rice paddies, shacks, billboards, and endless miles of fields in all directions, mud puddles, and then casinos. It is *Viva Las Vegas* meets *Gone with the Wind*.

Once in Tunica, the four of us set up the Golden Touch Blackjack class at a non-casino hotel. We set up blackjack tables, chips, and shoes for cards. It took a couple of hours, and then Dom and I headed over to the Grand so I could check in. He had already checked in.

The Grand (subsequently Harrah's, which has since closed) was the premier property in Tunica at the time, with three hotels, a golf course, a shooting range, a spa and salon, a Kid's Quest child-care center, and a convention hall. The property was huge, with small lakes throughout. The views from the Terrace Hotel were beautiful. Supposedly the Terrace was the best of three hotels on the property. I have to take that on faith, since I never stayed at any of the others.

When I checked in, I told the desk clerk that the last three nights of my stay were comped with a room comp coupon. The first three nights had also been comped with a different three-night coupon. I had avoided doing the host-RFB thing because I didn't want to have to give any casino four hours of action per day, which is usually what they want in return for RFB. Instead, I wanted to spread my action around all the casinos in Tunica. I was also somewhat concerned by the rumors I had heard about Tunica changing its attitude toward advantage players. It would be better if I didn't bring too much attention to myself.

That was my thought. Unfortunately for me, everyone in the Tunica casinos knew me.

I had made an 11-day reservation at the Grand over the Internet. The room rates were ridiculously low, and then I started to get coupon comp offers that didn't require any set amount of play. It was my second time staying at the Grand's Terrace Hotel. I substituted the free offers for the first three days and I wanted to substitute another free offer for the last three days of the trip. "We got you for those days already," the clerk said.

"Yes, I know, but I want to use a free coupon for them and not pay for them," I said.

She looked at me as if I were speaking some strange dialect, or maybe my New York accent was hard to fathom, but I could tell she didn't understand what I was saying, as her eyes looked like a deer I once *almost* hit on the Garden State Parkway on my way to Atlantic City. I figured I would come back once I was registered in the hotel and explain to someone else who could understand me that I wanted to substitute my paid days with the free days.

That night we ate at Murano's, an Italian restaurant, at the Grand Casino. Murano's was the only Italian restaurant in all of the Tunica casinos, so we frequented it a lot. Dom wasn't that hungry, so he just had salad. Stickman ate like a horse, and Tamburin and I also ate full meals.

Then we hit the craps tables. I took up the position at the end of the table so that Dom could throw without chips in his landing zone. Dom was throwing from SR1, and Stickman was shooting from SL1. Tamburin was on the other side of the table, opposite me, to protect Stickman's landing zone.

Dominator had a decent roll—we made some money on it, which is the definition of *decent*. Then Stickman had a decent roll. Then the dice made their way from one random roller to another random roller.

When the dice returned to Dom, he established a point and then immediately sevened out. Billy "the Kid" believes that we dice controllers tend to do the point/seven-out (PSO) more often than normal random rollers because we are trying to protect against the 7, and when we are the least off in our throws—*bam!* Seven-out! He might be right.

It was Stickman's turn with the dice. Stickman had looked good in his previous roll, so I went right up on him with $150 on the 6 and 8. Here was Stickman's roll: 4, 6, 6, 6, 6, 6, 6, 4, 6, 6, 9, 6, 6, 6, 10, 6, 6, 8, 6, 6, 6, 6, 8, 6, 6, 6, 6, 6, 7-out.

The Grand's box man would occasionally pick up the dice and look at them, and then look suspiciously at Stickman, then put the dice down. That was weird. Usually the Grand's box people were pleasant. Maybe he thought we had substituted our own dice.

After Stickman's extraordinary hand, hitting 22 6s in 28 rolls, we colored up and called it a night. One thing I have learned in my casino-playing career is not to be greedy at the casinos where I enjoy playing. I love playing the games, but I also know that in many casinos my identity is no secret.

In Tunica I wrote for several magazines and newspapers, and I also did a weekly radio show from Memphis, largely sponsored by the casinos. So I tried to keep my winnings within the realm of tolerance. At least I thought that I did that. Even with my advantage-play teams, I usually directed them to casinos that had banned me. I took it easy in casinos where I liked to play, and I liked playing at the Grand.

Foolish me, as you will see. The Tunica I was in was not the great player-friendly Tunica of the past, but a new Tunica—a darker place.

That night when Dom got back to his room, he called room service. Then he called me. "Can you believe it?" He was quite agitated.

"What?" I asked.

"The damn room service is closed because of bad weather."

"Bad weather? What bad weather?" I asked, looking out the picture window at the clear, star-studded sky. "It's not bad outside. And how would that affect room service, even if it were bad outside?"

"It's supposed to be bad tomorrow," he said.

"Tomorrow? So what?"

"So there's no room service tonight."

Saturday, February 18

The next morning an ice storm hit Mississippi and Tennessee. It wasn't a particularly bad ice storm, and some salt and sand would make the roads drivable. I called down for room service, and the phone rang interminably until finally someone answered. "I want to get in touch with room service," I said.

"They ain't no room service. It's closed," said a female voice, before hanging up.

I went downstairs to get a newspaper and found that the gift shop was also closed. A crudely scrawled sign taped to the front door announced that fact: *We Close.* Then I went to get some coffee and a muffin in the Java Grand shop. It was closed.

I went back to my room and drank some water and took my vitamins.

An hour later Dom and I headed for the Golden Touch Blackjack class. We groused about the fact that nothing was open because people hadn't come to work. When we arrived at the class, we asked Stickman, a resident of Tennessee, about the fact that no one seemed to have gone to work at the Grand's Terrace Hotel. He laughed. "People here don't go to work in the bad weather," Stickman explained.

"We drove here, and the road was ice. They haven't salted yet," I said. "We could have been killed it was so slippery."

"They don't have salt," Stickman said. "It'll melt on its own. God brought the storm; God will take it away. That's the thinking."

After the class Dom and I drove back to the hotel, in fear I must say, since the roads were still icy. It was 5:00. We stopped at the valet parking in the front of the Terrace and waited.

And waited.

And waited.

No one came over. Finally we saw a woman who looked like a worker, and we called to her.

"Hey, hey!" Dominator yelled. "We want to valet the car!"

She ambled slowly toward us and after a decades-long wait said, "They ain't no valet parking now."

"What?" I asked.

"You're kidding," Dom said.

"You got to park yourself," she said.

"You mean we have to go into that icy self-parking lot and park the fucking car ourselves?" Dom yelled.

"Yup," she said, and started to amble away, as if to say, "That's that, boys."

"Did the valet parkers come to work?" I asked.

"No, we a different department," she stated.

"What the fuck does that mean?" Dom asked.

"We a different department," she said gently, ignoring his use of the word *fuck* and speaking to us as if we were lunatics. "You got to park the car. Over there." She pointed to the parking lot about 400 miles away.

So we drove the car into the icy parking lot—it was a sheet of ice, there were no non-icy spots, and we had to park in the very back of the lot, which looked to be about 410 miles away from our hotel. As I got out of the SUV on the driver's side, I slipped, caught myself on the door, and luckily didn't fall and kill myself. My Indiana Jones hat fell off my head, however. I reached and grabbed it just before it could blow away across the ice, and I put it back on.

"God almighty," I said. "Be careful, Dom. We can kill ourselves trying to get to the hotel."

So we walked like hockey fans going onto an ice-hockey rink. We slid along the ice. It was scary and dangerous. "You park the car," the woman had said as she walked away from us. You come to a hotel for services and amenities; you don't come to a hotel so that you have to park your own car on an iceberg because the valet attendants don't show up for work on bad-weather days.

Inside the hotel there was no bartender at the bar. I could have used a drink, but the bar was closed. Why would that be surprising? *No one comes to work in bad weather.*

In the elevator, Dom rattled off, "No room service, no gift shop, no coffee shop, no valet, no bar, no salt or sand on the roads. What the hell? Does it get worse than this?"

Sunday, February 19

Sunday was worse.

I looked out my window, and there was ice everywhere. I didn't bother with room service. I drank some water, took my vitamins, showered, dressed, knocked on Dominator's door—we had adjoining rooms—and off we went to the Golden Touch Blackjack class.

Of course, we first had to negotiate our way into the parking lot to get our SUV—it was like walking over the frozen steppes. We needed a Sherpa.

As we inched through the Grand's property, the ice glistened every-where, except on the roads that the shuttles use in order to take the players from the hotels to the Grand Casino; there was *plenty* of sand on those roads. Trying to exit the Grand property was hair-raising; I drove about 10 miles per hour.

"Do they want their fucking players to die?" screamed Dom as the SUV did a little skid to the side of the road. Luckily we didn't go into the ditch.

"They are trapped on the property," I said, as I righted the SUV. "You have a hard time getting out of here, so the players have to play here." The SUV skidded again. "I hope we get out of here alive."

There was no sand or salt on any of the exit roads, and just about all the blackjack students came to class late. The common refrain from the students who flew in from other areas of the country was: "What the hell is wrong with these people? Don't they know how to handle ice?"

The answer to that was, "No."

We taught the class and at 5:00 PM headed back to the Grand along the same icy roads. We parked in the guest lot, which now seemed about 8 million miles from the Terrace Hotel, and walked—no, *snowshoed*—our way to the hotel. It was worse than the previous day, as frozen winds had covered everything in ice—even the sides of the building. Cars that had remained in the parking lot during the storm looked like ice sculptures.

Once safely inside, I went to the front desk to explain about my three free room nights the next weekend. Again the desk person, a different person than before, didn't understand what I was saying. I explained it three times, in three different ways, all three ways engendering looks as if I were talking gibberish. "You nights in already," said the desk clerk, looking at the computer behind the reservation desk.

I gave up. "Never mind, I'll take care of it some other time," I said.

"You haff a good evenin', sir," said the desk clerk.

"Thanks," I said.

The people you meet in Tunica are universally friendly, but there's a slowness there that can drive a New Yorker crazy—a slowness, and no sand or salt on the roads, and no one coming to work in bad weather.

We called the restaurant line to make reservations from Dom's room, and finally someone answered. The woman didn't know if any restaurants would be open that night. "Depends if anyone's coming to work," she said.

"If they salt the damn roads, people could drive!" shouted Dominator into the phone. Dom looked at me. "She hung up."

"Crap."

Miracle of miracles that night at the Grand Casino: all the restaurants were open. A few people made it to work after all. We ate at the steakhouse, and while service was slow—service is always slow in Tunica, but you get used to that after many visits—we had a fine meal.

We went to the craps tables, but they were filled, and then we checked out the blackjack games, but they were not very good. When you use Speed Count, the most important thing is depth of penetration. We wanted about 60 percent or more.

The Grand was giving about 50 percent penetration on their double-deck games, and while we still had an edge at that level, it wasn't big enough to waste our time playing. We were also tired. But we'd have a whole week to play the games starting the next day—as long as the forecasted sun came out and melted the ice so we could check out other casinos.

I had in mind hitting Fitzgerald's casino, which our team had hammered the previous November.

Monday, February 20

I went down to the Bellissimo Spa at 7:00 AM to work out. It was closed. It was supposed to open at 7:00 AM. I went back to my room and came down at 8:00 AM. It was open, thank the Lord! I worked out for an hour on the treadmill and then did a half hour of weight training. Dom came down about a half hour into my workout and did his workout as well. Dom is a very strong guy and lifts monumental weight compared to me.

I could finally jettison the hat and the gloves, as 72 hours had passed and I wasn't susceptible to light anymore. My eye was also getting a little better. And the sun was out, strong and bright, and melting all the ice. God had brought the storm and God was getting rid of the storm's remnants.

All was right with the world.

Or so I thought.

The ice was melting rapidly, and the valet parking was open. After our showers, we took the shuttle to the Grand Casino to eat at the buffet. Of course, the gift shop was still closed, as was the Java Grand, but it looked as if they would open later that day, since the hand-made signs were no longer posted.

At the buffet there was no butter until the waiter found some in the kitchen. The toast turned cold during the five-month waiting time.

"They didn't put it out," he said by way of explanation.

"I know that," I said.

Obviously they didn't put it out! That's why I asked you to go find some! But rather than being nasty to him and saying that out loud, I said "Thank you." I also left him a decent tip for bringing the butter.

After breakfast we went into the casino to play craps. That day, in four turns with the dice, Dom and I each had 50+ rolls. Not to put too fine an edge on it, we were *spectacular*. During our turns with the dice, a huge *suit* conference was held in the craps pit—with what I took to be floor people and pit bosses and whoever else wears a suit in the casinos. Every one of them occasionally glanced at us. The suits were nodding to each other, looking at the computer screens, nodding some more to each other, and then surreptitiously looking over at us.

They didn't look friendly. We carted a boatload of chips from the craps table that morning.

Tuesday, February 21

The Bellissimo Spa opened at 7:00 AM, and I worked out for an hour, just doing the treadmill. I went back to my room, showered, shaved, and knocked on Dom's door. We headed to the buffet.

After breakfast I tried to explain to the new desk person at the Terrace about my three free nights for the upcoming weekend.

That clerk too looked at me as if I spoke some space-alien tongue. We stood there and looked at each other. Time passed. Ice floes in Antarctica melted. She was silent. I was silent.

"Never mind," I finally said, and left.

At noon, Dominator wanted to send out a rush overnight FedEx package to one of his clients. But the staff at the desk said that the package couldn't be delivered until the next day. "What are you talking about?" Dom asked. "FedEx picks up at 5:00 PM; it's noon now, for God's sake." The desk clerk took the FedEx package.

That afternoon Dom had to take care of some business, so we decided to hold off on playing until after dinner when we would go to Fitzgerald's to play their delicious double-deck blackjack games.

After dinner we each went into our rooms to wash up, get our money, and prepare to tackle Fitzgerald's. In my room I suddenly heard a scream from Dom's room. "Aaaaarrrrrggghhhhh! You stupid fucks!"

I knocked on his door, and he opened it. He looked like a madman. The *rush* FedEx package had been returned to his room while we had dinner—it was sitting right on the bed—because the Terrace staff thought it was addressed to him. "They delivered the package to me!" he screamed. "They delivered the fucking package *back* to me!"

Fitzgerald's had the second-biggest property of all the hotel-casinos, behind the mighty Grand. The casino was not very large, but it tended to be crowded all the time. I think they had a cheap buffet that players flocked to, but the casino itself didn't really appeal to me. It seemed kind of dingy. Or maybe that is just a particularly bad experience clouding my general memory of the place. You decide.

The Dominator and I were playing blackjack in the high-roller room. Dom was wearing one of his disguises. He looked like a really dopey, nerdy type of guy, complete with a penholder in his top pocket. In fact, I put just a smudge of ink on his shirt to make it look even more realistic. He wore these thick-framed Barry Goldwater glasses.

Before this incident, we had been told at the craps table that we were not allowed to shoot the dice anymore. We could bet on other shooters, but our shooting days at Fitzgerald's were over. Dom got annoyed. "You mean to tell me you want us to bet our money at craps but not shoot the dice? Shooting is the most fun."

We had probably played through two shuffles when a sour-faced woman showed up at the table. There was nothing subtle about her approach. She did not ask us to leave the table, as would be done in Vegas. Instead, she yelled at Dom, "You don't think I know who you are? You don't fool me. I know who you are!"

"What?" asked Dom, feigning ignorance. His acting skills would not be effective with her. She had nailed him. I ignored her harangue and put out my bet. After all, I wasn't with this ink-stained-pocket and thick-glasses Barry Goldwater man. She pushed my bets back. "Everyone knows who *you* are!" she screamed at me.

I took my chips. We'd been made.

"I don't know what you're talking about," Dom said.

"You two are together. Frank and Dom, we know who you are. I am now going to tell you that you will be considered trespassing the very next time you set foot on Fitzgerald's property. That is *anywhere* on our property."

Dom scooped up his chips.

"Let me color you up," said the dealer. Dom sneered at her. I put my chips back on the table and let her color me up.

The sour-faced executive then went into the trespassing thing again. A woman at the table said, "What are you doing? These men are very nice. They weren't cheating. Why are you treating them this way?"

"This is *none* of *your* business," the casino employee said to the woman.

"I would just like to know what's going on," said the woman.

"This is none of your business."

"You just do this to players who have done nothing wrong?"

"This is none of your business."

Dom said to the nice woman, "We can beat their fucking game, and she doesn't want us to play. They did it at craps and now they're doing it at blackjack. We can't come back here." He snarled at the supervisor, "This place is a fucking shithouse anyway."

Four security guards came over. Dom had his chips in his hand and a big security guard on each side of him. They walked him to the cage to cash out. I had a security guard on each side of me as well, though one seemed so old I thought he would die before we got to the cage. None of the guards said anything to us.

Once we had cashed out, my old, withered security guard said, "We will walk you down the road to the gate and see you leave the property. You are never to come back."

I held up my hand. "We have a friend here. He can drive us." That was best-selling author Henry Tamburin. I wasn't going to his table (that might get him booted), so when we exited the building, Dom gave Henry a call on his cell phone. The old security guard said, "Normally we would walk you out, but your friend can pick you up down there, near the gate."

And so our trespassing at Fitzgerald's started us on the road to ruin in Tunica, Mississippi. Thankfully Henry was there to ride us off into the sunset—actually moonlight, since it was nighttime.

We headed over to Horseshoe to check out the craps and blackjack games. Horseshoe was crowded. In those days the Horseshoe was always crowded. But something had changed—the craps tables were like trampolines, and the dice would often bounce off them. The tables reminded me of those at the Flamingo Hilton in Vegas. Why had they messed with their tables? The Horseshoe had made the most money from the table games of any casino in Tunica—why screw around with what worked?

Dom went to the high-roller room to play blackjack, and I was to follow in a few minutes. Except that I didn't have to follow because he came walking back over to me and whispered, "Let's get out of here." So we went to valet and silently got the van, and then Dom said, "They stopped me from playing. They knew who I was, and they mentioned you too. Just like that. This place used to be the friendliest casino on earth."

"It was the best casino in the country," I said.

"Harrah's fucked this place good," Dom reflected.

"So we are out at Fitzgerald's and Horseshoe," I mused. "I never expected anything like this."

"Fuck," said Dom, who then lit a cigarette.

"I thought you were cutting down on the smoking?"

"Fuck," said Dom, inhaling.

Wednesday, February 22

I had a great workout in the spa. That wound up being the highlight of my day.

After breakfast Dom and I went down to play some craps. We were the only two at the craps table. Dom would roll first from SR1, and I would roll from SL1. We had our Pass Line bets up, and Dom established his point and we placed our numbers, and then a loud holler came from across the casino.

"Stop! Stop!" yelled a voice. At first I thought it was a player wanting to get into the game—sometimes the players don't know the rules of how and when to enter a craps game. It was a Grand executive. "Frank, I'm really sorry," he said, a little out of breath, "but we don't want you to play blackjack or craps in our casino anymore. You too," he said to Dom.

"What the fuck?" Dom said. "Do you think we're going to break you? What the fuck is this?"

"It isn't me," said the executive to me, "and I am sorry, but that's how it is." Then he turned to the dealers and said, "Give them all their bets back."

"You can keep your tips," I said to them.

The dealers pushed all of our bets back to us but deposited their tips in the toke box.

"This is really fucking stupid," said Dom, his face red, the veins in his neck bulging.

"We're leaving," I said. "We're not going to give you any trouble."

"Fuck!" Dom said.

"Hey, it wasn't me, guys, it wasn't," said the Grand executive.

Several days later a friendly executive in the Harrah's empire who shall remain nameless called me and said, "Frank, you just won too much money, and you teach those classes. No one wants you to play in Tunica anymore. That's coming from above." I asked him about the countless thousands of people I had sent to Tunica, but all he could say was, "That's the way it is for now."

After getting the boot at the Grand, we went over to Sam's Town. I had been invited to speak at Sam's Town twice in the past by their executives, and I was very friendly with some of the suits there.

The one open craps table was crowded, so we went to a Pai Gow Poker table to play while waiting for our spots to open at the craps table.

Pai Gow Poker is a great game, and you can get an edge if you structure your betting properly. [The complete strategy to beat Pai Gow is in my book *Everything Casino Poker*.]

Sam's Town did not let you bank 50 percent of the time, so it was not even theoretically a beatable game. That didn't matter. Dom and I were just wasting time with $5 bets. There were only two other people at the table—both $5 bettors—so even if it had been a good game, it would not have been a moneymaker for us.

Except none of that mattered, because we got tapped. Tapped at Pai Gow Poker! That had to be a first.

The executive who tapped us out was one of the guys who had hired me to speak to his players several years before. He had been very friendly then. But this time he said coldly, "We don't want you playing in our casino, Frank. Take your chips and cash them."

It looked to me as if Dom was ready to take his chips and shove them down this executive's throat. But after saying a few "fucks," he picked up his chips and we left.

That night we had dinner at the Chicago Steakhouse at Gold Strike, a casino that had become insane about players shooting the dice and allowing their arms to extend past the stickman. Many of the Golden Touch dice-control instructors were coming in that night, and we arranged to have a meal for all of us. At dinner one of our instructors said, "It was weird at the table tonight. I was rolling the dice, was at 21 rolls, and the pit boss came over and said, 'You know that's all bullshit about being able to control the dice. That Scoblete is full of shit.'

"I ignored him and rolled," said the instructor, "but then he said, 'And Scoblete is banned from every casino in Mississippi, you know; he can't play here anymore. He's been banned everywhere.'

"One of the players at the table said, 'Well, if it doesn't work, why is he banned?' And the pit boss walked away saying something like, 'Scoblete gives players crazy ideas that they can beat the house.'"

I looked at Dom, and Dom looked at me. Then we told our tales of being asked to leave the casinos and being trespassed at Fitzgerald's. Evidently we were banned from every casino in Tunica if that casino guy was correct—maybe every casino in Mississippi.

Just to keep you savvy about advantage-play backoffs and bannings, the casino has two ways to stop a player who has an edge. The first is to simply tell him not to play certain games, but that means the player can come back to the casino to play other games. The other, more drastic way is to trespass the player, which is to tell that player the next time he comes on the property he will be arrested for trespassing.

There is a third, illegal and immoral way, too. And that is to backroom the advantage player and seriously abuse his civil rights by holding him against his will, filing false charges, and sometimes beating him up. I had never been beaten up, but I did have a gun put into my back in a downtown Las Vegas casino by a steroidal, muscle-bound security guard. I walked right out the front door, praying that my wife and playing partner, the Beautiful AP, and I would not be shot down in the casino.

Since I never cheated at games and since my partners and team players never cheated at games, we were not doing anything illegal. But the whole thing is still unpleasant.

Unfortunately, the casinos' executives had the right to stop you from playing their games because, again, casinos are private property. So that was, as they say, that. The Tunica casinos were dead to me.

Tunica has, sadly, become a gaming venue that sweats the action but wants to soak the players. Casinos are closing, too. The Grand (which changed its name to Harrah's) is gone.

The Tunica I used to love, that I used to write so glowingly about, that I used to advertise any chance I got because of its great games and friendly attitude, has dimmed to the point of being a dump.

But I still had five more days there, as we were giving our Golden Touch dice-control classes that weekend. What was I going to do in those five days?

Thursday, February 23

I started this day with a great workout in the spa. Then I went over to the front desk to see if I could get someone to understand about my free rooms. The supervisor at the front desk understood that I wanted to substitute the three free room nights that I had with the three paid ones that I had booked over the Internet. He said, "It's all taken care of, sir." I was at last happy. I thanked him.

After breakfast I went to Elvis Presley's Graceland mansion in Tennessee.

Friday, February 24

I walked 3.5 miles on the treadmill and I lifted weights. I had little 10-pound weights, and an old lady, an *ancient* lady, was lifting 20-pounders—the show-off!

Dom was really frustrated by his stay at the Grand's Terrace Hotel, too, so we both decided to talk to the manager. The time had come to complain. I wrote a list of what had happened during our stay.

Dom explained all about how his FedEx package wound up back in his room.

"I heard about it," said the manager.

I then read my list: "No room service during storm, no gift shop during storm, no coffee shop during storm, no valet during storm, no bar during storm, no salt or sand on the exit roads, no understanding on the part of the check-in clerks about my rooms, no wash cloths, restaurant was closed when it was supposed to be open and no butter at the buffet and no wheat toast either, and the damn toaster puts the bread on the counter, and today it shot the bread into the floor."

"I am not responsible for the buffet," said the manager.

I looked at the manager. Dom looked at the manager.

"You come to a hotel," I said calmly, "to enjoy amenities like room service and the other things. That's why we're here. And we didn't get any of the amenities."

"There was a storm," he said.

"So what? So *fucking* what?" Dom screamed.

"People don't come to work in storms," said the manager.

We all stood there silently.

"How about you pick up the rooms we have paid for to make up for the lousy service?" Dom asked. "A sign of good faith."

"I'd have to talk to the president," stated the manager.

"Great, talk to him," I said.

Dom and I walked away. In the elevator, Dom shouted, "Motherfucker!"

We drove over to the hotel for our dice-control class. We were renting two rooms there and we had a lot of setting up to do—two full-size casino craps tables, eight practice tables, in addition to all sorts of dice paraphernalia. The moving of all this stuff to the hotel took a lot of time.

"Let's relax," I said to Dom as we pulled up to the hotel. "We relax and set up the banquet rooms. You did call to remind them to clean the rooms?"

"No, they know they have to do that. They can't be that stupid not to clean the fucking meeting rooms," said Dom.

Both rooms were filthy. There was garbage all over the big banquet room. The smaller room, where we do the lecture part of the class, was being painted by two scrawny guys who looked as if they had smoked five packs a day since they were toddlers.

We talked to the manager of the hotel and informed him we had to have both rooms set up immediately for the next day's class. We needed that second room now. "I didn't think you needed it," explained the manager slowly, "so we went ahead to paint the molding."

He assured us that he would personally set up the room for the next day.

Dom offered to pay for the meeting rooms in advance. The manager explained we could pay on Sunday, saying, "There ain't no rush. I trust you guys."

Then the manager asked, "How many students should we set the room for?"

"Set it up for 32 students," said Dom.

Saturday, February 25

The room was set up for 62 students. We had to quickly remove chairs and rearrange things. The front part of the room's wallpaper was starting to peel onto the new paint.

The class went well, and we headed back to the Grand's Terrace Hotel. In my room the phone rang. It was the manager of the hotel where we had done the Golden Touch class. "We want payment for the banquet rooms right now!" he screamed.

"Didn't you say Sunday was fine?" I asked.

"My boss wants it now!" he screamed.

We drove back and paid him for the two banquet rooms. Dom reminded him to clean up so that when we started the next day the rooms would be ready to use.

That night Stickman, the Sainted Tres, Rock 'n' Roller, Dominator, and I ate at Sheraton's steakhouse. Stickman ordered a Belvedere martini, dry, straight-up, no vermouth, and Dom ordered Kettle One on the rocks with an olive. About 10 hours later, long after we'd ordered our meal (which hadn't yet arrived either), the waiter brought over one of those round glasses you get in hotel rooms with some vodka in it and put it in front of Stickman.

"What's this?" Stickman asked.

"That's your drink," said the waiter.

"I ordered a martini," Stickman said.

"That bartender, he says that this is what it is, and he must be kidding me because..." and the waiter went on and on as to why Stickman's drink wasn't his drink. Maybe the bartender was playing a joke? Maybe aliens from another planet had kidnapped his drink? Maybe I couldn't understand what he was saying half the time, but it was the *longest* excuse I have heard in my life.

"Please go back and get me what I ordered," Stickman said.

"Bring my drink too," added Dom, looking disgusted. "How hard is it to get a drink order right?"

The waiter finally brought over our dinners with Stickman's drink, this time made properly, but he didn't have Dom's drink.

"Where's my drink?" Dominator asked.

"Your drink?"

"Jesus Christ. Forget my drink. I don't want it now," Dom said.

"I'll get your drink right away, sir," the waiter said.

"Forget my drink."

"What did you order?" the waiter asked.

"Forget my drink."

The waiter walked away, checking his notepad.

"You know I think they are trained in school to make excuses," I said. "They are always polite, but when they screw up, they just make excuses."

"Even if the excuses make no sense," Dominator said.

Sunday, February 26

I called room service at 6:30 AM and ordered some eggs and whole-wheat toast with a small pot of coffee.

"It will be right up, sir," said the woman on the phone. I called down at 7:00 AM to check to see if my order was ready.

"It will be right up, sir," said the woman on the phone.

I called down at 7:30 to see what was taking so long.

"The cook didn't come in. We got no cook," said the woman on the phone.

At 8:00, five minutes before I left for class, my cold, cardboardy eggs and cold *white* toast arrived. I wolfed down everything and headed out the door.

At the hotel where we were holding our class, the rooms had not been cleaned—so we cleaned them up. "I told the fucking guy to clean the damn room!" shouted Dom into the air.

That night we ate at the Grand's Murano's, and Rock 'n' Roller ordered some penne pasta to go with his meal. After the table was cleared of our desserts and our coffees, the pasta was brought to him.

"What's this?" Rock 'n' Roller asked.

"Pasta," the waiter said.

"We had our meal, we had our coffee, we had our desert," Rock 'n' Roller said.

"You ordered pasta," the waiter said.

"As a part of my meal," Rock 'n' Roller said.

The waiter just stood there. "All right," Rock 'n' Roller said, "I'll eat it now."

So with the table cleared, with Stickman, Dominator, and I totally finished with our evening of dining, poor Rock 'n' Roller ate his pasta. "It's good," he said, "at least the pasta is good."

Dom, angry as all hell over the week, over the service, over every damn thing, said as we left the Grand, "I want to play one more time."

"You're out of your mind," I said. "You don't want to get arrested, do you? You saw *My Cousin Vinny*, right?"

"Marisa Tomei was beautiful, a real Brooklyn girl," Rock 'n' Roller said.

"Look, I think it's a big mistake," I said.

"If you play, I'll go with you," Stickman said.

"Great, you're going to get poor Dom arrested," I said.

"I'll go too," Rock 'n' Roller said. "I really liked Marisa Tomei."

"I'm not going; I'm going back to my room, watch a movie, and go to sleep," I said. "You will be sleeping with Big Bubba in a Mississippi jail."

"Frank, I'm telling you, we were hotter than hell last weekend. We hammered them until they kicked our asses out. I feel it tonight, my friend. I am ready to bust them wide open," Dom said.

"I think you just want to gamble," I said. That's one of the ways I get Dom to see that I am right. I call him a gambler. And he hates to be called a gambler because before I met him he had more gambler in him than was good for him.

"I didn't gamble all week. I visited the museum, I saw Elvis's house, you know, I held back, but this is the last night, and I know I'am going to be hot. I can feel it. I won't be gambling," he said.

"I'm going back to my room," I said.

"You don't understand," Dom explained, "I made myself a costume. Nobody will recognize me. We'll go to a casino that we haven't been to very much, and I won't be recognized. I'll take the dice once, and that's it. I'll hammer the bastards and leave. I want one more shot at these fucks."

"I did the costume thing in Vegas for a whole summer. It could work, but if it doesn't, there's a Big Bubba in your future," I said.

"Wasn't President Clinton called Bubba?" Rock 'n' Roller asked.

"What are you going to be?" Stickman asked.

"I got it in the trunk of the SUV," Dom said.

"Good luck," I said. "I'm going back to my room."

"You know, Frank, you're smart," Stickman said. "Because your face is really well-known down here. But Dom might be able to get away with it. I think you have more of a chance to be identified."

"I'll get away with it," Dominator said. "I know I'll get away with it."

When I got back to my room I called the airlines and changed my flight back home from Tuesday to Monday afternoon. I was anxious to get home to my Beautiful AP after having the worst week I ever spent in a casino hotel and a casino town—ever.

About two hours later, I heard a knock on the door between Dom's and my rooms. I was just falling asleep and I was a little foggy. I opened the door. I wish I could tell you that Dom had a good roll and won a little money; I can't tell you that, unfortunately.

Instead, he had a *monstrous* hand that was over the 50-roll mark! He hit so many numbers that the casino suits held a convention behind the table. No one knew it was the remarkable Dominator "kicking ass" as he said he would.

He pulled out a pile of $100 bills and laid them on the table. He pointed to them dramatically. "I'm adding this to the pile we already have."

"We? You're letting me share in your winnings?" I asked.

"Hey, we were partners on this trip and we're partners now. In our last playing trip to Tunica, we beat the crap out of them," he said.

"That we did," I agreed. "And tonight I didn't even have to do anything."

Monday, February 27

It was time to leave the Grand, and boy was I glad to be going home to my AP. At the front desk I checked out my bill, and there it was in black and white—they charged me for the three *free* nights. I told the woman at the desk that the last three nights were supposed to be free. She was in the process of training a man to be a reservation agent. He looked dumbfounded as I spoke. She looked dumbfounded, too. Her training regimen was obviously going quite well because there were two dumbfounded people looking at me as if there were something wrong with *me*.

I repeated the fact that my last three nights were free. She looked me up on the computer. "You didn't use them nights. You stayed in the room you was in."

I had a choice to argue or to just sign the bill and get the hell away. I signed the bill.

It was a beautiful day in Tunica. The air was crisp and clean. I headed to the airport. I just kept thinking I would get on the plane and head back to New York and home and I would put the rotten week behind me.

Unfortunately Northwest Airlines was delayed, and my flight took off an hour and 20 minutes late.

I was seated in the aisle seat, and next to me was an elderly woman who fell asleep as soon as the plane lifted off. While she slept, she snored really loudly and then started to rip the most wicked-sounding and horrendous-smelling farts.

When the stewardess came by for drinks, the woman woke up and ordered orange juice. The stewardess handed it to her, but the old woman dropped the glass and all the orange juice in my lap.

"Give me another, this one spilled on this man."

This man asked for some napkins to wipe himself off.

"I live in Connecticut," said the old woman, and, finishing her orange juice, she promptly fell back asleep, again snoring and farting.

About 50 miles from LaGuardia Airport, the pilot said over the intercom, "You probably noticed that we just made a 180-degree turn. The tower has told us it will be another 20 minutes for us to land. So we've been delayed again. I'll keep you posted."

We finally landed in New York.

Of course, my limo service wasn't there at the airport. I stood outside, and there was no one to pick me up. I called my wife and she called the limo service.

Five minutes later my limo arrived. I had been waiting on the departure level of the airport—where I always wait—and he had been waiting for me on the arrival level. He was a new driver.

And we took off for Long Island and home.

Except there were three accidents on New York's busy highways, which stalled me getting home. It took another hour and when I finally arrived home I felt like kissing the ground. Instead I kissed AP, my beautiful wife. When we disengaged, she said, "You smell like oranges."

Sometime in March

I'd been doing a radio show from Memphis, Tennessee, for about 12 years. The Tunica casinos and some other non-casino advertisers supported it. A few weeks after my disastrous trip to Tunica, I got a phone call from the jolly owner/host of the show. "Hey, hey, Frank, my boy," he started.

"What's up?" I asked.

"Frank, we got some bad problems on the show. You see, some of the casinos are pulling back their advertising, and I am just not going to be able to pay you to do your segment of the show anymore. We had a pretty good run, ha ha."

"Twelve years," I said. I had been with the show almost 12 years, and he was cutting me loose just like that?

Of course, the situation didn't surprise me—it seemed that Tunica's casinos had gone to war against me because they thought I was winning too much money and teaching people advantage play in my Golden Touch classes. These were no-nos. The fact that tens of thousands of non-advantage players had discovered Tunica thanks to my writing was never a factor. Suits are suits. The next logical step would be for them to put pressure on the radio show to dump me. "Good luck in the future," I said to the radio show's owner. But I felt betrayed. In my casino gambling life, there had been three people who I felt betrayed me, the radio show owner/host being one of them. Soon I would have a fourth, the *worst betrayal* of all. "If things get better, I'll let you know," he said.

"Sure," I said, "Are you keeping John on the show?"

"Yeah, yeah, I can still afford to pay him," laughed the owner.

Years earlier I had made a deal with the radio show owner that I would never ask for a raise if he started to pay John Robison, the show's slots expert, because up to that time, John was working gratis. The owner and I agreed to that, and John received a stipend from that point on to do his weekly stint on the show. And I never asked for another raise.

But I was out, and John was still in. I guess that's the way of the world. No good deed goes unpunished. To make matters even more ridiculous, months after my exit from the show, this owner/host wrote to me and asked if he could put his name to an unpublished book I wrote, publish it under his name, and not pay me!

Yes, it is possible that those of you reading this are discovering that Tunica has returned to being the best gaming destination in America. It's also possible that the Tunica casino executives, some of whom had been very friendly to me over the years, have called me and welcomed me back to what had been my favorite place to play in the entire country.

I'm not betting any of that will happen.

Sadly, the great Tunica, Mississippi, that I loved is now gone with the wind.

Mississippi Goes After Golden Touch

Some years later, on April 9, two weeks before the Tunica Golden Touch dice-control class, Dom called me. "Frank, I have a bad feeling about Tunica. I don't know why or what it is," he said.

Even though Dom and I had been trespassed and banned, we still could do our dice-control classes since we used non-casino hotels.

"Dom, it's because you've been playing in Vegas for three weeks in a row and you've been hot. Now we go down there and we can't play," I counseled. "That's all it is. It's depressing for you not to play."

"Yeah, maybe," he said. I could tell he wasn't convinced.

On Wednesday evening, April 21, my phone rang at 6:00. "Fuck, shit, fuck, piss, fuck!" It was Dom.

"What's wrong, Dom?"

"The Mississippi Gaming Commission just called me. They are going to stop us from having the class this weekend."

"What?" I said. "We won that case in 2004."

"Isn't it enough those fucking casinos have banned us from playing?

We won the free speech case against the gaming commission, for God's sake."

"Call our lawyer," I said. "He can straighten this out. The gaming commission has to have made a mistake."

"Yeah, okay, fine, fucking jerks!"

"And just in case we have to 'get out of Dodge,' I will start looking up hotels in Memphis. Just in case," I said. "And get all the info from our lawyer, so we know what's going on." Our lawyer, Steve Lacy, had handled our previous case against the State of Mississippi and had won it handily. The guy was a good lawyer.

I went to the computer and started making a list of Memphis hotels that had banquet and meeting rooms big enough to accommodate us. Our Tunica class was sold out. We had 33 students; normally Tunica ran about 25 to 28. In comparison we usually got between 50 and 60 in Las Vegas and Atlantic City, which were far bigger venues. With the number of our instructors we only had room for 60 students in the big venues.

I made a list and called Stickman, who lives in Memphis, to have him go over the list. He was familiar with the locations of many of the Memphis hotels.

"Tomorrow morning when you get into Memphis," Stickman said, "we go to all the hotels and see which ones are good and which of those we can book. I'll also check out the computer listings." Stickman was picking me up at the airport at 8:45 Thursday morning. Instead of going directly to Tunica, we would make the Memphis hotel tour.

Dom called again. "Fuck."

"What is it?"

"I left a message for Steve, but then I spoke again to the jerk from the gaming commission. I told him again that we already won the free speech case. So he told me it is not a free speech case this time. It's a table case."

"What the hell is that?" I asked.

"They have a law in Mississippi that you can't have gaming tables outside of casinos," he said.

"Did they just invent that law?"

"No, no, those fucks say the law started around Wyatt Earp's time. It was a law to stop the game of Faro."

"Faro? That hasn't been played for decades, maybe 60 years or so," I said.

"What the fuck is a gaming table?" Dom asked. "I play cards on my kitchen table. Is that a gaming table now?"

"Well, our tables have never been gambled on, so how can they be gaming tables? What if I use our blackjack tables as bars and our craps table as a practice area for throwing dice, but I never gamble on those throws? Is there a law against practicing dice throws on a non-gaming table?"

"Stupid fucks!" Dom screamed.

"Well, Stickman and I have a list of hotels, and we'll visit them tomorrow to see what we can get."

"Steve is going to talk to them and explain how stupid they are," Dom said. "Maybe by tomorrow morning it will all be straightened out."

"Maybe," I said

I went to sleep that night, tossing, turning, and awake almost the whole time before I had to leave my bed at 4:30 AM to be picked up by my car service to be taken to LaGuardia Airport.

When I got to the airport I was pumped with anticipation about the class and simultaneously exhausted from worrying about how we would solve our problem with the Mississippi Gaming Commission. Knowing Dom, he had probably not slept well either. Class weekends are intense and tiring; I didn't want Dom and me to be exhausted the whole time.

On the plane, I closed my eyes to sleep, and then two monstrous girls started talking *into* each other's faces. It was not an argument; it was merely face-to-face screaming between two monsters seated in the seats behind me on the plane.

Next to me was a woman who incessantly drank coffee, burped loud coffee-scented burps, and yelled at her junior high school daughter for being stupid until she dropped her empty cup to leap up and run to the bathroom because she had diarrhea—a fact she proclaimed to the whole plane on her way back: "Boy, I had some diarrhea there."

I closed my eyes to sleep. Then in the seats in front of me two dirt-encrusted backwoods types, a man and a woman, started to explain to each other how itchy they were. "Man, I itchy," he said. "My hair is itchy," she said and started scratching like mad. She had weird black hair, really straight but with gray strands here and there sticking straight up, making her look like the Bride of Frankenstein. I was just hoping their scratching didn't catapult several legions of little bugs behind them onto me.

I closed my eyes and slept a little until the two monsters in back of me started screaming at the stewardess and some passenger behind her. "I talk just as I wants!" screamed one girl.

"We be doin' what we wants, and you ain't doin' nothing!" screamed the second girl.

"You shut up, you old..."

I hazily thought, *Are all of these people seated around me an omen of bad things coming?* I drifted off and slept for an hour until the plane landed.

Stickman picked me up, and we had breakfast at Brother Juniper's. Then we headed out to look for hotels. Nothing. The ones that had big enough meeting rooms were filled; the others had rooms that were too small. We needed two rooms, one a classroom and one a practice room where we put all of our tables.

About 10:30 AM Dom called. "Steve is talking to the commission. You are not going to believe this. They have lost the records of our case in 2004."

"You have to be kidding."

"Steve has everything from 2004, and he is faxing everything to those jerks at the commission," Dom said. "I didn't sleep at all last night."

"If we have to move the class to Memphis, we'll need to get a bus to bring the students from Tunica."

"And a truck to move all the stuff too," Dom said.

"You know, I actually hope we get the hell out of Tunica for good," I said. "I hate it down there."

"I hate it too. How's the hotel search going?" Dom asked.

"So far, not so good. We've visited six so far. The best one was the Marriott, but it was sold out. We'll spend all day looking until we find one."

"I'll keep you posted on Steve and the commission," Dom said.

At the very next hotel we hit pay dirt. It was the Hilton in Memphis. They had two meeting rooms left for the weekend. This is an *A* level hotel similar to the ones we use at other venues. The hotel we had been using in Tunica was not an *A* or even *a B*; it was more toward the end of the alphabet.

We asked the woman in charge of catering at the Hilton if they would hold the rooms until 5:00 PM. She was gracious and said she would. The hotel was quite large and had many giant banquet rooms and conventions that weekend. Getting two empty rooms was a miracle.

Then Stickman and I headed to Tunica. I was staying at Harrah's (formerly the Grand). Although I was not allowed to play at the property, I was able to get a room thanks to Skinny, who had gotten a major comp for that weekend. So I was going to pay nothing and stay at a property that certainly did not want me staying at it. Stickman was comped there too—thanks to Skinny.

So we split up and went to our rooms. Since Stickman was in Harrah's Casino Hotel that evening and I was at the Terrace, I was able to get a room right away, but he had to wait. So he and Skinny went to a casino to shoot some dice.

At 2:00 PM Dom called. "Our lawyer said to get out of Mississippi. They intend to arrest us tomorrow and fine us $10,000 if we use our tables—which are actually called exhibits since they are not used as gaming tables, whatever gaming tables means."

"Okay, let's get a bus company. The woman at Hilton gave us the name of a company," I said.

"Call them," said Dom. "Can you get Stickman to call and try to find a storage facility?"

"Yeah, okay." I called Stickman, and he started calling storage facilities in Memphis as close to the Hilton as we could get. We were figuring on making the Hilton our new home for our Southern classes. Tunica is only 30 minutes from Memphis, so it would not be a big deal to hold our classes in a classy Memphis hotel near the casinos.

Then Stickman, Skinny, and I made calls to 22 students to tell them of the change of plans and what time for them to catch the bus. Dom called the other 11. We were set to move our business to a fine property.

On Friday morning all the instructors and interns showed up at our Tunica storage facility, and we explained the situation to them. They unanimously agreed that getting out of Tunica was the right move. None of them liked doing our classes there—and those who wished to play could do so at the few casinos that still had decent games.

We packed up the rental truck and drove to Memphis. Dom and Stickman visited the storage facilities near the Hilton and found one about two miles away that would suit our needs. Dom negotiated with several bus companies to get us a fair deal. Both Stickman and I canceled our reservations at Harrah's.

We then set up our class at the Hilton.

Saturday morning from 1:00 to 4:00, there was a tremendous storm. My room was on the 10th floor of the Hilton, and I had a panoramic view of the constant lightning and the roaring thunder. It was an impressive storm, and the local stations predicted tornadoes for Mississippi.

That Saturday morning the rain poured from a blackened sky, and the bus didn't get the students to the Hilton until 9:30. But the class went well, and the students were in good spirits. They fully understood what had happened. As one of them put it, "The casinos are afraid of you guys, and the gaming commission works for them!"

At lunchtime, the hotel alarm went off, and a female voice announced that there was a tornado warning for our area of Memphis. She explained where we would go should there be a final announcement to protect ourselves. The restaurant we were eating in had floor-to-ceiling windows and the wind was bending the trees into horseshoe shapes and whipping the fountains into whitecaps.

We survived it all and had a great class.

And now the irony of ironies, Tunica was totally blacked out by the vicious storm that Saturday. We would not have been able to hold our class in Tunica had the Mississippi Gaming Commission not forced us out of the state. For that, we thank them.

CHAPTER 4

Betrayal

By the 10th anniversary of Golden Touch Craps, I knew I was resigning and that I would sell my shares to Dom. Dom did not yet know this, nor did anyone in Golden Touch, including my close friend Jerry "Stickman." After our Vegas class (my last) in October 2012, we held a great party to celebrate 10 years of the most successful dice-control school in the country

After the 10th anniversary party, Stickman, his wife the Sainted Tres, the Beautiful AP, and I headed to Hawaii. A great start to my new life.

Since my retirement from Golden Touch, the Beautiful AP and I have traveled America and many parts of the world. On a 16-day trip to Japan, AP and I went to a Tokyo Giants game. (Jerry "Stickman" and I are visiting all the baseball parks in the country over the next few years and writing about our experiences for my website, frankscoblete.com.) We've also visited England, Ireland, Scotland, and France. While you are reading this, I have traveled still more, making up for lost time for the quarter century I made the casinos my second home.

In December 2012 I invited Dom to the Arno Ristorante in Manhattan. I told him I was leaving Golden Touch. We'd had a great partnership, a great friendship, and built a great company. We experienced great adventures at the tables, some of which I have documented in this book and others. Naturally, our teachers were the foundation upon which we constructed everything. Without good teachers, a school is just a word. We had a *real* school.

Dom was shaken that I was leaving. We agreed on a price for my shares. I didn't need to make money, especially off Dom, so I priced my shares far lower than their worth. In fact, he could pay me over time. With each class, he would make double the money (my salary *and* his salary), so he'd easily be able to pay me. We shook hands on the deal—that's all I needed, a handshake.

On December 4, 2012, I called American Express and told them I would no longer be the primary cardholder or even be on the card; I was leaving Golden Touch. The representative told me to have Dom call within five days to put him on as the primary.

A couple of days later Dom called me and said, "All done. I took care of it."

"It's like cutting the umbilical cord," I said.

And that was that...or so I thought.

Despite Dom's regular flare-ups at the tables, his conflicts with hotel supervisors, and his outrage at various instructors...and despite the times when customers called to complain that Dom owed them money and never returned calls or emails...and despite the occasions when New York State contacted me about Dom's debt, I liked and appreciated Dom.

I had totally dismissed those website claims that he had taken markers from the casinos and never paid them back. I also pushed out of my mind that Dom never took markers or used his real name in the casinos when he checked in. I had dismissed Howard "Rock 'n' Roller's" sense that Dom was screwing him.

Make no mistake, Dom was an excellent partner. His creativity, charisma, and business sense helped to make Golden Touch the gold standard in dice control. Bottom line: he was a close and, I thought, *loyal* friend.

Then it all came tumbling down.

On July 2, 2014, my *personal* American Express credit card was frozen. How could it be frozen? I always paid my bill in full.

I called American Express, and they told me I was overdue on two business cards and that they would not allow me to use any American Express credit card until minimum payments were made on those cards.

"I don't have any other credit cards," I said.

"You are the primary on two cards," said the representative.

The two cards were a business cash rebate card and a business platinum card with *unlimited credit*. Both cards were for Golden Touch Craps.

I told the representative that there had to be some mistake. I was taken off those cards in early December 2012. My former partner, Dominic, had put himself on as primary. "I am sorry, sir, no one did that," said the representative. "You have been primary and are totally responsible for the payment of the debt."

"What debt?"

"You owe $8,752.57 on the cash rebate card and $42,089.32 on the platinum card."

"What?"

"It's a total of $50,841.89 on those two cards, sir. You have to pay that, sir."

Over the years Dom received all the bills and statements. I never saw any of the American Express bills. So I had American Express send me all the bills from December 2012 forward.

I explained that I had made no purchases on those cards. "All the purchases were made by Dominic, sir," agreed the representative. "But you are personally responsible for everything he put on those cards."

I also discovered when I looked at the bills that not all the expenses on those cards were for Golden Touch; there were Dom's *personal* charges too, which meant that he had purposely made me responsible not only for the Golden Touch debt he had run up but for some of his own debt.

How could Golden Touch be in the red?

I had no idea.

How could the American Express cards show a debt of almost $51,000? What had Dom done with all the money from the classes, which made between $45,000 and $110,000, depending on the venue? Plus sales of craps tables, books, DVDs?

Money was *obviously* coming in, yet he had deliberately made me responsible for paying the business debt and his personal debt on those credit cards. So where was the class money going?

I had no idea.

My credit rating, which had been perfect before I became involved with Dom and Golden Touch, suddenly barely made it to the top 25 percent.

Could Dom be in debt? Was he taking the Golden Touch money for himself and sticking me with the bills? Well, he was obviously sticking me with the bills; certainly a sly way of stealing money without it being a criminal offense.

Dom was an advantage player at craps. Had he some other problem? Was he losing big at some other forms of gambling? Had his gambling nature reasserted itself? Were his other businesses losing money? Is that why he was taking the Golden Touch money and strapping me with almost $51,000 on two credit cards?

I really don't know. I just don't know.

Dom handled all the Golden Touch money. Where had all that money gone since it was not being used to pay any bills?

His failure to put himself on as primary on the two credit cards—which he claimed he had done ("I took care of it") devastated me. How could he do this to a friend he claimed he admired? He certainly could not have forgotten that I was primary—my name, in large print, was on the top of the bills, so he saw it every time a statement came to his home. Once he knew that I knew about the credit cards, he stopped paying me for my shares of the company.

And we had shaken hands!

I talked to the Beautiful AP. "Look at what you did for him," she said. "You got him on television and radio. You created *The Dice Dominator* show that wasn't even going to be about him, and you got History Channel to change the whole thing to make him the star. You wrote a DVD with him in it. You put his picture on two covers of your books. You wrote articles for him. You wrote articles about him. You even put him as coauthor of three craps books, and he didn't write a thing. You *made* him. The Dominator was nobody until you created him. You even dedicated a book to him. Why would he do such a thing to you?"

"I don't know," I said.

Dom made no effort to pay off the cards. After all, he didn't have to pay them. He didn't pay me for my shares. But he kept holding classes. Where was all the money going?

When we realized Dom would not pay his business and personal debt, we tried to lower what was owed. The Beautiful AP and I tried to negotiate a partial payment with American Express—even going directly to the

CEO. American Express wouldn't hear of it. They wanted payment in full, even though I had nothing to do with Golden Touch Craps, Dominic, or with charging anything on those cards.

In the end I paid off both cards for $50,841.89.

I thought of what the Captain said when his friend and business partner had deserted him, leaving him with massive debt: "It was horrible, that betrayal by a friend."

"Why is Dom doing this to us?" asked the Beautiful AP.

I shook my head.

I didn't know why then and I don't know why now. But I do know, it is horrible, that betrayal by a friend.

CHAPTER 5

Good-Bye

J erry "Stickman" and I were walking the Boardwalk in Atlantic City on the Ides of March, the day Julius Caesar was betrayed and assassinated by his close friend Brutus—a gray, wet day, and a sad day in many ways. I looked at the Claridge, where it all started for me.

Except for Satch and me, the Captain's Crew members are gone. Jimmy P. died in the late 1990s from lung cancer. He had been a three-packs-a-day smoker. It did him in. He went from being a large, robust, energetic man to a shriveled husk. The Captain spent many days at Jimmy P.'s bedside as Jimmy P. slowly withered and passed on. Jimmy P. had been a loyal friend to the Captain, and vice versa.

The Arm retired at the end of the 1990s, but I hadn't seen her play for a couple of years before her death. She had severe arthritis by that time and soon developed Alzheimer's disease, which stripped her of her self and soul. The greatest dice controller of all time, the scourge of the casinos, did not go out with a "bang but a whimper," to quote W.B. Yeats' "The Second Coming." I don't think there will ever be a "second coming" of a shooter such as the Arm. She was a once-in-a-lifetime giant; I was lucky to have seen her.

The last time I played with the Captain was 2008. I had the good fortune to be on his epic 147-number roll in 2005. The Captain died on February 10, 2010, during that monster snowstorm that heralded his passing. In myth great men die while nature reflects their deaths. That cold day, with snow whipping throughout New York City, was the sign that the greatest craps player in history would be no more. Anyway, that's how I saw it and still see it to this day.

His death was peaceful. As a World War II veteran and a "wounded warrior" in today's parlance, he was given a complete military farewell.

Yes, it is over. That time, those men and women, they are gone now. Still I remember it all and long to take a time machine and say hi to them.

I *see* them in my mind's eye.

The Beautiful AP and I walk into the Claridge. I can smell the casino from the lobby—that cigarette-adrenaline-alcohol-hopeful smell unique to casinos. I walk into the casino, and there they are—the Captain's Crew—standing at the tables, cheering, clapping, joking, and laughing.

The Arm smiles at me as she sets the dice. People are crowding around the table, two-deep. "The Arm is rolling! The Arm is rolling!" goes the chant seemingly throughout the casino. Jimmy P., smoking a cigarette and laughing loudly—a big man and the Captain's first mate—yells out, "Hey, Frankie, good to see ya!" Russ the Breather inhales his oxygen and nods to me. Russ has been a close friend of the Captain's for many decades.

The Doctor, a surgeon, makes a fist in my direction as if to say, "Let's get 'em!" There are Little Vic the blackjack player, Joe, Joey, Paul, John the Tailor, John the Analyzer; these guys slap me on the back or hug me or shake my hand and they all give the Beautiful AP a hug and kiss on the cheek.

There is Phil the Forgetful, wondering what bets he has made. "Is that my Hard 8?" There is fretful Frank T. who looks sad (he always looked sad) because he feels he has no luck and is known for yelling "Turn off my bets!" even when the dice are in the air. And there is Sal the Staller, taking his time, asking questions, slowing down the games and the meals because "he wants to know" something. He lives his life in slow motion while his wife is a cyclone. Add the two of them together and you get a normal pace.

There's the Judge, debonair, a Douglas Fairbanks Jr. There's my friend Satch and his wife, Annette, my wife's best friend since kindergarten. I recruited them for the Crew. Actually I recruited myself for the Crew, too. Satch was the best man at my two weddings to the Beautiful AP. Oh, yes,

I married my lovely bride twice—once by a Protestant minister and once by a Catholic priest. I was hedging my bets there, something you should never do in craps. Annette was, naturally, the matron of honor at both weddings.

The women are there: Rose and Connie and Jo the Wanderer; and Ellen, Eileen, Mary, and Denise. They all give me big hugs and kisses on the cheek. "Great to see you, great to see you!" they say.

There are others around that table; their main host, Mike, is there too, some hangers-on are there, some curious folks are there to see such a bunch of players throwing purple, orange, and higher chips onto the layout. The Captain's Crew can dominate a casino craps pit. They are a force, a tidal wave, a loud, boisterous tornado. These men and women have come to play and to play big. More often than not they can be found at two and three tables when the whole Crew comes to play.

I can hear their voices even after all these years. I see them standing there—the Crew, that one-of-a-kind Captain's Crew. I *see* them.

And there is the Captain, the leader, one of the greatest craps players of all time, enjoying the scene, enjoying his friends, enjoying his steady victories in a world ruled by Dame Fortune—a woman the Captain made his mistress. He smiles at me and gives me that nod, which says, *Are you ready to take the casino's money?*

Yes, Captain, yes I am, I nod back.

The Claridge, back in those long-long-ago days when I first learned it all; *that* Claridge I will never forget. There they are, in memory, the Crew, each of them as real to me now as they were to me then. I'm smiling as I look back at that part of my life; I'm smiling because I remember them well and I was in a small way a part of it all, a part of something great.

The Claridge casino is closed now. I stood on the Boardwalk and looked at the building where I was conceived. The wind was picking up; it was getting colder, damper, a depressing gray day. It had been been sold to a non-casino company.

Jerry "Stickman" and I walked down to the front doors. Interesting enough, they were open. The two entrances within the lobby to the casino were boarded up. Dust was everywhere in the lobby. Outside the front doors pigeon droppings colored the entranceway, the sidewalk, and the driveway. Ghosts of valet parkers shuffled through time. "Are you checking in, sir? Do you want help with your luggage, sir?"

Windblown papers, candy wrappers, and feathers; grains of sand and dust; that was the Claridge on that Ides of March. Across the street sat an empty lot that used to house the long-gone Sands.

Atlantic City is in old age now. When I first came to this seaside resort town it was booming, an adolescent full of energy and a bright future. New casinos such as Taj Mahal were being built; old hotels were being remodeled and new additions were being added.

The ACH (Atlantic City Hilton)—which was the original Golden Nugget, then became Bally's Grand, then Grand, and then ACH—has closed. Showboat has closed. Trump Plaza has closed. Revel has closed. Yes, that old glorious Atlantic City is now wheezing its way from day-to-day to death.

The Crew is gone.
Jimmy P. is gone.
The Arm is gone.
The Captain is gone.
That world is gone.
I have this to say to the Captain:
I did it, Captain.
I took it to them.
I won!
Thank you.

Previous Works

BOOKS

Armada Strategies for Spanish 21 [Bonus Books]

Baccarat Battle Book [Bonus Books, Taylor Trade Publishing]

Beat Blackjack Now!: The Easiest Way to Get the Edge! [Triumph Books]

Beat the Craps Out of the Casinos: How to Play Craps and Win! [Bonus Books, collectors' item only]

Beat the Craps Out of the Casinos: How to Play Craps and Win! (expanded edition) [Bonus Books, collector's item only]

Best Blackjack [Bonus Books, Taylor Trade Publishing]

Best Blackjack (expanded edition) [Bonus Books]

Bold Card Play!: Best Strategies for Caribbean Stud, Let It Ride & Three Card Poker [Bonus Books]

Break the One-Armed Bandits: How to Come Out Ahead When You Play the Slots [Bonus Books, out of print]

The Captain's Craps Revolution [Paone Press, collector's edition only]

The Captain's Special Report: How to Win at Tournament Craps [Paone Press, out of print]

Casino Conquest: Beat the Casinos at Their Own Games! [Triumph Books]

Casino Craps: Shoot to Win! (with DVD) [Triumph Books]

Casino Gambling: Play Like a Pro in 10 Minutes or Less! [Bonus Books, Taylor Trade Publishing]

Confessions of a Wayward Catholic [FSE Publishing]

The Craps Underground: The Inside Story of How Dice Controllers Are Winning Millions from the Casinos [Bonus Books, Taylor Trade Publishing]

Cutting Edge Craps: Advanced Strategies for Serious Players [Triumph Books]

Everything Casino Poker: Get the Edge at Video Poker, Texas Hold'em, Omaha Hi-Lo, and Pai Gow Poker [Triumph Books]

Forever Craps: The Five-Step Advantage-Play Method [Bonus Books, Taylor Trade Publishing]

Golden Touch Blackjack Revolution! [Research Services Unlimited, out of print]

Golden Touch Dice Control Revolution! [Research Services Unlimited, out of print]

Guerrilla Gambling: How to Beat the Casinos at Their Own Games! [Bonus Books, Taylor Trade Publishing]

Guerrilla Gambling: How to Beat the Casinos at Their Own Games! (updated edition) [Bonus Books, Taylor Trade Publishing]

I Am a Card Counter Controller: *Inside the World of Advantage-Play Blackjack!* [Triumph Books, winter 2014]

The Morons of Blackjack and Other Monsters! (as King Scobe) [Paone Press]

Slots Conquest: How to Beat the Slot Machines! [Triumph Books]

Spin Roulette Gold: Secrets of Beating the Wheel [Bonus Books, Taylor Trade Publishing]

Trev: A Novel [FSE Publishing, winter 2015]

Victory at Video Poker [Bonus Books, outdated]

The Virgin Kiss and Other Stories [Research Services Unlimited]

FRANK CONTRIBUTED CHAPTERS OR FOREWORDS TO:

109 Ways to Beat the Casinos, edited by Walter Thomason [Bonus Books]

American Casino Guide, edited by Steve Bourie [Casino Vacations Press]

Blackjack for the Clueless by Walter Thomason [Lyle Stuart]

The Casino Answer Book by John Grochowski [Taylor Trade Publishing]

The Experts' Guide to Casino Games, edited by Walter Thomason [Lyle Stuart]

Gambler's Digest, edited by Dennis Thornton [Krause Publications]

Twenty-First Century Blackjack by Walter Thomason [Bonus Books]

FRANK SCOBLETE'S VIDEOTAPES, HOSTED BY JAMES COBURN:

Winning Strategies: Blackjack [outdated format]
Winning Strategies: Craps [outdated format]
Winning Strategies: Slots with Video Poker [outdated format]

FRANK SCOBLETE'S DVDs:

Breaking Vegas: Dice Dominator [History Channel]
Golden Touch: Beat Craps by Controlling the Dice written and hosted by Frank Scoblete [Golden Touch Publishing]
Special Online Series with Video Jug [http://www.videojug.com/interview/gambling-basics-2]

FRANK SCOBLETE'S AUDIO TAPES:

Power of Positive Playing! [outdated format]
Sharpshooter Craps! [outdated format]
Slot Conquest! [outdated format]

FRANK SCOBLETE'S GET THE EDGE GUIDES:

77 Ways to Get the Edge at Casino Poker by Fred Renzey [Bonus Books, Taylor Trade Publishing]
Get the Edge at Blackjack: Revolutionary Advantage Play Methods That Work! by John May [Bonus Books]
Get the Edge at Craps by Chris Pawlicki (as Sharpshooter) [Bonus Books]
Get the Edge at Low-Limit Texas Hold'em by Bill Burton [Bonus Books, Taylor Trade Publishing]
Get the Edge at Roulette: How to Predict Where the Ball Will Land! by Christopher Pawlicki [Bonus Books, Taylor Trade Publishing]
How to Win Millions Playing Slot Machines...or Lose Trying by Frank Legato [Bonus Books, Taylor Trade Publishing]
Insider's Guide to Internet Gambling by John G. Brokopp [Bonus Books, out of print]
The Lottery Book: The Truth Behind the Numbers by Don Catlin [Bonus Books, Taylor Trade Publishing]
Thrifty Gambling by John G. Brokopp [Bonus Books]

PRODUCED PLAYS:
Dracula's Blind Date
The Virgin Kiss

Frank's books are available at bookstores and on Amazon.com. Many are available in e-book editions for Kindle and other e-readers.